WORD HERO

WORD HERO

A FIENDISHLY CLEVER GUIDE
TO CRAFTING THE LINES THAT
GET LAUGHS, GO VIRAL, AND
LIVE FOREVER

JAY HEINRICHS

THREE RIVERS PRESS
NEW YORK

www.crownpublishing.com

Three Rivers Press and the Tugboat design are registered trademarks of
Random House, Inc.

Library of Congress Cataloging-in-Publication Data is available.

ISBN 978-0-307-71636-1
eISBN 978-0-307-71637-8

4764 1039 1/12

PRINTED IN THE UNITED STATES OF AMERICA

Book design by Mauna Eichner and Lee Fukui
Cover design by Jessie Sayward Bright

10 9 8 7 6 5 4 3 2 1

First Edition

To Sherry,
who proves that every bad vacation
can become the stuff of immortality

CONTENTS

PART IV

WORD WIZARD

PART V

WORD HERO

PREFACE
THE LEGEND OF QUOTE BOY

**WIT IS THE ONLY WALL
BETWEEN US AND THE DARK.**
Mark Van Doren

WHEN A FRIEND ASKED what I was writing these days, I replied, "I'm going to teach you to come up with the words they'll quote in your obituary."

She recoiled as if I'd offered to design her coffin. So I added, "Ever see the musical *Fame*? Where the song says, 'Baby, remember my name'?"

She nodded. "'I'm going to live forever.'"

"My book will help you do that. Only with words instead of singing and dancing."

I meant it too, having had experience with immortality—not my own, but the lasting words in an important book. When I got into college, I celebrated by buying a copy of Bartlett's *Familiar Quotations* for the breathtaking sum of fifteen dollars. Every day I switched on my new electric typewriter, typed a quote onto an index card, and taped the card outside my dorm room door. Naturally, classmates started calling me Quote Boy. I didn't mind; a guy on our hall threw up on a dean and earned the name "Booter" for the rest of his life.

Besides, the quotes were a conversation piece and a way to meet women.

Even better, the words in Bartlett's were the stuff of immortality. One of the cards I put up bore a quote from the Hindu Upanishads that was almost three thousand years old: "The gods love the obscure and hate the obvious." Whatever that meant, I felt jealous. Imagine making anything that lasts three thousand years! I taped up the work of other immortals, like Ogden Nash.

NASH: A door is what a dog is perpetually on the wrong side of.

And Mark Twain.

TWAIN: When angry, count four; when very angry, swear.

And Cornelia Otis Skinner.

SKINNER: Woman's virtue is man's greatest invention.

Each time I taped up a card, I wondered how that person did it. What was the magic behind words that went viral and stayed viral?

Many years later, I discovered the means: tools that produce brilliant words in striking order or that shift our view of reality. I share them in this book in the hope that there's a Quote Boy or Girl—or even a Word Hero—in you.

PART I

WORD APPRENTICE

You have the motive but not the knowledge.

Take heart: in this section we explore the secrets

of memorability—focusing your thoughts, tapping

into inspiration, gaining an audience's attention,

and making your words stick.

1

PRACTICE WITCRAFT

THE SQUARE ROOT OF RAINBOWS
Formulas for Memorability

My FIRST REAL LESSON in what I call "witcraft" came off a loading dock in Philadelphia. I was sixteen and just starting my first summer job at a department store. My assigned mentor, Al, was a man of the world at least two years my senior. He led me onto a semitrailer and pulled a thousand-dollar dress from a hanging rack.

"Observe."

Al ripped the fabric down the middle, recorded the dress as damaged, and turned significantly to me. "With responsibility," he said, "comes great power."

I had heard the old chestnut about power and responsibility, but it had never occurred to me that a cliché could be corrupted so deliciously. From that day on, I hung on to everything the guy said.

In retrospect, he wasn't all that witty, and his bon mot certainly wasn't worth a designer gown. Needless to say, Al proved to be a dubious moral guide; next day he taught me how to surf the roof of a moving delivery van. But that summer he became my first living Word Hero.

In the years since, I've studied witcraft as an effective way to change people's emotions, their minds, and their willingness to act. I learned how to get people's attention and make a good impression, even better than the one Al made on me. I wrote a book, *Thank You for Arguing,* and went on to coach rhetoric, the art of persuasion, with students, lawyers, corporate execs, and aerospace engineers. I read all the ancient and modern rhetorical wisdom I could find and have employed the advice and help of hundreds of experts.

But Al was the first to teach me the essence of word heroism: with a very little wit comes great power.

THE SHAPE AND FORM OF HEROISM

Since then I've had some terrific mentors. The great Roman orator Marcus Tullius Cicero—lowborn, stubby, turnip-nosed Cicero—stood on words and led the Roman republic. He and other rhetoricians through history, from Joan of Arc to Barack Obama, grasped the secrets of image crafting through witcraft. They set their words in stone, sometimes literally. They were Word Heroes. I'd like to help make you, too, into a Word Hero; maybe not on the order of a Shakespeare or Churchill, but someone who holds a share of immortality.

Word heroism takes very few words—no more than a dozen or so. Few of us remember Franklin Roosevelt's speeches, but many of us remember the memorable, the *characteristic* parts, that made FDR FDR. "The only thing we have to fear is fear itself." ". . . a date which will live in infamy."

To create memorable words yourself, you simply need to discover a set of techniques—forty-three in all—that have been used by masters from Winston Churchill to Jimmy Kimmel.

These tools will help you focus on the few words that count the most in a conversation, argument, important e-mail, blog post, thank-you letter, college paper, or presentation.

This book does far more than merely list the techniques, though. Consider it a course in self-taught heroism, and use it to develop your own unforgettability. From the next chapter on, you will progress through the stages of phrase-making mastery, beginning with Word Apprentice and working up to Word Hero, that rarified state where your witcraft compels people to remember your name. By the time you achieve word heroism, you will have gained:

- Confidence in your ability to write and speak

- Knowledge of what makes a memorable expression memorable

- Prowess in producing the right words in just the right order for maximum effect

- Skill in the techniques used (consciously or instinctively) by the most unforgettable personalities in history and pop culture

You'll project a strong, articulate personality, the kind people like and respect. But we're talking about more than image polishing. We're talking about a *lasting* image, one that lingers after you leave the room—or this mortal coil, for that matter. The right words, arranged perfectly, leave a lasting impression in an audience's brain. And what are the techniques to create this magic? Figures of speech.

Word sounds and rhythms, puns and wordplay qualify as *figures*—the term rhetoricians give words in unusual context or order.

You know the expression "That's just a figure of speech." Personally, I object to the "just." Figures can do for speech what architectural forms do for a cityscape, or the female human form does to your average randy male. A figure in the physical world composes the shape or form of something; look at the Washington Monument on a foggy day and you'll make out the figure of a column. Less monumentally, we traditionally call a woman's shape or form her *figure*. A figure of speech works the same way, usually without the obsession over phallic architecture and weight loss. This rhetorical figure constitutes the shape or form of words in a sentence.

Figures get an audience's attention because they stand out from the rest of language. Take this head-snapping hyperbole from the TV show *Glee*:

SUE: You have enough product in your hair to season a wok.

An unexpected ending to an ordinary line (again, in *Glee*) can get an audience's attention.

KURT: He's cheating off a girl who thinks the square root of four is rainbows.

You can raise eyebrows by ironically agreeing with your interlocutor.

WILL: Who's to say everything I do is one hundred percent on the ball?
SUE: No one would say that.

It's all about delivering the unexpected. The audience unconsciously hyperfocuses on your words and makes its own links to the familiar. The effort makes people more than passive listeners. They become active participants in your words. (If you're witty enough, you hear this participation in the form of laughter.) The links the brain makes between the familiar and the less familiar take place in electrochemical connections called *synapses*. Imagine if you ran into Angelina Jolie on an elevator. Even if you had never met her before, your brain has linked up enough synapses that you would have no trouble recognizing her. *Stranger who doesn't know me*, the brain says, while the synapses fire like crazy: Movies. Dark-haired women. Fat lips. Hollywood beauties. Eighty-seven adopted kids. Brangelina And so on. What got your attention in the first place was the shock of seeing this familiar-looking woman. Your brain did the rest. Memorability comes in part from linking the familiar (Angelina!) with the unfamiliar (Hollywood star in my elevator!). The utterly familiar, on the other hand (same creepy guy you see every day, inspection sticker), gets ignored.

You know how camouflage works, using patterns and colors to fade into the background. Similarly, a good spy looks perfectly ordinary and speaks in perfectly ordinary ways. To rouse someone's awareness, you do the opposite: go for the unusual and unexpected. Later on, you'll see figures that help you sneak up on an audience and give it a rhetorical knock on the head. The more surprising figures mug the audience's expectations, twist grammar or logic, or marry unlike things. You can use them to look witty, tell a memorable story, get a laugh, or change the emotions in the room. But all figures deliver something out of the ordinary. Every good figure is an attention-getting figure.

I selected the best figures for the tools in this book. The easiest and most fun part of rhetoric, figures compose the core of my language blog, Figarospeech.com, where I take on the guise of Figaro (last name "Speech"), a committed, even obsessive, "figurist," or coiner of figures. Figaro explores the tricks and pratfalls of language in politics and the media. Owing to our national ignorance of rhetoric, I tend to find more pratfalls than tricks.

But knowing your figures can turn you from someone of the pratfall variety into a skilled practitioner of the art. With the right tools, you will gain the ability to compose beautiful prose, express irrefutable anger, proclaim your love, get people on your side, or thank them as they have never been thanked.

Figures can do all that. The Greeks believed in them so much that the philosopher Plato actually wanted to ban them. If Plato had had his way, Athens might have had a figure czar just as we have a drug czar. He had a point. Figures in the wrong hands can be powerful forces for evil as well as for good. In fact, your ability to spot their use will let you see through the tricks of marketers and politicians.

In your own hands, well, make sure you act the hero.

A warning: too much of this good thing—this witcraft and clever wording—can become an embarrassment of riches, overwhelming your audience or turning it off. Not even Churchill and MLK came up with a blockbuster in every sentence. Their audiences' heads would have exploded. Use the tools in the book for a few great memorable words, and then build your other, simpler words around them.

WORD IT LIKE WARREN

In fact, born Word Heroes use figures instinctively without sounding overly ornate. Take Warren Buffett. Investors read his annual Berkshire Hathaway chairman's letter as if it came from the oracle of Delphi. They savor his wit while they glean the secrets of the world's savviest investor. OK, they read mostly for the investment secrets; but how many investment letters get quoted for decades afterward? Warren Buffett's do, because he proves himself to be a wizard at figures, the rhetorical as well as the business kind.

For instance, Buffett clearly likes one of my own favorite devices: taking clichés literally. Look at this quote from a panel discussion he did in 2008:

> BUFFETT: I try to buy stock in businesses that are so wonderful that an idiot can run them. Because sooner or later, one will.

See what he did? He took the cliché "an idiot can run it" and imagined it wasn't a cliché at all. Why prefer something that an idiot can run, if an idiot will never run it?

Buffett even instinctively knows the figure that defines terms to get the upper hand in an argument.

> BUFFETT: Price is what you pay. Value is what you get.

The quote reminds me of the late, lamented cartoon "Shoe." In one strip the son asks his journalist dad, "Why are you staring out the window? You should be typing." Dad answers, "Typists type. Writers stare out windows." This device, which chapter 8 covers, lets you redefine an issue in one short expression.

If you really want to achieve immortality, though, talk like Yogi Berra, the immortal logic buster who said, "If you find a fork in the road, take it," and "Nobody goes there anymore. It's too crowded." When you abandon logic to achieve a higher wisdom, you coin a figure called a *Yogism* (chapter 12). Warren Buffett is good at this, too.

> BUFFETT: Occasionally, a man must rise above principles.

You have to love a wit like that—and people do. Easy for Warren to say, right? Well, speaking figuratively does take practice. It also takes a bit of studying. I make the studying part easier with a method for examining memorable words. Called *unwriting*, it works like this: to see how a quote you like varies from plain ordinary speech, write it as you or I would normally say it, without the wit. You'll learn this technique in chapter 3.

To get the general idea of unwriting, grab this Buffett quote:

BUFFETT: Beware of geeks bearing formulas.

Next, put it in plain, unmemorable language:

UNWRITTEN: You should be skeptical of number crunchers and their computer models.

Now ask yourself how Buffett's quote varies from the unwritten version. As he often does, he twisted a cliché—"Beware of Greeks bearing gifts." The old saying probably occurred to him when he was thinking of computer geeks. Hmmm. Beware of geeks . . . Beware of geeks bearing . . . um, formulas! All you have to do to complete the picture is to become an investment wizard and make more money than anybody in the world. Personally, I still find mutual funds a mystery. But you have to start somewhere. Besides, while Word Heroes like Buffett are to the mannerisms born, the rest of us must be made. We have to learn the tools.

NAMING THE TOOLS

In ancient Rome, students learned their figures after they learned grammar, considering them to be the next step in training the sophisticated mind. While schools still teach some grammar, modern education tends to stop at that point. It's as if our education ground to a halt in the sixth grade, as if our society limited mathematics to arithmetic and ignored the calculus and finite math behind our bridges and computers. An education in figurative language actually helps you move beyond grammar. Some people—the kind who see grammar as the equivalent of the laws of Moses—need to get used to some figures. Logic lovers may not like the more fallacious aspects of figures either. But as you shall see, there are good, persuasive reasons to bend the rules.

The same urge that drives some of us to know the rules also makes us want to learn the names for the tools. It certainly helps to know the difference between an adjective and an adverb, and a pronoun's missing antecedent can be difficult to spot when you don't know your antecedent from your elbow. For similar reasons, you will find names for the figurative tools in this book, in the chapters that describe them as well as in an appended glossary. Not only can the terms help you remember the techniques themselves, but they also help prove that I have some serious scholarly backup—that the figures did not spring newborn out of my head.

The problem is, most of the official terms for these techniques happen to come in the form of unpronounceable ancient Greek. Take, for instance, this old joke:

> You said you wanted to play football in the worst way.
> Well, you're playing it in the worst way.

The joke uses a remarkably useful device that repeats words while changing their meaning. The figure has an official name, *antistasis* (an-TIH-sta-sis), but in the text I call it the *repeat changer*. If you once happened to be the kind of curious child who memorized the names of dinosaurs, rest assured that you will find the official name wherever one exists. For those of us who find the tools more important than the names, my informal labels should make the tools easier to remember. After all, it's what the tools *do* that counts.

I believe that most thoughtful people have the stuff of great words within them. The inspiration—wit, even genius—lies buried in our unconscious. For most of us, that fire burns too deep for ready use. We sense something witty or wise approaching the tip of our tongue but never quite getting there. Figures help narrow the gap between inspiration and expression. While they may not put the words in your mouth, they will bring your inspiration closer to your expression—making the gap small enough to let the spark leap across. I've chosen the ones that help you go from inspiration to memorable phrase as easily as possible.

Still, the sheer number of figures here may sound overwhelming at first. There are just so many of them—and I left out a couple hundred others that rhetoricians have defined over the centuries. Besides, how can you whip out a device on demand? Are you supposed to memorize all the tools in this book and sort through them like a computer to find the right one?

No, and let me count the reasons why.

1. **A few tools will take you a long way.** Which ones you use will depend on your personal predilections. I suggest you read this book through and then scan the list in the back for the tools you like the best. Your own life situation will have you sticking to a few purposes. You may give presentations a lot. You may be a storyteller in search of good endings. Or a hospice nurse in search of comforting words. Or a shy person who wants to sound witty at parties. Your situation or predilections will have you reaching into that part of the toolbox that suits you. (Go to this book's website, wordhero.org, for a tool that helps you find your oratorical type.)

2. **When in doubt, cheat**. In the next chapter, I show a method that lets you simply insert words into other people's memorable expressions.

3. **It helps to know what you're talking about**. Half of figurative brilliance consists of brilliant boiling down. In the preface, I quoted Cornelia Otis Skinner's wonderful line.

    SKINNER: Woman's virtue is man's greatest invention.

    A rhetorician will find the quote packed with great devices—a figure of definition (*this* is *this*), a piercing analogy (woman's virtue is like electricity and telephones, only more ingenious), irony (she pretends to admire the invention), and a trope—a kind of nonliteral language—that equates "man" with the male gender. But essentially, the quote's effectiveness comes from a distillation process. Skinner took a complex interpretation of relations between the sexes and reduced it to two words: "greatest invention." Feminine virtue doesn't exist in the natural state; men had to make it up ("invention"). This fiction has been used to keep women in their subservient place, an impressive feat of rhetorical dominance ("greatest"). Cleverness, and some tools you'll find in this book, took the sentence over the top. But the sentence started with some serious boiling down to what I call the *pith*. You'll find that, and more, in the next chapter.

2

FOCUS YOUR THOUGHTS

THE PITH METHOD
Creating the Core of Wit

FIGURES DO MORE than create flashy language. They underlie many, maybe most, creative acts. Words themselves can serve as catalysts for thought. At the core of every great anecdote, punch line, comeback, love letter, thank-you note, e-mail, essay, college paper, proposal, or presentation lies a compact, magnetic set of words that makes everything else fall into place. It's the climax, the payoff, the takeaway. That's what I call the **pith**. Again, it rarely consists of more than a dozen words. Get your pith right, and it bookmarks your thoughts in people's minds. It works whether you plan to speak it aloud, print it out, or send it into the data cloud.

I first learned this principle as a freshman in college, when I wrote two words that helped launch my career as a writer and editor. The phrase itself did not change my life—I can't even remember whether I wrote "seismic copulation" or "fornicational geology"—but the effect it had made all the difference.

I used the phrase to sum up the famous sleeping bag scene in Hemingway's *For Whom the Bell Tolls.* Like many other immature readers, I found the passage both titillating ("He felt her trembling as he kissed her and he held the length of her body tight to him and felt her breasts against the chest through the two khaki shirts . . .") and hilarious ("And then the earth moved"). My paper was mediocre, and I knew it; so I received a double surprise when the instructor gave it an A-plus and circled my seismic phrase in red ink. "Gemlike!" he wrote in the margin.

The prof liked to grade papers during the five-cent-beer hour at a dive called the Alibi, which may have had a lot to do with his generosity. But his comment gave me a flash of insight: *My professor was a phrase man.* For the rest of the semester, I made an effort to write one memorable phrase into every paper, and I ended up with an "A" for the course. Having discovered one of the secrets of gaming the academic system, I diligently crafted key phrases right up through senior year. You could say I was cheating, that I was giving my education short shrift. But four years of concentrated rewriting of phrases and short sentences did more for my eventual career than the courses themselves. After all, every memorable set of words contains a pith.

This chapter will show you how to produce a pith from a jumble of thoughts. We will look at ways to produce memorable lines that help fuel the rest of your thinking. You will see what makes people remember your words, and you'll learn a method that lets you steal the best techniques from others. Then, in the following chapter, we look at the three basic elements that underlie memorable expressions. You'll spot the techniques in a fun or profound quote; by the end of the section, you'll be co-opting those techniques for your own expressions. To put it pithily, you'll go from pithy to peerless, concise to catchy, succinct to striking in just two chapters.

OK. That wasn't pithy.

LET THE PITH SPEAK

Do not mistake pithiness for bumper sticker writing. After all, how many bumper stickers have you read that really say something?

MY OTHER CAR IS A HORSE

IMAGINE WHIRLED PEAS

I ♥ WOLFHOUNDS

EAT BERTHA'S MUSSELS

Actually, as you'll see, some bumper stickers really do have an effect, but only because they use techniques that you'll acquire in the chapters to come. (I'm a big fan of "whirled peas," which uses a pun to misdirect our peace-loving brains.) Most bumper stickers, on the other hand, fail to deliver *any* point other than self-expression. But the fault lies in empty-headedness, not pithiness. You can express a lot in a few words, and those few words can help direct your thinking into greater complexity and originality. Focus on a few words or so, and you focus your thoughts as well. When you prepare to argue with someone, or present a proposal, or give a talk, this kind of focus helps frame your point. Coming up with those few words also makes for a first-class exercise in rewriting, a skill that schools should teach more. You might find pithy writing useful if you're on Twitter— you can even find a site, besttweets.com, devoted to the art of microelegance—but this book isn't about short writing for the sake of short writing either. Nor am I talking about writing, exactly. I'm talking about a way to think.

Pith Method

Our education can get in the way when we prepare to say some-thing important. In our memos, formal e-mails, and the like, many of us put our thoughts down using the method we were taught in school, with a topic sentence at the beginning of each paragraph. The remaining sentences serve to support that first one. This is not a bad way to think. Chances improve for your paragraph having a thought behind it, which ranks it far above most people's. And learning to write this way helps you orga-nize your spoken thoughts as well. But this pyramid approach—putting the important stuff first—rarely creates memorable words. Your best takeaway. the expression people can't get out of their heads, might come at the end as a surprising punch line, or in the middle.

We also learned in school that words invariably are a product of thinking. *Thoughts first, then words.* Our teachers told us to get down whatever was in our heads, and clean it up later. Again, this isn't a bad method; it certainly helps relieve writer's block. But it's not the only method, or even necessarily the best one. When you want to come up with something memorable—not just orig-inal phrasing but an original thought—sometimes you should start with the words. *Words first, then thought.*

That's because there are times when we can only suss out the best of our thoughts—dig them out of our unconscious—by labeling them. If that sounds counterintuitive, well, of course it is. Still, try it sometime with something you have to write, such as an important memo, a "Dear John" letter, or a big paper for a class. Instead of working out your thoughts in your head or scrib-bling them down, start instead with a key line. Write it down and then, before you write any other line, perfect that one. It doesn't have to be the first line. Think of it instead as a tag line for a movie. "Houston, we have a problem." "Sometimes love means never having to say you're sorry." "In space, no one can hear you scream." Then use that line to inform the others.

In fact, a single phrase helped me focus and structure this book. I knew I wanted to take the ancient principles of figures and tropes, updating them for modern life. The problem was, I had no idea how I was going to structure the book itself. Instead of writing an outline, as my schooling taught me to do, I worked first on a title. I scribbled all the terms that might help, and even tried to invent some of my own. Here's what I came up with:

SET YOURSELF IN STONE

WITCRAFT

AWECRAFT

VERB, NOUN, RENOWN

SHORT, SWEET, DURABLE WORDS

None of these titles quite did it for me, though. Only one, *Set Yourself in Stone,* focused on the reader or even on the outcome of reading the book. I wanted something playful, words that might riff off a pop-culture phenomenon. My editor wanted a book that makes the reader feel she's progressing from piker to wizard in one volume. Pretty daunting, from a title-writing standpoint.

Then one day, while visiting in-laws in Cincinnati, my nephew, Clay, invited me to play *Guitar Hero.* He handed me a fake guitar and fired up "Love in an Elevator." I was terrible. But having recently bought a real guitar, I loved the feeling of being actually capable of jamming with the likes of Joe Perry and Steven Tyler. And then it occurred to me: *Word Hero* was the perfect title. It messed with a common expression, which many successful figures do. Plus it had all the qualities I was looking for in a title: playfulness, pop reference, focus on the reader.

What's more, the phrase helped *me* focus. I would write a book that helped people take one step toward immortality. The book wouldn't merely introduce people to the wonders of figures; it would be about making you memorable If I hadn't been thinking about the pith of my book, I doubt that my game with Clay would have led to more than a sense of humiliation (Perry and Tyler shook their heads in disgust on the screen as I mangled their song). And the book would have been very different.

In short, figures do more than fancy up your language. Like Shakespeare's Prospero, they can endow your purposes with words that make them known. A well-turned phrase can inform your thoughts and help you decide what you really want to accomplish.

I'm not just talking about writing, by the way. Figures can also make you sound witty and spontaneous in front of other people. As someone who speaks frequently in front of people, I try to avoid notes and to give the impression that everything I say is extemporaneous. But in actuality, I prepare furiously. During that preparation, I do the opposite of what writing classes teach. Before I write a single thought down, I try to come up with a few great key lines—memorable words that I can build out from. If I come up with a great pith—or two or three in a long talk—then the rest of my presentation simply supports this core. I memorize those words, along with an outline, and convey more spontaneous wit than I actually have. (Chapter 15 gives the details on figurative speech making.)

TRIED AND TRUE CONFESSIONS

You can apply the same method, using the tools in this book, even if you never speak professionally. Whether or not you have focused your thoughts already, you can start by zeroing in on the key words that mean the most for your purposes. To find the pith, simply ask yourself what it's about. By "it" I mean your proposal or argument or description or story—whatever sums up what you're trying to say. Narrow "it" down to three or fewer items.

At an early age, my daughter, Dorothy Jr., showed a scary knack for zeroing in on what it's all about. When she was eleven, I took on a freelance assignment to write a book of home remedies for the Rodale publishing company, which produces health-oriented books (*South Beach Diet*) and magazines (*Men's Health*). To give me a sense of the style they wanted, the editors sent me a box of *Men's Health* back issues. The magazine is notorious for its covers of shirtless, abdominally awesome men, and headlines promising better sex. After perusing the stack of magazines, Dorothy Jr. asked innocently, "Hey, Dad. How come every issue of *Men's Health* is about sex and abs?"

"Because men mistakenly equate the two," I answered, a little embarrassed by the question.

Years later, I went to work for Rodale, supervising a group of sports magazines. The CEO told me to lead each magazine through what he called "true confessions," asking the editors what the contents were really about. People who work at a magazine like *Men's Health* like to think their work is about great storytelling, or empowerment, or fine journalism. "But everybody knows that *Men's Health* is about sex and abs," the CEO said.

"They sure do," I replied, thinking of Dorothy Jr.

To use the tools in this book effectively in any situation, you need to lead yourself through a similar process of "true confessions," boiling the matter down to the solid core. What's it really about? Let me give you a real-world example.

In our little town, we have a problem with what the state euphemistically calls "off highway recreational vehicles," or

OHRVs. They include snowmobiles, all-terrain vehicles, dirt bikes, and any other excuse to burn fossil fuels instead of calories. (Readers of my last book will recognize this issue; snowmobiles reared their ugly engines in our town a few years ago, and we managed to keep them off our roads for a while. Rhetoric is like a long-lasting pesticide. You have to spray again every once in a while. Beware of toxic environmental effects.)

The three members of the "select board," or town council, held a public meeting to decide whether to allow these nasty things on town roads. My wife and I did our homework and came up with some jargon to make it sound as if we knew what we were talking about: "auditory footprint," "premises liability law," and "statute S-1202-R." But those words weren't true-confession words. What was this issue really about—not just to me but to the audience? I scribbled some key words at random.

ENVIRONMENT

NOISE

COST

I crossed out "Environment." The word is beloved of touchy-feely liberal types, which in our town compose only a third of the electorate. To most of the audience, the issue isn't really about the environment.

I circled "Noise." Residents like to talk about this being a quiet town.

Then I circled "Cost" twice. I'm proud to say that besides being a libertarian state, we're also traditionally the most frugal state in the nation. Our town is no exception. Besides, I had a good argument to make: allowing off-highway recreational vehicles on our roads would cause expensive damage while subjecting the town to possible lawsuits. In case anyone challenged me on the lawsuits, I found a list of liability attorneys who specialize in all-terrain vehicles. Before we allowed those things on our roads, the town would need to consult one of those lawyers, at a cost about equivalent to fixing the town's dirt-road rake—an item the select board had cut from the budget.

That left me with:

NOISE

COST

Then I spoke the words aloud in a sentence.

ME: We shouldn't put up with the noise, and we can't afford the cost.

Not perfect, but the process was working:

(a) Ask, What's it all about?

(b) Put those "true confessions" in a sentence.

Next comes (c), Apply a tool to make the words stick. In the Word Wizard section you'll learn about tropes, techniques that allow you to change your audience's perception of reality. One of these tools, which I call the *belonging trope*, takes someone who belongs to a group and makes that person stand for the whole group. While lots of people use ATVs and snowmobiles for legitimate work, I would choose one lazy goofball to represent the whole lot.

ME: A person's fun shouldn't cost the rest of us money.

Whoa, what happened to noise? The snappy line helped me distill it out. Self-editing is a brutal process, heroically throwing away hard work and good thinking for the sake of memorability. Once you put your key words into a sentence, you're not done. Editors often dispense an old piece of advice: "Murder your babies." After you give birth to your lovely thoughts, you must kill some of them. Why murder two of my key words, "noise" and "tradition"? I figured that plenty of people at the meeting would be talking about noise; and as someone who has lived in the town only seven years, I might sound presumptuous talking about traditions.

See what happened? I didn't simply come up with an argument and a catchy way to express it. I gathered my thoughts, tried to distill them in one expression, then used that expression to focus my argument.

Duly armed, I stood up at the meeting, used my jargon words, spoke about expensive legal counsel, and concluded with my sentence about one person's fun costing the rest of us money. The line won't be carved on my gravestone, but it did the job. In fact, one of the officers of a nearby snowmobile club repeated it back to me after the meeting: "I agree that my fun shouldn't cost you money," he said. And since then I've heard townsfolk speak about "the cost of other people's fun." Hardly immortal words, but they worked. For a moment, I almost felt like a hero.

Now You

While you haven't yet tried most of the tools, you can apply the pith method to come up with a pretty good line on your own. Boil down, and boil down some more, until you have two or three key words. Then use those words in a sentence. You're talking sports, say, and two players famous for their sportsmanship on and off the field get into a brief fight. You want to say something memorable to your friends, or at least get a laugh. Time for "true confessions": What is this topic really about, at least from the storytelling standpoint? Think of some key words.

FIGHT

ATHLETES

POLITENESS

What are the words that grab you? "Fight" certainly does. Athletes? Yeah, it's about athletes. Nothing unusual there. "Politeness" doesn't scintillate either, usually; but "politeness" and "fight" make a surprising combination. So let's delete "athletes" and try to use the other two words, or some form of them, in a sentence.

YOU: It was the politest fight of the weekend.

OK, it won't get a laugh, but it's a start. *Sports Illustrated* writer Brant James took the idea of polite fighting a step further in a National Public Radio interview about two gentlemanly NASCAR drivers who got into a tussle after a race. ("Sort of an aggressive hug" is how James described it.) He took the concept of "the politest fight of the weekend" and turned it into an analogy.

JAMES: This was Switzerland and Sweden goin' at it.

The notion of two of the politest, most neutral countries in the world getting into a tussle: in a certain crowd, that would get a laugh. What's impressive is that James seemed to have come up with the line spontaneously. As a professional sportswriter, he has had plenty of practice applying analogies to sports events. What about the rest of us? How can we come up with great stuff like that? Well, practice helps.

——————— *EXERCISE* ———————

One of the most fun exercises is to write a six-word review of your favorite movie. Use the pith method to help you boil down the plot, characters, and setting.

> *Ocean's Eleven*: Clooney robs Vegas. Ten guys help.
> *Toy Story*: Outgrown toys speak witty product lines.
> *Avatar*: An out-of-body planet rescue.

Six-word exercises have grown popular since Smith College's alumni magazine began a contest for best six-word memoirs. Their slogan: "One life. Six words. What's yours?" The magazine runs the challenge to honor Ernest Hemingway, who mastered the extremely short story genre years ago with, "For sale: baby shoes. Never worn." You may surprise yourself with your own wit and possible profundity. To sum it up in six words: half of witcraft is boiling down.

THE TOOLS

The Pith Method. Write down what you want to say, then find the two or three key words that sum up your points. Use these words in a fabulous new sentence. You'll see the pith method throughout the book as we use it to ready your thoughts for tools to come.

3

CAPTURE THE SECRETS

THE MAD LIB PROTOCOL
A Tool for Accessing the Brain's Three Memory Keepers

HAVING LEARNED TO FIND the pith in your thoughts, you have the raw material. Now you want to apply the tools of memorability. To understand how, we will conjure up some neuroscience and Sue Sylvester:

SUE: You think this is hard? I'm passing a gallstone as we speak. *That* is hard.

If you own a television, have spent more than ten minutes with a nerdy teenager, or like musicals, you probably know that Sue Sylvester is the genially vicious villain on the TV series *Glee*. In which case, you also know that a significant demographic comprising epidermically challenged self-described "Gleeks" love to memorize lines from the show.

Without the memorable lines, frankly, the show would hardly be all that memorable—a few hotties lip-syncing Top Forties, for the most part. For future Word Heroes, though, the script is solid gold. Its best lines neatly illustrate well-established scientific principles—not to mention ancient rhetoric, which intuited the stuff of memorability before the first electrode got taped to a scalp. So let us look at what makes a line irresistibly memorable and use that knowledge for our own immortal purposes. In this chapter we'll look at the three building blocks of "stickiness," the ability to make your words memorable. And we'll use a technique that imitates the Mad Libs game to copy the techniques behind your favorite quotes. If I do my job right, you'll find yourself seeing self-expression in a whole new light.

People's memory tends to work alike, mechanically, whether the brain belongs to a middle-aged guy who writes for a living or to a self-conscious adolescent Gleek who fantasizes taking a Spanish class with the adorable Mr. Schu. In either case, three kinds of recording mechanisms hold words in the memory. Collectively, I call them the SPA: **sounds, pictures, and associations**. Just about all figures and tropes employ one or more of these memory keepers. You'll find some overlap among all three. Tools that create sounds may also create pictures; the picture tools often have associative qualities; puns employ both sounds and associations; and a trope like metaphor may have entire SPAs dancing in your head. Still, the organization closely follows the current theory of cognitive neuroscience. People file memories under these three elements.

SOUNDS: TAP-DANCING HORSES

The *sounds* memory keeper converts names, phone numbers, and other abstractions into mental audio tracks and plays them over as a kind of sound loop. Music makes a great mnemonic for this reason. You probably learned the alphabet along with your little classmates by singing "elemenopee" as two notes. Commercial jingles take advantage of the brain's sound recording apparatus by setting words to tunes. Readers of a certain age can sing along to "Double your pleasure, double your fun with double good, double good, Doublemint gum!" (In fact, if you're of a certain age, you probably hate me right now because you will be singing that stupid jingle in your head for the rest of the day.)

Rhetoric uses more hip-hop than jingle, marshalling repetition, wordplay, and what the poet Robert Frost called the "sound of sense" to lay down its memory track in people's brains. Take this line from *Glee*:

> JESSE: You guys need to stop being such asses and start being badasses.

Jesse sets up some nice hip-hop syncopation here. YOU guys NEED to STOP BEING ASSES. Pause. And START BE-ing BAD-asses. The repetition of "asses," with the surprising change in meaning second time around, helps make the line memorable. And rather funny.

The very sounds of words can make a passage unforgettable. One of my indelible memories of high school is a junior-year English class during which our teacher recited a poem by Lord Byron. Normally, Mrs. Appleton spoke in a high, soft voice; but when she quoted from memory it seemed as if Byron's demon had taken over her body. "ROLL ONNNN, DEEP AND DARK BLUE OCEAN, ROLLLL ONNNNNNNNN." The teacher had intended the recital to demonstrate onomatopoeia, I think. But it literally made me sit up and take notice, and not just because this birdlike woman suddenly channeled a famously randy poet. Like Mrs. Appleton, you can use sound effects—popping consonants, lugubriously drawn-out vowels, the exploding onomatopoeia—to get your audience to pay attention.

ARTIE: I sound like someone put tap shoes on a horse and shot it.

While this *Glee* line makes little logical sense, look at the two critical words, "tap" and "shot." Both of them qualify as onomatopoeias, words that mimic the sounds they describe.

Besides the mimicry, the sentence also plays with the length of words: "Put tap shoes on a horse and shot it." What do those words have in common? They all contain just one syllable. That second half of the sentence has a taplike sound to it. Monosyllables make for great punch lines, because the choppy effect puts the stress on every word, increasing the audience's focus on them.

Now listen to the sound stylings of Sue Sylvester:

SUE: Some people like to film themselves getting physical with their partner. I happen to enjoy revisiting the impeccable form of my Jazzercise routines.

Is that the language of someone you love to hate, or what? The brilliant insertion of "impeccable" makes the line especially maddening. You will find few more impeccable-sounding words than "impeccable." Say it aloud: "impeccable." The word has a punlike quality, as if it means "not susceptible to pecking" instead of "flawless."

Imagine if Sue had used "flawless" instead.

UNWRITTEN: I happen to enjoy revisiting the flawless form of my Jazzercise routines.

While alliteration may make things marvelously memorable, in this case, "flawless" is flawed. Why? Because it contains a "flaw." That's where sound contributes to, and takes away from, the sense of a sentence. You want to be impeccable? Then avoid the flawless—avoid the sound or meaning you deny.

Use the sounds memory keeper to enhance your storytelling, offering a soundtrack to make scenes come alive. Sounds also work to change people's mood, through humorous noises or lugubrious lamentation. And you can even use sounds to link things that don't naturally go together. They don't seem alike until you make them sound alike. Finally, sounds help you label people, things, or ideas. The ways words play in the ear can let you shrink or grow almost anything. You can make something seem important or unimportant, calming or alarming—all with the sound of your voice.

Or you will be able to, soon. The chapters to come cover a variety of sound tools, from the whizz-bang onomatopoeia to the word-mashing portmanteau. In fact, the next three sections after this chapter take you through all the memory keepers and the tools to go with them. First, though, let's look at *pictures*.

PICTURES: SPRAYING CATS AND SMELL-O-VISION

The second memory keeper renders thoughts visually, as if storing memories on tall shelves in an unconscious warehouse. The Greeks could memorize vast amounts of information by deliberately "putting" concepts into mental rooms. World-champion memorizers use this method today. Instead of remembering facts and numbers, they simply reserve imaginary rooms for them and then mentally walk around and pick them up. Words that create pictures for your audience do much the same thing, providing a setting for thoughts and emotions. Observe Santana, one of the evil cheerleaders, gossiping about a fellow Glee Club member.

SANTANA: She's like a cat in heat. She talked about him yesterday and practically sprayed the choir room.

UNWRITTEN: She is so horny. She could barely contain herself when she was talking about him yesterday.

Talk about catty. It's cruel enough to talk smack about another girl, but to describe her so vividly will earn Santana at least another eon in purgatory. If you're going to be evil, *that's* the way to be evil. The unwritten version would just engender an eye roll of agreement from her listeners. The *Glee* version gets quoted by middle-school students across the land. Why? Because of Santana's masterful use of imagery here. Not stopping at comparing her colleague to a hormonal cat, she puts a little video clip in her listeners' heads of girl-as-cat spraying the choir room.

I call this technique *special effects*—details that employ a variety of senses to make life appear before your very eyes, the way computer graphics work magic in movies. (Rhetoricians call the phenomenon *enargia*, but I like my term better, and find it far easier to pronounce.) Special effects can implant a vision in people's brains even more indelible than a scene in a video game. That's because rhetorical special effects make people form the image themselves. It's second only to experiencing the scene in life—an impossibility in this case, thank goodness.

Sue Sylvester, a master of special effects, loves to use the perfect hair of her nemesis, Will, to create unflattering pictures.

SUE: I don't trust a man with curly hair. I can't help but picture little birds laying sulfurous eggs in there, and it disgusts me.

Image making at its best, in the form of an analogy. (Both of my kids recited that line to me at separate times.) From the moment she said it, Will's hair was spoiled. Those birds will be laying their rotten eggs amid those curly locks for years to come.

Special effects can also cover other senses, such as smell.

SUE: I thought I smelled cookies from the tears of elves weeping that live in your hair.

Here you have a combination of senses, including sound. Sue loves to use the word "weeping" when she refers to other people crying. (Sue herself doesn't cry; she had her tear ducts removed because, she said, she "wasn't using 'em.") Why choose "weeping" over "crying"? Because "weeping" sounds wimpy and weak; the word makes the victim seem like a wuss.

Having implanted the soundtrack, Sue turns on the figurative Smell-O-Vision with the baking cookies. The fact that the line doesn't make any sense only shows that its memorability comes from one direction: the senses. This is purely right-brained stuff. And the brain's right hemisphere—the side less interested in logic—happens to be where the most important memory keepers reside.

ASSOCIATIONS: BOWELS AND CONSONANTS

While sounds and pictures can convey just the sensual effects you want—effects that extend far beyond the meaning of the words themselves—they can also create links with other parts of the brain. Which leads us to the third memory keeper. *Associations* put thoughts in the context of previous experiences, or they link one concept with another.

Look what happens when *Glee* characters employ puns, intentionally or otherwise.

BRITTANY: When I pulled my hamstring, I went to a misogynist.

Brittany happens to be the most delightfully stupid *Glee* character, and I'm grateful to her for teaching vocabulary words to young people (assuming someone's around to explain "misogynist" to the lexigraphically clueless). The malapropism comprises a kind of unintended pun, and puns make for a great associational device. Brittany's addlebrained talk could turn any massage therapist into a blonde hater, making her statement quite accurate.

Glee's Puck, on the other hand, puns on purpose.

PUCK: Dude, my bowels have better moves than you.

Ah, the pure pun. It does what the ancient Roman rhetorician Cicero said rhetoric itself does, delighting, moving, and instructing the audience. Puck's line certainly handles the moving part. His pun connects bad dancing with fecal matter in a way that records in the audience's memory far more effectively than a more direct line.

UNWRITTEN: Dude, you dance like crap.

Only one subject enhances memorability better than scat, and that's sex.

WILL: Hold on a second, Sue.
SUE: I resent being told to hold on to anything.

After that episode ran, kids across the nation could not wait to try Sue Sylvester's line on each other. For better or worse, this kind of pun teaches children the ancient art of the sexual innuendo. You'll find the identical device in the first *Wayne's World* movie.

GARTH: I'm gettin' tired of holding this.
WAYNE: That's what she said.

In each case, the sound of the word attaches itself to a different meaning, making the line dirty, funny—and memorable.

Associations also work when you compare things side by side, such as in an analogy. Managing the American economy is like driving a car with no windshield, and with a speedometer that only tells you how fast you're going every three months. That's an analogy. You can also make memorable associations simply by weighing one thing against another and noting the differences. There's an old expression that Republicans love people and hate humanity, while Democrats love humanity and hate people. Many comparisons, like this one, point out differences while still making links. Republicans and Democrats are both flawed political types.

An even more powerful kind of association, the trope, creates a mental alternative reality. You're already familiar with metaphor, the best-known trope. If you call the earth a marble, your audience receives the mental picture of a marble against the dark background of space. Besides triggering the picture memory keeper, though, the metaphorical marble creates an association in people's brains: Earth equals marble.

Another kind of trope associates the members of a group with the whole group. Most Norman Rockwell paintings use this trope: the kindly doctor, the young brave soldier, the teenage couple at the classic soda fountain. These pictures make you associate the groups with their representative characters: the medical profession equals kindly doctor, the military equals young brave soldier, and so on.

Any kind of nonliteral language or symbol constitutes a trope. We'll get to more tropes later. Meanwhile, remember this: if it isn't literally true, and still isn't a lie, it's probably a trope. Why should you care? Because while tropes constitute fancy rhetoric, they often don't look fancy. Few people recognize politicians' use of "Main Street" as a trope—a tricky way of making us think we all live in small-town America. That's not literally true, and it's not actually a lie; but it's pretty darn misleading. Typical of your slick, sound-bitten, hair-done politico. (Yes, that's a trope, too.)

And there we have it. All figurative language falls under one of those three categories: sounds, pictures and associations. When you want to speak memorably, visit the SPA. This next part shows you how.

NOW START UNWRITING

To find the SPA in a great line, you can employ **unwriting** as a rhetorical magnifying glass. You met it in the first chapter, and you'll see it throughout the book. The technique works whether you want to suss out the eloquence in a piece of writing or spot a public speaker's rhetorical trick. I first thought of unwriting years ago, when my wife and I were homeschooling our children in New Mexico. George had a plug-and-play sixth-grade correspondence curriculum. As a ninth grader, on the other hand, Dorothy Jr. was too advanced for remote schooling. So it fell to me to teach her literature. At one point, we studied short stories. I had her read a variety of authors and choose the one she liked best. She surprised me with Edgar Allan Poe—not the cheeriest of authors, and I didn't expect Dorothy to appreciate his Victorian prose. Nonetheless, we read a collection of the man's stories, and she surprised me further by choosing "The Cask of Amontillado," a grim tale of murder by brick wall, as her favorite.

"OK," I said. "Now read the story over two or three more times. Then type it."

"You mean, just copy it by typing?"

"Right. Pretend you're Poe while you do it. Only of course you'll use a computer instead of a pen; might as well practice your typing while you're at it. And unlike Poe, you'll be sober."

The following day, I had her type the story all over again, without looking at it.

"From memory?"

"From memory. Now you can really pretend you're Poe."

"You're going to drive me to drink," she said. But she seemed jazzed at the thought of channeling a famous writer; and as an astonishingly accurate reciter of song lyrics, she was likely to come pretty close to the original.

The next day, we printed out both versions: the one she had copied while looking, and the one she had done from memory. Then we examined the ways they differed. Why had Poe done those passages his way? In some cases, we actually liked Dorothy Jr.'s version better. She wrote in a style more suitable for her day. But in other cases, we found marvelous figures of speech that took a little time to absorb. Dorothy still remembers that exercise as the highlight of my literary tutoring.

Since then I've occasionally done a simpler version of that exercise myself. I'll download podcasts like the storytelling series "The Moth," write down the memorable expressions, and look at the difference. Let's see how you can use the method on your own.

DISSECTING THE LITTLE OLD LADY

Unwriting

You come across a great quote and want to know how it works, so you can steal the technique and produce a great quote of your own. As an experiment, we'll take an actual quote that has proven its memorability over the years; that is, people have clearly remembered it because it continues to get quoted

HAROLD ROSS: *The New Yorker* will be the magazine which is not edited for the old lady from Dubuque.

Having gotten past the sexism, ageism, and annoying New York snobbery behind this quote by the magazine's founder—and when you finish picturing the sizable number of female over-sixty subscribers living in Dubuque today—you begin the first step of unwriting: **translate.** What does the passage mean? Well, Dubuque is in Iowa, a rural state allegedly filled with country folk in 1925, when the passage was written. So Ross doesn't intend for *The New Yorker* to appeal to rubes—to unsophisticated rural types.

Now **write your translation in the simplest possible terms.**

TRANSLATION: *The New Yorker* will be edited only for sophisticated readers.

Good. Next, **compare your translation with the original.** We can see two differences. First, Ross's version states the negative: the magazine will *not* be edited for the old lady. But that just leads to the second difference: the old lady herself. Ross put the sentence in the negative so that he could have the magazine reject her.

Clearly, that poor senior lies at the heart of whatever technique Ross is using. Is he referring to a specific old lady—an aunt who always sent him scratchy knitted pullovers for Christmas when he was a child? Presumably not. So we **zero in on the key difference**: the category of humanity represented by old ladies, expressed in terms of a single hapless woman.

That's unwriting.

1. Translate the quote. What does it mean?

2. Put that meaning into the simplest terms.

3. Compare your simplified translation with the original.

4. Zero in on the key difference.

Now you're ready to spot the technique hidden in that key. Remember that memorability comes in three varieties: sounds, pictures, or associations. So, having zeroed in on the old lady, we need to ask ourselves where her memorability lies.

Does the **sound** of the words make the quote memorable? Is the old lady a play on words, forming a new word or a pun of some sort?

Do the words draw a memorable **picture**—create a vision in the audience's head?

Does the old lady link one thing to another in an **association**? Does she weigh things side by side? Are the words literally true, or do they seem ridiculous if you take them at face value? In other words, does she associate with a different reality?

Hmmm. "Old lady from Dubuque" does sort of trip off the tongue, but the sound of her doesn't really make the quote memorable. I don't see a hit song being written about her until she moves to Pasadena. No wordplay there, either.

What about forming a picture? She does, doesn't she? If you squint, you can see her rocking away on her farmhouse porch, glaring at a *New Yorker* cartoon and muttering, "That doesn't seem so funny." But she isn't entirely literal, either. Harold Ross presumably wasn't banning the editorial from a specific old lady, Mrs. Bona Fyed of 108 Podunk Road, Dubuque, Iowa.

So we have two possible secrets to that old lady: she both forms a picture and makes a nonliteral association. No worries. The choice is not some critical dilemma. We're not taking an exam, here; we're discovering the secret to the quote's memorability. If you see more than one source of memorability, just pick one and explore. When you're done, you can always go back and look at the other.

Since the old lady seems slightly more of an association with the nonliteral than a picture, we'll choose the nonliteral path for now. But exactly what kind of trick are we talking about? Non-literal language almost always means tropes—special language that shifts reality. A metaphor is a trope, for example, because it claims that one thing is another thing.

Example: This fragile blue marble, the Earth.

The old lady from Dubuque doesn't work this way. If you called the earth "the old lady from Dubuque"—*that* would be a metaphor. But *The New Yorker*'s use of the old lady entails a different kind of nonliteral language, which I call the belonging trope. (I mentioned it in the first chapter; you'll see much more of this kind of trope in chapter 11.) The old lady belongs to a group of people: unsophisticated readers. Instead of saying, "*The New Yorker* won't be edited for unsophisticated readers," Ross takes one character and makes it represent the group.

Now you have a way to find the SPA in a great sentence. Take a quote you love, unwrite it, and compare the two to find a sound, picture, or association. In this case, after unwriting the Ross quote, we isolated a nonliteral link between unsophisticated readers and a representative, fictional Iowan.

Now you. Go to Bartlett's.com or find the actual hardcover John Bartlett's *Familiar Quotations* in the library. You could use any other book of quotations, but Bartlett's works best in this exercise because the paper version arranges quotes by author in chronological order. Flip through it and you'll see how the styles change from one century to the next. And yet, reassuringly, the SPA remains the same throughout. Most of the quotes rely for their memorability on sounds, pictures, or associations. Take half a dozen gems from half a dozen eras, and unwrite them. You should start to see the essence of witcraft.

Having done the drilling down, we need to ask what we'll do with this little nugget of information. A professional wordsmith would instantly know what to do: steal it. Use the technique as your own. You can even steal most of the words themselves. The theft—perfectly legal, with no real old ladies harmed in the process—constitutes a kind of Mad Lib.

MAD LIBERATION

Have you ever played Mad Libs? That's the game where the players supply parts of speech—noun, adjective, whatever—while one person writes them into blanks in a little story. (There's now an official Mad Libs app for the iPhone.) Teachers find the game one of the best ways to teach parts of speech. Kids find Mad Libs hilarious; flashbacking stoners from the sixties, for their part, may find them strangely profound.

To steal a quote's technique, unwrite it. Before you begin Mad Libbing, it helps to get a sense of what makes the words so great; and you'll get insights into the occasions that suit the technique. By unwriting the Ross quote, we discovered that it would work well whenever we wanted to exclude a class of people. Unwriting also helps us discover the key words essential to any Mad Lib. Having found the key words, just write the parts of speech they represent. There's your Mad Lib.

MAD-LIBBED HAROLD ROSS: [Noun] will not be [verb]ed for the [generalized person].

Mad Lib Protocol

A politician could use the Mad Libbed Ross, stealing the technique in order to stand against corruption.

POLITICIAN: My office will not be run for the Armani-suited lobbyist on K Street.

A bride-to-be could use the same Mad Lib to argue against her father's suggestion for a tribute band at her reception.

DAUGHTER: My reception will not be for the mullet-haired Aerosmith fan.

You get the picture. Or the trope, I mean. Stealing the techniques of others will seem easier after you have progressed all the way to Word Hero. In the meantime, though, the **Mad Lib protocol** can help you practice the tools as you learn them. So let's see if we can unwrite and Mad Lib our way through one of the great lines that inspired me in the preface.

OGDEN NASH: A door is what a dog is perpetually on the wrong side of.

It's hard to make a complete theft of a superb line like that. The ending preposition ("on the wrong side of") makes it sound quirky and fun, and that might be hard to reproduce. But let's see whether there's any way we can hijack the expression. Start by unwriting it, translating it into the plainest, most obvious language. What, exactly, did Ogden Nash mean?

UNWRITTEN: A typical dog can never decide whether to be inside or out.

You could come up with other interpretations, but I think this is what Nash meant. When a dog is inside, it wants to be out, and vice versa. Now compare the two versions, and zero in on the key difference. Well, the difference is obvious: the subject of Nash's sentence is the door, while in the unwritten version it's the dog. This helps us spot the technique. Instead of telling us that dogs are never satisfied with the side of door they are on, Nash *gives the definition of a door*. He uses a definition for humor. (See chapter 8 if you can't wait to learn more about using definitions rhetorically.)

Great. We know the key element, we spotted the technique, now all we have to do is Mad Lib it.

MAD LIB: A [noun] is what a [noun] is perpetually on the wrong side of.

You could use it to make a statement about your spouse.

YOU: Politics is what my husband is perpetually on the wrong side of.

Not brilliant, but not bad, either. When you get used to Mad Libbing quotations, you can play with the technique without literally transcribing the words. Look at the Mad Lib version of Nash's quote, and you can see that it has to do with a noun's relationship to another noun. That relationship comes in the form of a definition. So whenever you want to describe a relationship in a witty way, try turning it into a definition. Start with the plain vanilla version.

UNWRITTEN: My wife can't keep herself from yelling at the computer.

Now put it in the form of a definition.

YOU: A computer is what my wife yells at.

Or make it more general.

YOU: A computer is a device for making my wife lose her temper.

Among the quotes you've come across, have you seen one that you might want to steal? Don't worry, it's not plagiarism if you do it right, adding wit of your own. If you ever take it public, you can assuage your conscience by noting that you are paraphrasing the original author. But chances are pretty good that that author stole the technique from someone else. Like Newton, we all stand on the shoulders of giants. (Unlike Newton, we writers also pick their pockets.) Now that your conscience is clear, Mad Lib the best quote. You should already have an idea of what the key words are. Substitute your own relevant parts of speech. Were you brilliant? If that didn't work, take another expression; if necessary, unwrite it first. Now go get all witty on someone you love. Try unwriting every memorable quote you come across, and then Mad Lib it to suit your own memorable purposes. I've found this to be the best way to learn the tools that make your words, and you, stand out from the crowd. To make you, in short, a hero.

THE TOOLS

You know that Chinese saying, "Give a man a fish, and you'll feed him for a day; teach a man to fish and you'll feed him for a lifetime"? This book gives you both the fish and the fishing. The forty-three tools should give you a big figurative leg up on witcraft. But behind them all are a couple of metatechniques that let you take great quotes and transform them into your own memorable words.

Unwriting. Take a quotation you love, and rewrite it in the plainest possible language. Then compare this simple version with the original. What's the key difference that makes the quote work so well? If you look carefully, you should see the SPA within most memorable expressions: a sound, a picture, or an association. While sounds and pictures are relatively easy, associations take some practice. Often you'll find a trope—nonliteral language that associates the subject with an alternative reality.

Mad Lib Protocol. Take the key words in a favorite quote and "blank" them out with the relevant parts of speech: [noun] for *The New Yorker*, [verb] for *edited*. Now see if you can fill in blanks with relevant words of your own. Not all quotes lend themselves to this exercise. For instance, how could you possibly Mad Lib this great W. C. Fields line?

FIELDS: Water? Never touch the stuff. Fish fornicate in it.

Still, you'd have fun trying. "Tequila? Never touch the stuff. Worms fornicate in it."

PART II

WORD NOVICE

Having learned the basics of making words

stick and ferreting out the goodness in other

people's expressions, you're ready for some of

the specific tools. You'll start with sounds,

play with words, and even invent some of your own.

4

LAYER THE SOUND EFFECTS

THINGS THAT GO DOINK IN THE NIGHT
Crashing Symbols and Rapid Repeaters

Long before there were words, there were charades. Instead of words, people used sounds and gestures to convey threats, warnings, requests, and the like. Of course they still do, in activities like sex and international diplomacy. Meanwhile, those early attempts at communication morphed into words that imitate the sounds and gestures.

Listen to the words we use to describe something horrible and scary; to pronounce many of them, we have to gape as if we were horrified and scared ourselves. Say these words aloud, and try to overact a bit. (You may find this especially amusing if you happen to be reading this on a public conveyance.)

HORRIBLE!

SCARY!

TERRIBLE!

AWFUL!

VAMPIRE!

OHMYGAWD!

The sounds of words go a long way to convey their emotion and purpose. If you want to take all the color out of your language, make sure that the words fail to provide any sound effects. On the other hand, if you tell a story and want people to feel as if they're living it—experiencing it right before their very ears—then this chapter should help. After hearing a few useful sounds, we'll bring in the barking, exploding **onomatopoeia.** The word soundscape naturally leads to some useful devices like **alliteration**—repeating the first letter of words for rhetorical effect. Finally, we'll visit the people who coin those words for a living, turning hard-to-spell, made-up terms into multibillion-dollar corporate brands. Among the many ways I love rhetoric, this is one of the best: while poetry exists for its own sake—beauty, art, grants, tenure—rhetoric gets out there and makes itself a good living by manipulating people and stimulating our marketing-driven economy. A beautiful thing. So let's begin at the rhetorical beginning, with grunts and groans and rings and things.

Whether you're writing or speaking aloud, the sounds of your words will subtly affect your audience's attitude. The position of your jaw, lips, and tongue makes things seem large or little, dainty or gross. Sounds signify certain attitudes or moods. Linguists sibilantly refer to this mash-up of sound and sense as **sound symbolism**. In the TV show *The West Wing*, characters talked about how frumpy the word "frumpy" sounded. That's sound symbolism. "Cute," on the other hand, sounds kind of cute, doesn't it? And while "crisp" doesn't exactly imitate the sound of crispness, it makes a very crisp sound. Unlike "soggy," which sounds awfully damp. Or "damp," which seems moist. Or "moist" . . .

John Madden's "Boom!" didn't just provide color to his

football color commentary; it summed up the former lineman's whole philosophy of life and established his public character as the representative football fan. Football, after all, isn't about "biff" or "paff" or even "smack." ("Smack" could trigger an offensive foul.)

Sound Symbolism

So let's examine more frumpy, crispy, yawning sound symbols. Certain combinations of letters evoke moods or attitudes. To convey the large and gross, for instance, use words that open the audience's barbaric yawp (that's what Walt Whitman called his gargantuan, America-sized mouth). If you want to make something sound itty-bitty, on the other hand, use the "ih" sound. While giant slobs suck and chug their flagons of beer, fit Betties sip and fiddle their demitasses. Hear the difference? Petite words make the jaw open just a little if at all. A little robot could be a *robit*.

Suppose you want to make someone sound little.

YOU: He's the petty type.

UNWRITTEN: He's the kind who focuses on the small stuff.

"Small" isn't a small word; it opens your mouth too wide for Mini-Me'ing. Neither is "focus" too small. But "petty" is neatly petite, and "type" makes the lips do some prissy pursing. A petty type shrinks littler than small.

Now let's try to make the words sound like the opposite of what you're saying. We'll start with a couple nonsense lines. Imagine yourself in another room, unable to understand the actual words your neighbors are speaking. You hear only the sound of sense—the shape of the words bereft of their meaning.

Eeh, ist met isp ritty did.
Oy, ab reed oms ahls noll.

Read those lines aloud. (If you actually are on a public conveyance, this will practically ensure an empty seat next to you.)
Those lines refer to the same sort of creature—one little, one
large. Judging from the sound alone, which refers to the little
animal: the first or the second line?

Now imagine that you enter the room and ask the couple to
repeat their lines.

Eeh, ist met isp ritty did turns out to be:

Gee, this mutt is pretty big.

Oy, ab reed oms ahls noll becomes:

Boy, that breed comes awfully small.

In general, you talk expansively when you employ vowels that
open and widen the maw. To restrict the scope of what you're de-
picting, use teeth-gritting, tight syllables.

Itty-bitty vowel sounds: *ih, eh, ee, uh*
Large vowel sounds: *oh, ah, eye, ow*

Itty-bitty consonants: *b, d, t, p, d, k*
Large consonants: *f, hard g* (as in "gargantuan"), *l, m*

A good poet knows how to use word sounds like wind instruments to convey a tone. Look at this famous line from Carl Sandburg's poem "Fog."

SANDBURG: The fog comes on little cat feet.

"Fog" is big and expansive, right? Even "comes" has a foggy feel to it. "Little," "cat," and "feet" make tiny, pitty-pat sounds. What a great way to convey the sneaky side of the damp. Talk about the sounds of silence.

You see the advantages of pursing your lips versus opening them wide. When you want to describe a person, use words that match the description. Take an aggressive, talkative guy and capture that big mouth of his.

UNWRITTEN: He always talks too much.
YOU: He's always flapping that large jaw.

But suppose he doesn't have a large jaw and inclines more toward jibber-jabber?

YOU: He likes to flap that yapper.

The "p" sound makes his mouth seem more rapid-fire than ponderous, while the "ah" sound still keeps that loud pie-hole opening wide. Sound symbolism works whenever you want to mix words together and make them seem real. If you want to write a true-to-life poem about a tree, don't write like Joyce Kilmer.

KILMER: I think that I shall never see/A poem lovely as a tree.

Yes, that silly little couplet did somehow win Kilmer immortality. But not every effort deserves fame. (How else do you explain Carrot Top?) If you want to describe a tree, make like a tree and rustle your leaves.

YOU: The tree sighs its wish to the breeze.

Sounds have a lot to do with the audience's emotional response to a description. When our kids were young, the family climbed Mount Isolation, a peak in the White Mountains of New Hampshire. We hiked the long approach to the mountain through boggy land after several days of rain. The flat valley was a sea of mud, making for a long slog. I had to search for eight-year-old George's sneaker after he lost it in the goop. At the end of the day, when we were warming our feet with the car heater, George's older sister, Dorothy, gave the peak a name we still use today: Mount Suck. She wasn't referring to the quality of the hike; it was the sucking sound our feet made that inspired the name. Well, yes, and the quality of the hike also. She had pulled off a nice feat of sound symbolism, using sound effects to emphasize a descriptive name.

Now, what if Dorothy Jr. had renamed Isolation "Mount Schlup"? Then she would be employing that pure sound effect, the **onomatopoeia**—or, as I like to call it, the "ono."

WORDS THAT GO SPLAT

Onomatopoeia

The Greeks came up with the unspellable figure, which means "made-up name." The ono is an echo, imitating a sound or action. Kids are really good at this, aren't they? And those under age three adore hearing them. Where would Old MacDonald's farm be without his talkative animalia? (When I was little, the song made me uneasy; I assumed that "ee yi ee yi oh" was the sound the farmer himself made when his obviously rowdy livestock attacked him.)

Before Dorothy Jr. turned two, she and I liked to annoy my wife with this ono-logue.

ME: What does a cat say?
DOROTHY JR.: Meow.
ME: What does a dog say?
DOROTHY JR.: Arf arf arf.
ME: What does a duck say?
DOROTHY JR.: Quack quack quack.
ME: What does a mama say?
DOROTHY JR.: Not! Not! Not!

My wife, being a good sport, laughed the first couple hundred times we did it. But the ono makes for more than cute children; it's a great way of bringing life to your storytelling. Things do not go "oops" in the night; they go bump. Remember the special effects I talked about in the SPA chapter? A master storyteller uses onos to make an audience feel the action, whether they're hearing the word sounds or reading them. The teenage narrator in David Mitchell's novel *Black Swan Green* makes you listen to his story even when you're reading it. Iron gates don't simply close; they *clang* shut. A teacher's chalk *slaps and slides* across the blackboard. Young lovers' teeth *clunk* when they kiss. The lid of a tin container *guffs* when it opens. A massive fart *flubberdubbers*.

There's no reason why you can't include sound effects in your own stories. When telling an anecdote about a drunk, you should never let his head merely make contact with an obstacle—not in the story, at least. Instead, he must *donk* his head; or, if the drunk happens to be a rather cartoonlike sort, *doink* it. Leaving onos out of a funny tale is like making a movie action scene without the soundtrack. Not that onos work only with humor. A clanging gate isn't necessarily a funny one. An ono can lend drama, or turn up the volume. Compare these two sentences:

1. He hit his head on the beam.

2. He cracked his head on the beam.

"Cracked" makes the injury sound more serious. But it's the sound that makes the word more immediate. The sound of "hit" is whispery, a glancing blow. "Crack" is more sudden, violent, and, well, striking. CRACK! Man, you *feel* that.

In short, employ an ono in a story or anecdote when you want the reader to experience the action. "Show, don't tell": that's the command every journalism student learns. It means, don't merely state an account. Let the life spring out right in front of your audience. Don't just *tell* that a sound occurred. *Show* the sound—make them hear it inside their heads.

But don't pass up the opportunity to use the ono for humor or exaggeration—or humorous exaggeration. Not all onos even have to represent realistic sounds, any more than the slapsticking Three Stooges realistically represented American malehood. In fact, onos often imitate imitations—they recall the unrealistic sound effects from TV and cartoons. Throughout most of my childhood, I almost never used the verb "to snore." Instead, I said a sleeping man was "hawshooing," in loving reference to the hilariously fake nocturnal sounds of Stooges Larry and Moe. Similarly, the word "bling," coined by rap artists to denote diamond jewelry and tooth inserts, comes from cartoon land. It's a sound effect that accompanies the fake lens flare from something shiny. In other words, "bling" refers to diamonds by mimicking a sound that evokes the glare of a shiny object originally depicted in comic books. And it made perfect sense from the start. The first person to use the term as a noun (the hip-hop community disputes its origins) deserves a niche in the Neologism Hall of Fame. As does the first person—undoubtedly another comic book fan—who first thought of intercourse as "bonking."

When you want to lend a cartoonish feel to your language, the fake sound effects of comic books offer some whiz-bang possibilities. While most girls eventually outgrow this kind of nonsense, the majority of boys never lose their fondness for the special effects of comics. (Which, admittedly, says something about the state of the American male.) The immortal Budweiser frogs appealed directly to this manboy psychographic—I mean the beer drinker. The frogs separated "Budweiser" into individual syllables, each one pronounced on a separate lily pad. The scene just begged guys to imitate each croak. After the ad premiered in the 1995 Super Bowl, men were walking into supermarkets with the brand on the tip of their frog-inspired tongues. Brilliant. One of the best ways to imprint your words in people's brains is to get them to repeat the words themselves. The Holy Grail of advertising is the kind of viral moment when audiences repeat the name of your brand with affection and an appreciative belch.

If you're still skeptical about the ono's remunerative power, consider this: Marvel Comics, home of the Incredible Hulk and the X-Men, has actually trademarked a pair of onomatopoeias. *Thwip!* is the sound that Spider-Man's web shooter makes; and when Wolverine opens his claws, they go *snikt!* Of course they do. Can you just hear the exclamation point?! Many years ago, I heard a radio interview with the ageless genius behind Marvel, Stan Lee. The man's a walking comic book. He couldn't get a sentence out without verbally boldfacing every other word. Before the interview, I thought his comics overdid the exclamation points. But that's **actually** how the man **talks!** It's **absolutely incredible**! Comics have been Stan Lee's calling. You find very little subtlety, few quiet moments in a comic book worthy of the name. Take that to heart: when you want to ramp up the action, implying lots of figurative boldfacing and exclamation points, don't pass up an ono op.

TALKING LEATHER PANTS

Create your own croaking market gimmicks, snoring buffoons, and sound-enabled heroes. First, find an appropriate moment. If you're trying to turn the volume down—say, by diminishing the shock of a reported injury—then you might want to skip the ono. *Enargia*, the special effects of rhetoric, brings objects closer than they may first appear. Consider an ono when you're telling a story, upping the drama quotient of an argument, or using slapstick humor. ("Slap" itself happens to be an ono. A slapstick was one of the original sound-effect instruments, a pair of sticks that mimicked a slap.)

OK, so you want an ono. Think about the sound of the object, character, or scene you want to portray. For instance, an overdressed woman squeezes by you in the movie theater after the film has started. The movie happens to be in an especially quiet moment, and the sound the woman makes as she brushes by you seems especially annoying. Did she *whoosh*? Or *crinkle*? Or *creak*?

Finally, think about whether you want to convey the sound as a verb within the sentence or as a sound effect all its own.

VERB: She squelched by me in her overfilled leather pants.
SOUND EFFECT: SQUELCH SQUELCH SQUELCH. That's all you could hear.

Which works better? That depends on how loud you want to turn up the volume on those pants. The first version comes across as—well, not subtle, exactly, but more integral to the rest of your scene. The second, louder version makes the sound itself the centerpiece.

The Budweiser frogs eclipsed Snap Crackle and Pop as the all-time best marketing onomatopoeia. Nonetheless, those three sound effects were very, very good to Rice Krispies. Cereal-maker Kellogg and its agency knew the first rule of advertising: sell the sizzle, not the steak. What's wrong with just selling the steak? Well, how do you make your steak stand out from any other slab of beef? By describing its nutritional value? Telling the life story of each grass-fed cow? Far better to form an emotional connection. As I mentioned in my last book, to get someone to take an action—such as buying your product—a logical argument will not suffice. Your audience has to *want* the outcome, *desire* the product. So how do you sell a tiny puff of air surrounded by a shell of baked rice? You sell the sizzle—or, more specifically, the snap, crackle, and pop.

Besides serving as sound effects that evoke the cereal-eating experience, the slogan perfectly matched the name of the product. "Rice Krispies" itself sounds like—well, like Rice

Krispies. "Rice" and "Krispies" are sibilant words, surging with sizzlin', snappy "s" sounds. What's the difference between sound symbolism and an onomatopoeia? Not a lot, frankly. Sound symbolism works more subtly, implying a sound or emotion, while the ono makes a direct imitation of a sound; but there's a lot of overlap. "She squelched by me" is the equivalent of "Rice Krispies," using sound symbolism, but it's also an ono. "SQUELCH SQUELCH SQUELCH" is like "Snap Crackle Pop," a pure imitation of sound. The ono works best with storytelling, when you want a direct representation of sound. To reproduce the sound, you make the sound. A Yorkshire terrier doesn't woof, or even bark, exactly; it says "WARF WARF WARF WARF." Sound symbolism offers a wider variety of uses, applying to just about any kind of description, even when you aren't telling a story. And you can work sound symbolism into a sentence without completely dominating it.

YOU: The dogs in the pound jingled and snaffled around my outstretched hand.

EXERCISE

Flex your ono muscle by practicing it in the course of your day. Perform some basic chore—straightening out your briefcase or backpack, doing the dishes, whatever. As you work, imitate the sounds you hear. After you finish, describe the chore with as many onomatopoeias as you can. Did you gish the sponge across the squeaky dish?

Assuming you have sufficiently unself-conscious friends, use onos for a party game. Turn on some music to dance to. Then turn off the music suddenly. Take turns describing what people sound like when they dance. Have you ever sat up front at a ballet? The stomping and thumping and *huh*-ing provide a surprising soundtrack to the visual grace onstage. Adolescents, and a few immature writer types, find this hilarious.

If all that doesn't convince you of the power of word sounds, consider the greatest sound symbol of all time: the word "yawn." "Yawn" comes pretty close to being an onomatopoeia, but it does not quite qualify as an exact imitation of a sound. Instead, it symbolizes and evokes the act of yawning. And it does such a great job, doesn't it? Are you yawning right now? Go get some caffeine and then come back for the next section. It's a real eye-opener.

HOW TO NEGATIVIZE A NABOB

You have seen that certain letters convey the sense of big or small, loud or soft according to how they position your mouth. You know that the "p" word, for example, pinpoints pretty or petty properties. If you want to amplify the effect of sound symbolism, you can use your favored letters in consecutive words. Peter Piper, for instance, obviously was a pretty picky little piker. Suppose instead we had Mama Mallow mash a mess o' muskmelons: The "m" sounds in reference to food imply massiveness and mastication. When speechwriter William Safire wanted to convey the meaningless nihilism of the press, he put plenty of "n" words into the mouth of his boss, Vice President Spiro Agnew, who referred to the liberal media as "nattering nabobs of negativism." Those "n" words evoked an annoying background noise.

Safire employed **alliteration**, the technique of beginning each word with the same sound. When you want to sound silly, alliteration can take you a long way. *USA Today* used the technique nicely when it described the 2006 Olympics in Torino, Italy, as "a topsy-turvy mix of marvels and misadventures." By imitating the kind of alliteration favored by circus posters of yore, the reporter neatly captured the Games' circuslike atmosphere.

Alliteration like that constitutes real wit; but alliteration itself does not qualify as wit, any more than doing witty things with your eyebrows makes you witty. While figures spice up your language, they should not dominate it. Just because you like horseradish on your steak doesn't mean you enjoy a meal of horseradish. Again: a little figuring goes a long, witty way. The "nattering nabobs of negativism" line probably did more harm than good for Agnew, who happened to be one of the dimmer bulbs in the political spotlight. Coming out of the mouth of the barely articulate man, the phrase sounded like the recital of a trained parrot. While the alliteration helped make William Safire a legend among speechwriters the phrase made Agnew a fool among vice presidents.

Bad headline writers misuse alliteration far too often. A school fund-raising day becomes a "Fun, Fancy Festival." A Renaissance concert gets reduced to "Multitalented Musicians Make Merry." A headline like that akes e want to stop using that letter anyore.

Sound Repeaters

Occasionally, though, you'll want to use a particular sound to convey a mood about someone or something. Suppose you want to describe an evilly subtle character. It's hard to go wrong with the serpentine "s" sound. To construct an alliterative string, start by writing down words that describe the character—never mind the letters for a moment.

UNTRUSTWORTHY
BACKSTABBING
HYPOCRITICAL
FAKE

Now come up with synonyms that begin with "s." Although I like the challenge of thinking them up in my head, I'm not too proud to use a thesaurus. An excellent online resource, thesaurus.com, has a prominent place among my browser bookmarks. Let's see what the site can do for us.

Untrustworthy = shady, sharp, shifty, slippery, sneaky

Backstabbing = slanderous, smearing, spiteful, slimy, sly

Hypocritical = sanctimonious, smooth, snide, specious, slick, swindling, smarmy, sycophantic

Fake = pseudo, spurious

All you have left to do is to choose the words that work best.

YOU: A slippery, sly, smarmy pseudofriend.

You can also use alliteration to tie people or concepts together. Genealogist Chip Hughes made a deft alliteration in an interview with the online magazine *Slate*.

HUGHES: There's horse thieves and heroes in everybody's line.

I'd like to put Mr. Hughes in the hero category just for that "horse thieves and heroes" phrase. (I even applaud the ungrammatical "There's." The correct "There are" would throw off the rhythm of the sentence; and the "there's" makes the whole thing sound faintly comical in an anachronistic way. "There's horse thieves in them canyons.") This is a harder line to come up with than our sibilant sycophant was. I can imagine Mr. Hughes preparing for the interview by thinking about the broad range of characters he wanted to portray in our ancestry. He comes up with an unwritten version.

UNWRITTEN: Everybody has bad guys and good guys as ancestors.

But he thinks, "I've got to make these characters sound exciting. What's an exciting version of a good guy? A saint? No, a hero!" Being a clever man, he wants more than just another exciting term for the bad guy. An alliteration creates sound-symbolic relatives, while the "h" sound lends an air of breathlessness to the relationship. Mr. Hughes then presumably thought of synonyms for "scoundrels" that begin with an "H" sound. Unfortunately, thesaurus.com wouldn't have helped this time around. I typed in "villain" and got "heel," "hooligan," "highwayperson," "hijacker," and "holdup person," with nary a horse thief. But "heroes and hijackers" isn't so bad, is it?

RHYMIN' REASON

You can work the same magic with rhyming syllables as with consonants—either to connect things or concepts, or to emphasize sounds that amplify or diminish.

RHYMED: There's heroes and zeroes in everybody's line.

That's not bad, though not as good as Mr. Hughes's "horse thieves and heroes." To find the rhyme, I simply thought of what rhymes with "heroes." (You can also cheat by going to one of the online rhyming dictionaries at rhymezone.com or rhymer.com.) Sound repeaters like rhyming and alliteration offer a striking way to show a range of things. Whenever you're thinking of saying something that contains "from . . . to . . . ," you can substitute a sound repeater. Think up your "from . . . to . . ." line first, as your unwritten version.

UNWRITTEN: That little zoo boasts animals from lemurs to elephants.

Now think of small and big creatures that begin with the same letter or rhyme. I went on rhymer.com to see what rhymes with "elephant," and found "infant."

RHYMED: That little zoo boasts elephants and mouse infants.

Hmm. That's a little unclear, isn't it? The trick only works if you put in an additional rhyme that shows off the range of animals. So I thought of fun-sounding animals; "baboon" and "loon" popped up in my head. (Rhymer.com yielded "raccoon" as well, but a loon differs from a baboon more than a coon.) Then I just doubled up on the rhymes:

DOUBLE-RHYMED: That little zoo boasts loons and baboons, elephants and mouse infants.

Or I could find animals that begin with the same letter to achieve the same effect. Take an extreme species—such as the impossibly long giraffe—then think of a critter that begins with a "j" or soft "g." Gerbil! Assuming the zoo has those furry little rodents, "giraffes and gerbils" makes a memorable phrase.

Combine it with one of your rhyming pairs, and you have a winner.

ALLITERATIVE AND RHYMING: That little zoo boasts giraffes and gerbils, loons and baboons.

EXERCISE

Create a fun invitation for a girl's birthday party. To convey the range of activities, first do an easy unwritten version, listing the activities.

UNWRITTEN: There will be a treasure hunt, balloon animals, face glitter, barbecued hot dogs, s'mores, birthday cake, and Wii bowling.

The temptation to throw "b" words together will be strong, since several of the items on your list begin with that letter. But most kids prefer rhymes, so we'll get more ambitious and see if we can come up with a whole doggerel. Remember, you don't have to list everything at the party—just show the range of fun stuff. The recipient will get more of a sense of variety than if you included every last party favor and trick candle. So go through your mental database of rhymes, or grab hold of a rhyming dictionary.

"Treasure" rhymes with "measure" and "pleasure." Hmm. Phrases like "for good measure" and "for your pleasure" come to mind.

"Balloon animals" would be tough to rhyme. How about "balloon critters" instead? Ooh, that rhymes with "glitter"!

"Hot dogs" is another hard rhyme. Could we say "wieners" instead—assuming that word doesn't raise age-group eyebrows? The only decent rhyme I find online, though, s "gleaners." Skip that one?

"S'mores" rhymes with "explores." (Also "gore" and "deplore," but we'll save those for a Halloween party.) Oh, and "indoors."

"Bowl" rhymes with "charcoal," which could get your hot dogs back in the game. And for "Wii," I typed "wee" into the online rhyming dictionary and got "ennui." Never mind. But what about "Wii games and wieners"? They don't rhyme, precisely, but they begin with the same sound.

Now all you have to do is combine your matches in a way that sounds good.

YOU: Sarah's Birthday Party! Balloon critters and face glitter, s'moring and exploring, Wii games and wieners, and (for good measure) a pirate's buried treasure!

While no one will be setting your words to music in the near future, they make for a cute, original invitation.

And that covers just a bit of what sound repeaters can do for you. Use them to show a variety or range ("horse thieves and heroes," "loons and baboons"); to emphasize sound symbols ("mashed mushmelons" make an "m"-powered mess). In addition, sound symbols help make descriptions come alive, as you've seen.

What's the big deal? Think of the number of times you describe things during the day. As I write this, it's only three o'clock on a Sunday afternoon and already I have experienced things worth describing to my wife and grown children at cocktail hour this evening. (The kids happen to be home, a rare occurrence.) I'll tell them how I awakened last night just as our radio-powered clock set itself back to standard time, from 2:00 a.m. to 1:00 a.m. Weird! Then, at 3:45 the cat woke my wife and me by calling from the living room; her wake-up call sounds eerily like an old foreign lady yelling "hello" (Heh-ROW!). I managed to fall back asleep until five. After breakfast (scrambled eggs made with a splendid new *Cook's Illustrated* recipe), I went into our woods to build a bridge in subfreezing weather, wading up to my waist in cold mud. Just as I warmed myself before the woodstove indoors, a man showed up with an old bench our kids won at an auction for "only" twenty-five dollars. An hour ago, while I was taking a writerly gaze out the window, an enormous bull moose walked across our meadow.

Because my family values wit, and the kids are faster on their feet than I am, I'll spend a few minutes thinking of good descriptions to go with my stories of the day. To make the descriptions seem real or at least clever, I'll use sound symbols and word repeaters for emphasis. I may come up with an onomatopoeia to describe the feeling of watching the glowing numbers change on the clock. The time went back silently, but it was as if I'd broken the "time barrier," moving backward à la quantum physics. What does that sound like? An empty "click" or a barrier-busting "boom"?

The lush, luxuriant, matchless, mouthwatering eggs deserve a lot of "l" words—which subtly remind the audience of tasting or even licking—along with lip-smacking "m"'s.

The freezing mud implies sucking sounds, and I may pile on the wide-mouthed, disgusting syllables *uck* and *ish*. (Mucking, gishing sort of words, I mean.)

The bench I'll make clumsy ("a blundering heap of wood") and the big moose gi-normous, using wide-mouthed sounds for the big and grotesque, lip-smacking sounds for the meaty and delicious; *uck, ick*, and *eek* for the disgusting, and so on. I'll set my mouth in the emotional or descriptive direction I want to take. It's great witcraft practice, even if I never get a word in edgewise tonight. Which, to be honest, I probably won't. The kids will have their own stories to tell. It's a talkative family. Besides, they're better at storytelling and description, having grown up with them. Witcraft comes less naturally for me. But I find it helpful to have at the tip of my tongue the tantalizing sound tools ("T" makes a great tip-o'-tongue sound, does it not?).

THAT SOPHISTICATED BRONX TASTE!

If you think all this stuff about word sounds smacks of poetry and other revenue-poor ventures, consider Landor, one of the world's leading branding agencies. I once visited two of the company's top "namers" in their Manhattan office. "It's hard to know the profession exists, even if you're suited for it," conceded Landor naming and writing specialist Christian Turner. (His real name. Great, huh? "Christian Turner" seems the perfect namer's name; it adds a kind of sacred transformation to any branding opportunity. Or maybe I'm being rhetorically oversensitive.) "We had a hard time naming the naming group," Turner admitted. Namers are a brainy lot, with backgrounds in fields like linguistics, writing, ancient languages. So you can understand how making up names constitutes a glamorous assignment for this kind of person.

The namers who devised Verizon combined *veritas*, which is Latin for truth, with "horizon"—corporatese for "cool metaphor." Häagen-Dazs, an ice cream brand born in the Bronx and owned by General Mills, qualifies as a naming tour de force: two fake names that sound vaguely northern European but don't exist anywhere in Europe. "Americans associate Europe with quality ice cream," a Landor official explained.

We're talking big-time word sounds here—sounds worth millions and millions per syllable. So don't pooh-pooh your rhyming words. Don't snort or yawn or sniff at the namer's idea of glamorous work. Focus on your big and little sounds and your onomatopoeias in the service of our topsy-turvy language.

Having symbolized our sounds, let's get even more playful with them. In the next chapter, we begin practicing that most noble instrument, the pun.

THE TOOLS

Words stand for things. The word "rock" isn't a rock—it merely represents a rock. On the other hand, "pebble" doesn't just stand for a little rock—it *sounds* little, and even sort of cute. Unlike "boulder," which conjures a big old rock that's just beginning to rumble down a hill. The sounds of words create a virtual reality connected to parts of the brain that govern emotion. If you want to keep your prose purely logical, try not to use sound-symbolic words. But good luck—once alerted to sound effects, you may find it impossible to keep them out of your prose.

(Don't forget: in the back of this book you'll find a list of all the tools in one place, along with their descriptions and an index of examples for each one.)

Sound Symbolism. The position of your mouth makes things seem big or small, significant or unimportant.

Onomatopoeia. A sound effect that grew up and became a word.

Sound Repeaters. Uses the same sound at the beginning, middle, or end of consecutive words.

5

PLAY WITH WORDS

BRITANNIA WAIVES THE RULES
Puns, Near Puns, and Puns with a Restraining Order

PEOPLE MAY CLAIM TO HATE PUNS, but most true word lovers have groaned to like them. (I'm not sorry.) If you happen to be one of these lovers, you have good company. In ancient times and right up through Shakespeare's era, people did not look down on wordplay. They knew that a **pun** lets the speaker sound two meanings at once, like a musician striking a chord, or like a really good yodeler.

Wait: yodelers have always been annoying. Forget yodelers.

Personally, I'm quite fond of punning, especially when I'm the culprit. Why, just yesterday, I described a new, well-armed neighbor to my wife.

DOROTHY SENIOR: I hope he doesn't go after the turkeys on our land.

ME: He's not a turkey hunter, but moose are deer to him.

I got a patient smile for that one. Dorothy's indulgence of punsters contributed to her excellent mothering skills when our children were little. Every parent should consider punning to be an essential part of good child rearing, if only because kids' social hierarchy tends to slot young punsters in the nerdy, bookish, law-abiding, sexually late-blooming, high-SAT-score category. In other words, an appreciation for puns practically guarantees your child entry into a prestigious college and a career that supports you in your dotage. Or else she becomes a lifelong student/academic whose constant tuition demands leave you bankrupt. But every baby is a crapshoot. No pun intended.

Pun

When my kids were young, I was willing to take the chance. For years they thought that a little island in the Washington Monument's reflecting pool was named after an Indian chief named Nomannison. (Nomannison Island does sound familiar, right?) My family suffered—or enjoyed—a barrage of wordplay and triple entendres that the punaphobic might consider abusive. Here's a typical bit of dinner-table badinage when my kids were little.

> DOROTHY JR.: What is this? It looks gross.
>
> ME: Don't dish the dish.
>
> DOROTHY JR.: What's "dish"?
>
> ME: Dish is eggplant Farmer John.
>
> DOROTHY SR.: He means parmigiana.
>
> ME: Parm me?
>
> DOROTHY SR.: Parmigiana. It's a pasta dish. Only with eggplant.
>
> ME: It's the Zsa Zsa Gabor of dishes.
>
> DOROTHY SR.: You consider her a dish?
>
> ME: In the sense that she's pasta prime.

The kids put up with it. (So did my wife, of course, but my wife is a saint.) They knew that their dad talked like that when he was in high spirits—of the sober kind, I mean. A punning dinner increased the chance that they could cadge a favor or treat from me. And while no one wanted to see me in a bad mood, my off days were compensated by the relief from my constant punning. Win-win. Besides, only pun-ready kids could appreciate the old billboard outside of Boston for the restaurant Dante's Inferno, with its cannibalistic slogan "Children Served."

More important, they learned the delights of competitive wit. By the time our two kids turned twelve, each could pretty much keep up with me. They now outdo me a maddening amount of time. George called me from college recently and carried on a punning monologue about the socks I'd accused him of stealing from me. I was trying so hard to keep up with him that we hung up without my remembering to tell him to bring the socks when he came home from college the next week. As he learned early on, wit has its uses.

So groan away. Besides wordplay around the dinner table, puns work as word-powered chords, sounding two notes at once. Shakespeare was a master of the pun. At the beginning of *Hamlet*, a skittish guard says to the soldier relieving him, "For this relief much thanks." Later in the play, during the famous skull-contemplating Yorick scene, Hamlet manages to use the word "fine" with four different meanings.

HAMLET: . . . is this the fine of his fines, and the recovery of his recoveries, to have his fine pate full of fine dirt?

The first "fine" uses the archaic meaning of "the end," as in "le fin" concluding a French film. "Fines" refers to fees Yorick leveled as a lawyer, while his "fine pate" refers to his beautiful head, and "fine dirt" is the well-sifted soil that covered him. The overall effect is of a "fine man" reduced to nothing, as if his own fineness had buried him. While you might shy from achieving such a Shakespearean feat—people might think you're suffering

from a punning version of Tourette's—you can use puns yourself
to effect double meanings

LINKIN' MEMORIAL

The true power of a pun comes when it twins up concepts that
share the same word or sound. This makes for indelible labels,
whether you use them in promoting a concept or branding
a person. Words that normally have nothing to do with each
other suddenly find themselves acting as odd bedfellows. Take
just about any pair of homonyms at random, and you can see
the possibilities; say, "ground" (as in, "on the ground") and
"ground" (as in, "ground up"). A friend tells you he likes a politician because she's "grounded"—deeply connected to family
and community. You think the politician is the kind of vicious
and self-serving jerk who would walk over her grandmother in
Manolo Blahniks.

> YOU: Grounded? I wonder how many people in her way got
> grounded up.

Not the height of wit, let alone grammar; but the next time
your friend thinks of the politician's "groundedness," he'll find
it hard to keep a disgusting image out of his head. Let's use sound
links to make fun of Sarah Palin.

> FELLOW CITIZEN: Know what I like about Sarah Palin? She's
> one of us.
> YOU: Yeah, she strikes that golden mean among Americans.
> Or at least the "mean" part.

You might actually have an effect on your audience—
assuming you have one that's larger than your starstruck in-

terlocutor. Maybe someone will walk away thinking a little differently next time a politician pulls the "I'm just like you" stunt. The stranger the linguistic bedfellows, the better. I once got a satisfying eye roll from my wife when we were reading a holiday letter from our friends, the Klein family. Each member had gone on to accomplish impressively different things, and I concluded, "It takes all Kleins"—thus pulling off a bad pun while punishing my wife for reading holiday letters aloud. Whenever my wife hears the cliché "It takes all kinds," I imagine she'll be thinking of our friends.

Far more insidious is the bumper sticker IMAGINE WHIRLED PEAS, which just about destroyed the pretty sentiment "Imagine world peace." It was as if the joke bumper sticker had thrown a nasty green pie in the face of world peace. Most of us cannot think of the original expression without linking it to peas in a blender. The sound link makes the associations memorable.

You can use homonyms for positive reasons as well, mashing up words for double-entendre effect. America's fourth-largest corporation uses a complex pun for its slogan.

GE: We bring good things to life.

To "bring to life" means to invent, much as Dr. Frankenstein utilized electricity and some hasty surgery to enliven his monster. (Presumably, GE was thinking of less controversial inventions, such as the lightbulb.) But the expression also means that the company enhances your life by bringing good things to it. The combined meaning says "benevolent invention," or "inventions that help us, not scare us." Pretty efficient use of just five words.

In a bit, I'll show a simple method for coming up with puns of your own. But puns, along with other figures, tend to pop into your head all by themselves if you practice enough. I can entertain myself for hours this way. It wreaks havoc with my work schedule but makes for very companionable solo walks. My family will be astonished to learn this, given how many puns they hear me say, but I don't actually utter most of my puns aloud. Some of my wordplay might confuse people or insult them.

For example, the other day I was talking with a friend who's a fine artist; I mean "fine" to mean the type of art—he paints landscapes—as well as the quality of his paintings. My friend was arguing that artists in America should be subsidized by government, since art does so much to, well, bring good things to life.

> ME: But do you really want government determining what constitutes art?
> FRIEND: No, the art community should funnel the money. True art—the transgressive kind—only comes when you take it away from commerce
> ME: In other words, you beg to differ.

Actually, I said that last line only in my head while biting my tongue. Still, I was as proud of that line as I was of my restraint in keeping it to myself. "You beg to differ" means he disagrees with me. It also means he wants to maintain his difference, his status as a unique artist, by begging. The implication would be that all true artists are mere beggars. Of course, my friend may not have picked up on the pun, but I wasn't taking any chances.

Puns play essential two-sided roles in powerful realms like advertising, politics, and the journalism chattersphere. Take Andrew Rice's great phrase, "political panda-ring," to describe China's offer of a pair of pandas to Taiwan. Having tired of lobbing an occasional missile at its island neighbor, Beijing decided to use an even more nefarious psychological weapon: adorable wildlife. While 80 percent of the Taiwanese couldn't wait to get the animals, their government balked. "The pandas are a trick, just like the Trojan horse," fumed one politician. He accused mainland China of attempting to "destroy Taiwan's psychological defenses." Exactly. Rice's "political panda-ring" shows a journalistic pun at its best. Pandering is exactly what China was doing: offering a goodwill bribe. At the same time, "panda-ring" adds a conspiratorial air; "ring" in journalese implies an illegitimate cabal.

Most political puns don't quite measure up to Rice's pudding of wit, but they can help to stir up believers and get a laugh. When General David Petraeus first proposed a surge in Iraq, liberals were dismayed; they had considered the brainy general to be one of them, and therefore a sort of well-armed dove. So the left applied the label "General Betray-Us." During the 2008 presidential campaign, on the other hand, conservatives were hawking NObama buttons. Besides pleasing the party faithful, these puns had the added benefit of annoying opponents. Of course, they're also stupid and childish. NObama! Right on! Obama-lama-dingdong!

LET US HOMONIZE TOGETHER

I do wish the politically motivated would try a little harder. We Americans consider wit to be a form of trickery, which is why we tend to prefer apparently straight-talking (i.e., witless) politicians. But cleverness can help promote your cause. Because the Republicans consistently outdo Democrats in rhetoric, I often try to offer the liberals suggestions in my language blog.

Puns can make for good labels. For instance, Democrats should point out the hidden costs we pay when Republicans

propose tax cuts. Cut back road maintenance, and car maintenance costs go up. Slash park budgets, and you get slapped
with user fees. And so on. Democrats should call these charges
"sneak-a-tax." Your state legislature plans to cut aid to education? Parents will suddenly bear an added burden for text-
books; and without adequate music programs, private lessons
will have to replace high school marching band and orchestra.
Sneak-a-tax! It's like a tax . . . but sneaky!

So how do you make one of those things? By familiarizing
yourself with *homonyms*, words that sound the same but have
different meanings. Homonym means "same name" in ancient
Greek. It serves as the raw material of puns; a homonym is to
puns what gunpowder is to fireworks. "A tax" and "attacks" are
homonyms (well, close enough for government work). So, to
create "sneak attacks" out of the hidden costs of tax cuts, you follow the four-step **homonymnastics** approach.

1. Say what you mean. Find the pith and the key words:
   this so-called tax cut is really just a sneaky way to
   disguise more taxes.

2. List possible homonyms. What sounds like "tax"?
   Tacks, ax, acts, pax . . . attacks!

3. Put the homonyms in phrases, whether they make
   sense or not in this context. Thumb tax (on the seat of
   power!), ax cuts . . . tax attacks.

4. Try your homonyms in context. What's sneaky about
   a thumb tax, or a tax attack? A sneak tax attack . . . a
   sneak-a-tax!

Homonymnastics

———————— *E X E R C I S E S* ————————

1. Homonymnastics get easier when you have synonyms at your command and don't have to consult a thesaurus all the time. Here's a useful game for the dinner table. Come up with sentences that use as many synonyms as possible. Make sure everyone is willing to participate, though; otherwise you might find yourself stabbed, stuck, pricked, pierced, punctured, wounded, or transfixed by a fork, utensil, or pronged eating instrument.

2. Punning also gets easier with practice. Try it for yourself. Take a proposal you hate, tell it like it is in as few words as possible, homonize, put your homonyms in phrases, and then try them out in the context of telling it like it is. Suppose you're a conservative who didn't like the sneak-a-tax dodge. I'm just putting a liberal spin on tax cuts. Hmmm . . . What's a homonym for "spin"? Spend! As in, tax and spend! So that's just what Democrats do. They tax and spin.

Homonicely done.

WANTS A PUN A DIME

Another way to practice your punning skill is to fabricate a Feghoot, a short, shaggy-dog-style story that ends with an elaborate pun. Ferdinand Feghoot was a grotesque little science fiction character invented in the mid-1950s by Reginald Bretnor under the gnome de plume Grendel Briarton. Feghoot went on short intergalactic missions for the Society for the Aesthetic Re-Arrangement of History, with each tale ending in an outrageous, cliché-based pun. A website dedicated to the Feghoot, shaggy-dogs.briancombs.net, suggested a challenge for the hapless British prime minister shortly before the Labour Party faced the Conservatives ("Tories" in Brit parlance) in the 2010 election: "Chicken! Catch a Tory!"

The annual Bulwer-Lytton Fiction Contest for bad writing often rewards prizes to Feghoot-like entries. A few years ago, Mitsy Rae of Danbury, Nebraska, pulled off an instant classic.

> RAE: When Detective Riggs was called to investigate the theft of a trainload of Native American fish broth concentrate bound for market, he solved the case almost immediately, being that the trail of clues led straight to the trainmaster, who had both the locomotive and the Hopi tuna tea.

Time magazine managed to turn a news story into a Feghoot many years ago, when the United Nations let China join the Security Council. The headline said, "China in the Bull Shop." Oh, how I loved that headline! It helped inspire me to become a magazine editor myself. Perhaps as a result, I often think of stories as potential Feghoots. My biggest triumph came a long time ago, when an American named Hale had difficulty with the British government. After London finally relented, I wrote the headline, "Hale, Britannia? Britannia Waives the Rules." Unfortunately, the headline was almost as long as the (rather trivial) story. My boss rewrote it to something sensible, saying the pun made him nauseated.

Which just proved he was the bastard of his own ptomaine. As in, master of his own domain. See, he was being a bastard by letting the pun go to his stomach . . . Well, jeez! A Feghoot is *supposed* to make you moan. Or did that one make you nauseated?

Feghoots aren't the most useful form of pun; but they can help you end a story—a big problem for many of us. We tell a great anecdote to our friends, get some laughs, and things are going well until we realize we have no clue how to bring the thing to a close. What do you do? Give it a moral? An alternative, the Feghoot ending, summarizes your story in a way that makes people laugh—or, even more satisfying, groan appreciatively.

EXERCISE

Want easy immortality? Fabricate a Feghoot and submit it to the Bulwer-Lytton Fiction Contest (bulwer-lytton.com). To create one, start with the pun. Take a common expression—any cliché will do—and find puns and near puns for several of the words. Then dream up a story that leads to the conclusion. You'll probably find that the punning is harder than the storytelling. For instance, we could use the expression, "The more things change, the more they remain the same." That can become, oh, "L'amour sinks chains, l'amour remains insane." We could tell a story about the screen actress Dorothy L'Amour losing a bracelet, or construct a more elaborate tale about a crazy man who falls in love with a prisoner. Admittedly, a Feghoot won't get you promoted at work or have your words engraved on the post office building. But winning Bulwer-Lytton: that's an honor worth a Lytton-y of praise.

THE NOT-REALLY-A-PUN

If punning fails to come naturally to you, do not despair. Our standards for wit are so low in this culture, just hitting anywhere near a homonymic target will win you points. Look at James Scott, a retired lieutenant colonel who serves as the Pentagon's certified laughter training specialist. He told *USA Today* that his program "prevents hardening of the attitudes." That joke hardly counts as a laugh riot. It's more of a laugh invasion.

The point stands nonetheless: a near pun can be as memorable as a real pun. It can actually sound rather witty. A couple years ago, Sprint ran an ad in which it offered mobile broadband as a cure for "connectile dysfunction." "Connectile" is not exactly homonymic with "erectile," but any humor that implies penises will get a rise—I mean, a laugh—from at least half the audience. At any rate, the ad bested most of its competition in that Super Bowl; the other ads found their humor in people falling off cliffs, suffering car accidents, or getting beat up. Sprint at least chose sex over violence. Droopy guy sits in an airport with his laptop in his lap while the voiceover says, "You know the feeling: you can't take care of business the way others do."

Which leads to another form of pun, the double entendre. This is a kind of extended pun in which whole phrases, clauses, or sentences match up with a second meaning. "Taking care of business" supports Sprint Mobile Broadband's wink-and-nod slogan, "Power Up." The ad might have worked even better if it had used a former vice presidential candidate who became Viagra's spokesman. But that might have seemed too doleful.

Sex traditionally gets more double-entendre play than any other subject, because in olden days, open sexual conversation (the oral—verbal—kind, not the legal one) was forbidden in polite company. So, instead of talking about it nakedly, people learned to use double-entendre protection.

It's amazing how dirty everything can sound when you're in the mood. Or even when you're not. When I was in college, a woman wrote a tongue-in-cheek letter to the campus newspaper objecting to the "offensive" names of candy dispensed in dorm machines. Milky Way. Mounds. Payday. I've never been able to look at sweets the same way. I can't even bring myself to order a chocolate dessert in a restaurant when the waiter calls it "decadent." Who knows where that thing has been?

The double entendre serves as code language, a kind of irony in which a secret meaning underlies the open one. Code language happens to be one of the best ways to bring people together. Years ago, I worked in an office six hours' drive from home. The company rented me an apartment to use during the week. My wife surprised me on my birthday by showing up and taking me out to lunch, an occasion a coworker insisted on calling a "conjugal visit."

"Have a good time?" he leered when I got back to the office.

I nodded. "We ate Italian."

From then on, of course, "eating Italian" had a different meaning. Whenever someone mentions an Italian restaurant, it cracks my wife and me up. Especially if it's a deep-dish joint.

I probably don't even need to tell you how to double your entendres yourself. Practically all you have to do is to look dirty when you say something. If you really need practice, just do the "That's what she said" joke in your head. (Saying it aloud is usually a mistake.)

Enough with the sex. (That's what . . . never mind.) Let's create something new.

THE TOOLS

"Wordplay" is a perfect word. It means playing with words, or words at play. The Puritan strains of our culture make us suspect words that refuse to put their noses to the grindstone, that fail to straighten up and fly right. It's almost our moral duty to groan at wordplay. But scientists will tell you that play is an essential part of mammalian development. Cats bat around balls (do not even think of a double entendre here) and become better mousers. Similarly, wordplay makes us better at making our words work.

Pun. A device that uses homonyms—words that sound the same— to imply more than one meaning. While in our culture we employ them mostly as a crude form of humor, I believe that every kid should be encouraged to pun as often as possible. Puns' regular use in wordplay creates verbally sophisticated adults, if occasionally annoying ones. Puns do have their serious uses as well, as Shakespeare proved—not to mention Madison Avenue.

Homonymnastics. A technique for coming up with puns. Say what you mean in plain language. Narrow your thought down to one or more key words. Think of corresponding synonyms— words that mean the same thing. A thesaurus (such as the excellent website thesaurus.com) can help you find the synonyms. Now play with those alternative words, trying them out in various phrases. While the process sounds tedious, with some practice you'll find yourself thinking up synonyms and forming them into puns spontaneously.

6

INVENT NEW WORDS

THE WAITRON BLOGARATI
Portmantizing, Verbing, and Group Venereal Activity

WORDPLAY ISN'T JUST FOR PLAY. Puns and other techniques allow you to create whole new uses for words, and even to invent altogether new words. Called *neologisms*, they let you label issues and ideas. They carry out your desires and take on literal lives of their own. Call them wordbots. Or termingnators. I picked out four of the most fun and useful ways to create neologisms or to repurpose existing words.

The **portmanteau** combines two words to make a new word.

Verbing takes existing words and makes them serve a novel part of speech.

Venereal words name groups of animals or people. While many venereal terms already exist, the form cries out for witty new ones.

The **getting medieval** figure uses uncharacteristic words as objects of a sentence.

Let's pack our rhetorical bags and take a ride with the first neologizer.

EGGS AS BAGGAGE

Portmanteau

Mash up two (or sometimes three) words to make one with extra hybrid vigor. The result: a *portmanteau*. French for 'carpet bag," the term combines the French words for "to carry" and "mantel" or cloak; a luggage "portmanteau," therefore, qualifies as a rhetorical portmanteau. The device also serves as a means for packing witty baggage. The Lewis Carroll poem "Jabberwocky" is a portman-tour de force. Some of the poem's coinages, such as "burbled" (combining *babble*, *murmur*, and *warble*, presumably) and "chortled" (*chuckle*, *snort*) still decorate the fanciful sentences of word lovers. You may not see portmanteaus through the smog (*smoke* plus *fog*) or on a spork (*spoon-fork*), but that's exactly what "smog" and "spork" are. They're portmanteaus.

Realtors are big into portmanteaus these days as they try to hipnify neighborhoods à la SoHo (South of Houston Street in New York). So in Manhattan alone you have your NoHo (north of Houston) and NoLita (north of Little Italy) and MePa (meatpacking district). Denver's hippest area is LoDo, lower downtown. Being as how I live just west of Cardigan Mountain, I could dub my place Wedigain (which, given the weather here in the rainy Northwoods, I often am). But my neighbors might find such a sobriquet to be a bit pretentious. With only three hundred residents, this town is a nugapolis (a nugatory metropolis).

You already know how the media love to portmantize Hollywood and political couples (Brangelina, Billary). And you're probably as tired as I am at seeing "holic" behind every phony addiction and "gate" in back of every scandal. Only if that notable workaholic, Bill Gates, misappropriates his foundation's money to build a new security fence will I enjoy seeing a Watergate-style coinage, Gatesgatesgate. While these prefab portmanteaus tend to fall into cliché territory, they can be fun to use. Just add standard syllables like *-tron*, *-tastic*, *-ize*, *-athon*, *-holic*, or *-ati* at the end of appropriate words. The literati lent themselves to the Hollywood "glitterati," which became the "blogerati." People under thirty seem to be in love with *-tastic* and *-tron*. An ice-cream cone is "tastetastic," while a fumbler is "stupidtastic." A robotic-seeming waiter becomes a "waitron."

Still, portmanteaus make a good parlor game. Challenge friends and loved ones to portmantize phenomena in the news. We're not just talking mind games here. A good, well-punned portmanteau can serve as a powerful way to label issues. After Hurricane Katrina struck New Orleans, the graft of some contractors might have gotten more attention if the press had called the corruption "hurrigains." Better, rich bankers during the financial meltdown should be permanently labeled "villainaires." Perhaps these terms sound a tad archaic; who speaks in terms of "ill-gotten gains" anymore? And have you noticed that police spokespeople tend to refer to male suspects as "gentlemen"? *The gentleman threatened with a grenade launcher before hijacking the vehicle.* It makes me glad I'm not a gentleman. Such euphemized English demands a cleverly abusive label now and then. Like, I don't know, "perpetraitor" if a native-born gentleman were committing a terrorist act. (On the other hand, a nosy male relative could be a "yentleman.")

More seriously, the portmanteau allows you to link concepts that normally wouldn't go together. You can attach an unflattering picture to a person, company, or concept simply by combining it with a punning, unflattering word. The book *The Obama Nation* turned a politician into a portmanteau and earned a pretty terrible author some serious spending money.

Suppose you're an old-style liberal who objects to the tax breaks given the richest 1 percent in our society. Their wealth has indeed grown exponentially in the past twenty years. Point out that fact, though, and the tax-break-loving superrich are likely to accuse you of "class warfare." But tax breaks for the rich *are* class warfare, says the liberal! So the issue of tax breaks for the superwealthy comes down to bastards defending their class. Class and bastards: classtards.

MAKE YOUR OWN PERVINATOR

More practically, the device makes a great way to attach labels to issues, especially those you don't like. First, find the pith, boiling it down to several key words. If you don't like the phenomenon you're describing, feel free to boil down to negative words. For example, take those body scanners in airports (please). Find the pith of the issue—or, rather, the pith of what bothers you most about it. A few top-of-head examples:

SNOOP
PORN
NAKED
GENITALS
MACHINE

"Snoop porn" makes for a good label in itself, but it fails to qualify as a portmanteau. Can we combine our key words into a single great mash-up? To make the attempt, we need to engage in homonymnastics (see the previous chapter for a refresher). We have the key words; now collect some synonyms.

For "snoop," the thesaurus gives me "meddle," "pry," "spy," and "molest."

"Porn" yields riches like "smut" and "pervert."

"Naked" generates "bare," "buff," and "nude."

"Genitals" gets me "organs." Let's add "junk," which has recently entered the popular lexicon.

"Machine" brings "appliance," "thingamabob," and "utensil." Also, keep in mind syllables that turn things into machines, like -*izer*, -*inator*, and -*ater*. "Molestinator" and "pervinator" come to mind.

We have a lot to play with. Fun labeling phrases—"meddle shop," "buff cycle," "junk yard," "organ grinder"—pop up as I look at these words. But the point here is to create a portmanteau. That means finding a pun—working in a homonym or near homonym as a substitute for a syllable or two in another word. To focus this deal, we'll assume that a synonym for "machine," combined with one of the other categories, will produce a good portmanteau. So can we find any puns for one of the "machine" synonyms' syllables? This part may seem a bit tedious, but it's not that difficult: scan your lists to see if any puns crop up. Start with "snoop" and hold it up to "machine," "appliance," "thingamabob," and so on. Then do the same with "meddle," all the way through your whole set of synonyms. Someone with a lot of practice in puns may find instant connections, but in most cases you will find yourself working your way through the lists. My own slog through the terms produces:

Appryance, combining "pry" and "appliance."

Thingamabuse, merging "abuse" and "thingamabob."

Nudetensil, mashing "nude" up with "utensil."

Can you find others? As with every aspect of figuring, you get better with practice. Try writing a few sentences with as many portmanteaus as you can. Compete with your friends to create the most new words redlined by your computer.

EXERCISES

1. You can start by looking around the room and dreaming up some puns. For instance, I have a microphone on my desk that I've been planning for months to use in podcasts. ("Podcasts" being a sleek portmanteau itself.) The microphone makes me think of all the self-proclaimed experts doing podcasts. Phonies, in other words . . . microphonies! Why do microphonies like to wear sunglasses indoors? Hmmm. Can't think of a portmanteau for that until I look at a lampshade. A plump microphony wears lumpshades. Or clampshades. The file cabinet next to my desk has drawers jammed with unorganized clippings and back issues of magazines I've worked on; in other words, it's, um, a pile-cabinet. The couch in my office has big pillows—which, if I were the bachelor type, I could call thrillows or ay-yi-pads.

OK, I'll stop. Which is hard. Try it, and you'll find yourself constantly punologuing. Which is fine. Exercises like that keep you on your portmanteaus.

2. I'll bet people were wittier back before TV, when people played parlor games. Wordplay makes for good clean—and occasionally unclean—fun, requiring no special equipment. Great for long car rides. You can set the rules yourself; and, being the one with the rules, you can cheat by preparing in advance.

If your car contains a teenager or two, it might be tough to extract their earphones. You might try money: a dollar for each "win." And what constitutes a win? Depends on the game. If you want your family to keep up with the news, take a single item and come up with a portmanteau to describe it.

YOU: OK, let's come up with a portmanteau describing the Chinese currency policy.
TEENAGER: Oh, please.
YOU: It's important. The Chinese manage their currency so that their goods are cheap overseas, and our goods are expensive there.
SPOUSE: Chi-kneecapping.

A dollar for the spouse!

VERBIN' RENEWAL

Besides mashing up existing words to create new ones, you can take old words and deploy them in new ways. The technique, called *verbing*, earns condemnation from grammar police across the land. But Shakespeare did some major lexicographical gene-splicing using exactly this technique. Besides, "verbing" is itself a form of verbing, since the word "verb" was strictly a noun before it became a gerund with "verbing." (Its technical name, *anthimeria*, isn't an anthimeria. It means "part switch." Most people refer to the common name, "verbing.")

Verbing

Turning nouns into verbs is fun; you might find it surprising that most nouns remain virgins, as yet unverbed. Verbing often lets you say things more efficiently than if you used a standard dictionary. We once had a next-door neighbor who obsessed over his lawn to neurotic lengths. His lawn was sodded, greened, saplinged, lawnblown, chemicaled, and nitpicked to the point where a stray leaf, loosed from his pollarded and injected maple, would defy physics to make it onto my friendly, leaf-littered lawn.

Count the verbed nouns in that previous sentence. I hope it gave the impression of lawn victimization. with the guy's poor yard subjected to loving abuse. What if I had avoided verbing?

UNWRITTEN: His lawn was laid down with sod, sprayed with green dye, planted with young saplings, blown with a leafblower . . .

Not the same effect. is it? Not only does the description take longer, the lawn itself doesn't seem . . . verbed enough. Verbing packs the action into every green, perfectly cut square inch.

Verbing nouns can make a slogan or expression sound witty. When the Italian car company Fiat introduced the minuscule Fiat-500, the American ad campaign bore the slogan "You are, we car." The manufacturer offered "500,000 car combinations" to provide the perfect car for each buyer, thus coming close to physically turning a car into a verb. An active verb, at that.

Which raises the question: When would you want to verb a noun yourself? Consider using the tool when you're describing an unusual or extreme situation that lacks an existing verb to describe it—such as my obsessive neighbor's lawn. Verbing nouns also can help you exaggerate a complicated process. Stick on mechanical-sounding syllables like -*adize*, and you can produce a rhyming list of words.

YOU: At the hospital I was chemicalized, IV-ized, doctorized, and nursasized.

Besides making splendid verbs, nouns also convert nicely to adjectives. That's what Kevin Spacey did in *The Usual Suspects*. Playing a character named Verbal, Spacey described an obese man by turning a killer whale into an adjective.

VERBAL: The baritone was this guy named Kip Diskin, big fat guy, I mean, like, orca fat.

You've heard the expression "rail thin." Same thing, only with whales. But if we're talking about anorexic models, "stiletto thin" might be better. In fact, verbing offers novel ways to describe people. Follow the aptly named Verbal by making your verbing as specific as possible; not "whale fat" but "orca fat."

UNWRITTEN: He had a killer smile.
WRITTEN: He had a Doberman smile.

Here you simply compare a person's smile to that of a Doberman. Instead of saying, "His smile was like a Doberman's," you do a sort of rhetorical Photoshopping, grafting the dog's smile onto the person's face. More effective, don't you think? Use this kind of verbing—converting a noun into an adjective—whenever you want to go one step beyond a simile. (We'll be getting to similes in a few chapters.)

SIMILE: His fart was as loud as a firecracker.
VERBED: He had a firecracker-loud fart.

SIMILE: His feet were the size of pontoon boats.
VERBED: He had pontoon feet.

SIMILE: The boardroom has a table the size of Butte, Montana.
VERBED: The boardroom has a Butte-sized table.

You might like the simile version better, which is fine. Figures give you a breadth of choices as big as God's green Earth. Verbing alone can turn nouns into verbs, nouns into adjectives, nouns into adverbs ("Army Strong"), verbs into nouns ("She gave him a good eyebrow-raise"), and so on.

To come up with a good one, start with the pith method to find the key words. Ask yourself what you want to emphasize most—subject? Verb? Adjective? How clever do you want to sound? (If the answer is, "Not too clever," avoid verbing altogether.) Then try a variety of combinations to see if they work. Even the failures can be fun.

UNWRITTEN: I worked until I was thoroughly tuckered out.
FAILED VERBING: I worked until I got myself in a good tucker.

Ouch. What if you worked yourself into eyes-closed somnambulence instead? That's a bit much, but I can understand the overwriting. You were really tired.

EXERCISE

Take phenomena in nature and verb them to describe the things around you or in the media. H. L. Mencken, a towering early-twentieth-century political writer and lexicographer, was a master of this game. Wishing to dignify the profession of stripping, he called strippers "ecdysiasts," borrowing an entomological term, *ecdysis*, for the act of moulting. Medicine and pharmacology offer a pharmacopeia of verbable jargon. For example, *stents* are used in extremely uncomfortable ways to help men drain their bladders. Someone who relieves a political obstruction could be called a "stenter." Or the deadly myocardial infarction, aka heart attack, could be applied to any sudden breakdown of machinery or bureaucratic function. Say it "infarcted."

GET ALL MEDIEVAL

A cousin to verbing, *getting medieval*, takes a word or phrase and uses it as the object of a sentence.

Getting Medieval Figure

The commander of the military joint task force for Hurricane Katrina did just that in admonishing journalists at a press conference.

GENERAL RUSSEL HONORÉ: Don't get stuck on stupid, reporters.

All the reporters asked was where New Orleans's evacuees were being taken. The general, who must have been tired, got all military on them. He lined "stupid" up and directed his sentence's rhetorical firepower at it. I call the device the getting-medieval figure after the famous line uttered by Ving Rhames playing Marsellus in the movie *Pulp Fiction*.

MARSELLUS: I ain't through with you by a damn sight! I'm gonna get medieval on your ass!

UNWRITTEN MARSELLUS: I'm gonna hurt your ass as if I were a torturer in the Inquisition!

You can use the figure to your own advantage.

YOU: He stopped dating her after she got all kindergarten teacher on him.

The easiest way to come up with the getting-medieval figure is to insert an expression after "get" or "got." Insert "all" before the object if you want to make the figure obvious. Saying "she got all kindergarten teacher" instead of just "she got kindergarten teacher" lets the audience know you're describing a type—a patronizing, lecturing, baby-talking woman, say—instead of sounding like Tarzan reporting a kidnapping.

But General Honoré shows the way to another getting medieval. Just substitute a word for "stupid" in his sentence. Suppose you're bored with people saying "That's what she said" after every other line.

YOU: Let's not get stuck on "She saids."

A variation is "Don't give me any more 'She saids.'" I like the figure because it sounds direct and blunt, as if you don't have time to work your way through a complete grammatical sentence.

The getting-medieval figure helps you use commonplaces to your advantage. Take expressions people frequently use and stick them in the back of your sentence as an object.

YOU: He tried a but-I-didn't and got a yes-you-did.

Getting medieval acts as a rhetorical scavenger, taking dead expressions, old clichés, and rotting ideas and making them fresh again. And speaking of fresh, your better rap singers get as medieval as they can.

LIL'KIM: You want beef with I?
TRANSLATION: You want to have a beef with me?

SNOOP DOGG: Keep it gangsta.
TRANSLATION: Behave as though you were a gangsta.

Personally, Lil'Kim, I don't want beef with youse. But I like your medieval experimentation.

AN ORGY OF VENEREALS

If you want to get more clever about using words in novel ways, you can try a parlor game called *venereal language*. *Venery* is what people called hunting and management of wildlife a few centuries ago. Venereal language is the terminology for groups of animals. The geese you see on your local golf course compose a "flock," right? When they fly together, though, they form a "skein." A group of whales is a "pod" or "gam." A group of crows is a "murder," of owls, a "parliament." My family and I like to extend the game beyond animals to include other collections.

A cloister of penguins

A slick of oil-company flacks

A levy of tax collectors

A slouch of hipsters

A peck of editors

A leak of journalists

Venereal Language

To create a venereal word, think of a group you would like to describe—for example, a bunch of thirteen-year-old boys. Now come up with some words that capture the essence of this lot. What do they look like? What are their characteristic expressions, moods, movements, gestures, or habits?

PIMPLES
SHY
BOASTING
SCUFFLING
HANDS IN POCKETS

Next, take each of these descriptive words and find syllables that might make a witty group name. You may not have the crutch of a thesaurus during a parlor game; in which case, you really will have to rely on your wit. When I wrote down "pimples," the word "eruption" popped into my head. Thus . . .

ME: An eruption of thirteen-year-old boys.

Not very nice, or pleasant for that matter. Now what would you do with "shy"? Keep in mind that you need a noun, which means converting the adjectives on your list.

YOU: A bashfulness of boys.

Sweet! I like the alliteration. Now do something with "boasting" or a synonym thereof. A hyperbole of thirteen-year-olds? "Scuffling" produces a scuffle of boys. That's easy. For "hands in pockets," I can only think offhand of "a pocket lint of thirteen-year-olds."

While venereal language serves as one of the fun, wit-enhancing figures, it has its practical uses as well. Group names can help you attach a label to a phenomenon you like, or dislike. While calling oil-industry PR people a "slick" may seem like a rhetorical version of shooting fish in a barrel—it's just too easy a target—the device can help you gain the sympathy of your audience. Venereal language can also let you create a kind of opposition when you're telling an anecdote or giving your opinion.

> YOU: Frost's poetry survives despite being bowdlerized over the years by a slew of editors—or a peck of them, rather.

Now imagine what you can do with Democrats, Republicans, Libertarians (a moat?), Christian Rightists, tea partiers (a bag, cozy, or lemon?), radical environmentalists (a greenery?), or any other label-worthy group. Lovers of civil discourse may frown on the resulting cheap shots, but I personally find any genuine wit refreshing. If you're going to sermonize, don't sound like a drone of sermonizers. Sound like a wag of wits, a badinage or banter of bards, a sling of wags.

So we're getting the lyrics. In the next chapter, we go dancing.

THE TOOLS

Neologisms attract attention because they stand out from the familiar lexical crowd. If you want to look creative, create new words.

Portmanteau. Combines two words to make a new word. Portmanteau was originally a French word for carpet bag that combined two words—thus a portmanteau.

Verbing. Takes a word and uses it as a novel part of speech.

Getting Medieval. Takes various parts of speech and makes them the object of a sentence.

Venereal Language. Words that describe groups.

7

REPEAT YOURSELF

THE GREEN EGGS CONCOCTION
Repetition That Emphasizes, or Changes, Your Meaning

SO FAR, WE HAVE USED WORDPLAY—sound symbolism, puns, new words, and unusual uses of words—to activate the sounds and associations of memory keepers. Now, instead of creating spanking new words or using words in novel ways, we'll do a bit of recycling. Most of the time, people employ repetition the way a caveman used a club, hitting the same word again and again and again until it mashes thoroughly into people's brains. Crude but often effective. As you have seen, repetition bulks up synapses like a ballplayer on steroids. If you want to try a more artful form of repetition, though, you need to strike that repeated word more subtly, sculpting the results instead of merely banging away.

The easiest, and most common, form of repetition simply repeats a word in each consecutive group, usually at the beginning. While **word repeaters** serve a host of purposes, some of the most effective include **accusation**, **categorical denial**, and getting an audience to **finish your sentence**. You can also repeat a word in a way that **changes the meaning**. And, finally, you can **convey a process** by beginning each clause with a word that ended the last one.

Word Repeaters

ACCUSATION: BLAME! BLAME! I GOT YOU!

Word repeaters can help you make a dramatic accusation, "whereas" style. ("Whereas you have failed to clean your room for an entire week; and whereas you sassed your father yesterday; and whereas you dropped your peas down the heat register . . .") Each repetition lands another smack on the culprit. Watch Dayton sportswriter Hal McCoy swing at Barry Bonds after he was caught using performance enhancers.

> MCCOY: To me you never existed in the pantheon of baseball, you never hit more than 700 home runs, you never hit 73 home runs.

> UNWRITTEN: In my mind, you did not hit more than 700 home runs, nor did you hit 73.

See the difference between the written and unwritten versions? The one shows righteous anger, while the other merely dismisses. The repetition strikes one blow after another to chop limbs from the body of Bonds's work.

Repeating the beginning works great for conveying emotion, as the words come tumbling out like the great sentences in the Old Testament.

> YOU: What do you mean, "We all make mistakes like that"? I didn't get drunk at the trustees' luncheon. I didn't tell Alice Roquefort that if she wasn't over eighty I'd try to "make out with her." I didn't try to teach everyone an obscene sailor song.

You can hear the emotion.

Word repeaters also emphasize a particular word, whether to reflect on a person's character ("You never . . .") or to compare the guilty with the innocent ("I didn't . . ."). Either way, the alleged perpetrator looks nastier with each charge. But you don't have to repeat "I" or "you." You can also repeat an aspect of the person's character or attitude.

> YOU: Without a thought for other people, you went ahead and indulged yourself. Without a thought for the consequences, you caused grave damage . . .

Continuing this tone of righteous indignation, imagine that your loved one borrowed your shirt without telling you. To emphasize its value to you, boldface "shirt" by repeating it.

> YOU: You borrowed my shirt? My lucky shirt? The shirt I need for the presentation tomorrow? The shirt that needs a particular dry cleaner who understands how the cuff gets a wrinkle if they're not careful? My *good* shirt?

We're into the crudest, and simplest, kind of repetition. To create this particular figure, you need only think about the reasons the shirt means a lot to you before you begin your accusation, a matter of a second's quick cogitation.

No question about what that shirt meant to you, but be careful. You're starting to sound a little . . . obsessed. Still, a few repetitions never harmed anyone, especially when you want to get emotional about a particular word—whether "you," "I," or a beloved object. You often hear politicians use word repetitions for emotional effect, because public addresses are ripe for emotion. Aristotle noted that tête-à-tête conversations should be more rational, while an orator addressing the hoi polloi can get away with a little excitement.

CATEGORICAL DENIAL: ALL THE CATEGORY DETAILS

That's not to say you have to limit your repetition to emotional expression. You can also use the device unemotionally in an argument that categorically dismisses the opponent's points one by one. Here's writer Frank Legato at work on this kind of word repeater:

LEGATO: Regardless of which mechanical apparatus is added; regardless of how many funny cartoons there are; regardless of whether they play the song from a TV show, give the player a board game to play, play the overture from *Les Misérables*, or get down on one knee and sing "Mammy," all modern slot machines . . . are computers.

UNWRITTEN: They may show funny cartoons, play the song from a TV show, give the player a board game to play, play the overture from *Les Misérables*, or get down on one knee and sing "Mammy"; all modern slot machines are computers.

Legato's version shows an interesting use of repetition to build a sentence to a crescendo. While his clauses get more and more complicated, like the machines he describes, we don't get lost. "Regardless" provides a way marker before launching us into the comic chaos of slot machines giving us games, playing us tunes, and channeling Al Jolson. (In chapter 8, this kind of repetition will aid another kind of device, the catalog, which uses a list for rhetorical advantage.) Thanks to repetition, the first two clauses serve as booster rockets, letting the sentence boldly go into absurdity. Nice crescendo, Legato.

You can copy this ready-made device for yourself. Begin with an opponent's more reasonable points and build your way up—

or down—to the ridiculous. Use "Regardless" or its cousin, "No matter," to fuel your progress.

> YOU: No matter how much the competition sticks a fancy label on it, no matter how many claims that it slices and dices and does spreadsheets, no matter how sincere their money-back guarantee and offer of their firstborn child if you're not satisfied, their product is still inferior to ours.

To create this variation of a word repeater, you list all your opponent's arguments or advantages, put "regardless" or "no matter" in front of each, build to a crescendo of ridiculousness, and then wipe them all away with the superiority of your product or argument.

EXERCISE

When you speak directly to someone about an unemotional subject—say, whose turn it is to do the dishes (assuming that subject isn't emotional in your household)—experiment by using a repetitive argument and see what your audience's response is like.

> *YOU:* I did them last night. I did them the night before. I did them the night before last. I did them more times than I can count.

Your experiment should also assume a strong and lasting relationship that's relatively immune to obnoxious behavior.

Being the simplest of all figures, repetition of the first word also sounds the most clublike, and it gets its most annoying bashing use among politicians who want to sound biblical.

> *BLOWHARD:* And I will lower taxes. And I will increase Social Security for our seniors. And I will spend bajillions

on defense to honor our brave warriors. And I will cut out all government waste on the remaining 20 percent of the government. And I will eliminate all deficits by burning carbon fuels and protecting the environment. And verily I say unto you . . .

FINISHING YOUR SENTENCE: CHOOSE YOUR IDIOT

In the wrong mouths, beginning word repeaters can turn into a verbal tic. Less instinctive, but often more effective, are the repeaters that do the repetition at the end of phrases or sentences. Watch savvy old John Adams use an ending word repeater to get more out of an expression.

ADAMS: If your actions inspire others to dream more, learn more, do more and become more, you are a leader.

UNWRITTEN: The definition of a leader is that of a person who inspires greatness in people.

You can tell that Adams was used to giving speeches. His sentence repeats "more" to set up a rhythm that gets people thinking along with him: the audience hears "dream more, learn more," and starts finishing the following phrases: "do . . ." MORE! "become . . ." MORE! The listener begins to internalize the words, unconsciously gaining sympathy for the speaker.

Copy Adams's device if you want the same kind of filling-in-the-blank from your audience—particularly if you're holding out a juicy goal for the decision you want them to make. Suppose you want them to put some capital in a little Internet start-up you're forming. Dangle the money in front of their faces.

YOU: If you want to earn money, grow your money, end up with a serious amount of money, invest in ohmanwillthis evermakemoney.com.

A local politician employed the same technique—not to make money but to harsh Michael Brown, the feckless director of the Federal Emergency Management Agency who headed the response to Hurricane Katrina.

AARON BROUSSARD: Take whatever idiot they have at the top of whatever agency and give me a better idiot. Give me a caring idiot. Give me a sensitive idiot. Just don't give me the same idiot.

UNWRITTEN: Michael Brown is an idiot. Anybody would be better than that guy.

Remember that word repeaters emphasize your expression's most critical term. Any time you're stuck for words, find the key ones in advance using the pith method. In Broussard's case, it's clear he came up with one: "idiot." Repeating it again and again, each time with a variation, hits home the idiotic label of the FEMA director. Whether you put them at the beginning or the end, repeaters let you say "Any choice but that one" dramatically and memorably. Remember *Green Eggs and Ham*?

> I do not like them with a fox.
> I do not like them in a box.
> I do not like them here or there.
> I do not like them anywhere.

Essentially, that's what Mr. Broussard does in reverse.

I would take an agency idiot.
I would take a better idiot.
I would take a caring idiot.
I would take a sensitive idiot.

It would have been even better, rhetorically, if the idiots got more and more idiotic through their repetition.

BETTER: Give me a drooling idiot. Give me a five-year-old idiot.

Repeating the last, crucial word is ideal when you're asking for an alternative to the status quo. Imagine your son has an incompetent teacher. You could ask for a caring idiot, but you could also emphasize a more useful key word, like, say, "teacher."

YOU: Give him a scary teacher, a foul-smelling teacher, a militant, yardstick-wielding teacher. Just give him a *teacher*.

Instead of a teacher, you could be talking about a working transit system, or a bed that fits two people, or a child's haircut—anything different from the current state of things. Place your key word at the end, and repeat. You will sound sufficiently desperate, and your audience will want to do anything to stop you from repeating yourself again.

CHANGING MEANING: WHO IS NUMBER TWO?

Sure, even the best word repeaters can get pretty clublike. But watch what happens when you repeat a word only once. This single repetition allows you to set the word in two different contexts for comparison.

Repeat Changer

When Martha Stewart launched an abortive reality series, the show had an aggressive tag line.

> She didn't just invent the business . . . She IS the business.

A formal logician would declare the line guilty of being a tautology, a fallacy that essentially repeats itself to prove itself. But by repeating "business," the promoters got us to pay more attention to the word. So did the accompanying visual, a mean-looking Stewart who had just served a term in prison. Martha, we're made to think, didn't just invent the business, she not only IS the business, she MEANS business. "I don't want to lose my patience," she says in the promo, using another word repeater. "None of you want me to lose my patience." You get the sense that if she has to repeat herself one more time, there will be consequences. Serious consequences.

At its essence, a **repeat changer** is a subtle form of punning—the use of homonyms for wit or double meanings. For example, if a friend urges you to get behind a particular politician, you can reply by repeating the expression.

> YOU: Sure, I'd like to get behind the guy and push.

Yes, that's an old joke—a variation of "Take my wife . . . please!" But it still has its pleasures. Now, what if a pun isn't immediately apparent? Can you still use a repeat changer? Sure. In fact, you may want to try to concoct one if you plan to redefine an issue. Take a word that seems supportive of the other side, and twist it. That's what Derek Smalls says in *This Is Spinal Tap* of the miniature Stonehenge set that turns the band into a laughingstock.

IAN FAITH: I really think you're just making much too big a thing out of it.

DEREK SMALLS: Making a big thing out of it would have been a good idea.

In this case, the repeat changer was easy to pull off—a matter of listening for the opportunity. But in most cases, you have to come up with the appropriate synonyms to make the device work. The trick is to find the pith—the key words—and take it through homonymnastics by finding the synonyms. Suppose someone's husband wants to go on a cruise. On the last cruise, he got drunk and made a fool of himself. Now, the aggrieved wife could turn the conversation into an accusation, repeating the word "you" over and over until he retreated from the rhetorical bludgeoning. But a little wit might make the conversation a little more comfortable for everyone, and make the wife seem less, um, aggrieved. First, she should list the key words in the issue, such as "cruise," "trip," "vacation," "relaxation" . . . Ooh, no need for thesaurus.com here. "Relax" gives me an idea.

WIFE: Sure, you want a cruise because you need to relax. You want to relax your moral standards.

EXERCISE

Take a quote from the media—a good place to find one is Time .com, which offers Quotes of the Day. Try to respond to one of them with a repeat changer. Either take a key word directly from the quote and repeat it in a different context, or use homonymnastics to work off a punning synonym. For example, I just came across a quote by Senator Richard Lugar, a Republican who faces a challenge by tea partiers two years in advance of the election: "Get real," he said. If I were a tea partier myself, I would reply thusly.

MY TEA PARTY SELF: Get real is right, Senator. Get real scared.

Not every repeat changer comes from a pun, though. A still easier way of repeating a word and changing its meaning is the old "Boys will be boys" chestnut. The expression may sound like a mere truism. Boys by definition won't be girls. But one of the most important purposes of repetition is to change the connotation of a word. In this case, boys (individual boys, that is) will generally behave like boys (the entire generalized, puppy-dog-tailed gender). As with any cliché, "Boys will be boys" has exceptions that disprove the rule. Boys, for better or worse, will often be girls. Yet clichés will be clichés, and morons will be morons, which is why clichés often get taken for profound wisdom.

Besides, the form has its unmoronic uses. You can make something sound inevitable, even inescapable, by putting it in "blank is blank" form. Mary Matalin, a Republican operative and fine political commentator, deployed the device when she reviewed Sarah Palin's campaign memoir. Palin used her book to avenge the many slights that the staff of her boss, John McCain, perpetrated on her. Matalin responded with an Austin Powers–esque sentence.

MATALIN: Granted, Palin was a unique nominee, with uncommon charisma and firepower, but number two is number two.

UNWRITTEN: You gotta follow the boss.

She probably meant nothing scatological in her reference to "number two." But the implication is there. Compared to number one, number two is a worthless piece of—that is to say, a worthless mouthpiece.

Try the "boys will be boys" ploy sometime and see how it works for you. "Computers will be computers," you say, eye-rollingly, to a colleague whose PowerPoint presentation has just crashed, and he'll chuckle knowingly. Actually, he's more likely to throw a laptop at your head. But then, coworkers will be coworkers.

CONVEYING A PROCESS: LOSE A SHOE

Another figure lets you lay on words like overlapping tiles. You repeat the last word in a phrase, clause, or sentence by using it to begin the next one—as in Ben Franklin's "For want of a shoe the horse was lost, for want of a horse the rider was lost . . ." Let's call it the **for-want-of-a-shoe** figure.

For Want of a Shoe

This figure will serve you well when you're trying to explain a complex process.

> YOU: Boil the sugar to make a simple syrup, stir the simple syrup with gin, pour the sweetened gin onto ice . . .

Ugh. You'll drive your student to drink with that one. But you have to admit, it's easy to follow. The for-want-of-a-shoe figure works even better, rhetorically, the way Franklin used it: to describe a collapse or a series of accumulating mistakes.

> YOU: Because they didn't bring enough water, they got dehydrated. Being dehydrated, they got hypothermia. Hypothermia impaired their judgment, and bad judgment led to their getting tragically lost.

For want of a shoe packs some condensed wisdom in one figure. Many, perhaps most, tragedies arise from an accumulation of mistakes, one thing leading to another. So you can see two good uses for that shoe figure: to show a process, and to make the conclusion of a series of events sound inevitable—a et of falling dominoes. Watch the difference between these expressions.

> UNWRITTEN: Yeah, the Republicans were in charge when the banks went bust, but if the Democrats hadn't pushed to give loans to people who couldn't afford it, you wouldn't have had those balloon mortgages and the subsequent massive defaults that led to this disaster.

> FOR-WANT-OF-A-SHOE VERSION: Yeah, the Republicans were in charge when the banks went bust. But it was the Democrats, wanting loans for people who couldn't afford them, who pressured the banks. That pressure led to balloon mortgages, ballooning mortgages led to defaults, and the defaults led to the banks going bust.

The first version is clear enough, but it lacks the domino effect we achieve in the second version. The audience follows you through one logical door after another. If you don't like those particular doors—if you happen to be a Democrat, for instance—

then you can respond with your own for-want-of-a-shoe version of those events. Corporate lobbying begat lax regulation, which begat exotic credit default swaps . . . Layer your repetition and lead your audience through a whole different set of doors. Create your own rhetorical real estate.

EXERCISE

Has someone proposed an idea or plan that you don't like? Concoct a dire outcome. Now express it in terms of a for-want-of-a-shoe figure, making that outcome look inevitable. This leads to that, which leads to that, which leads . . .

THE TOOLS

Repetition tends to be the least subtle of all figures, and therefore the most overused. That's why you'll find repetition most in situations where subtlety isn't needed—such as in public speaking and emotional exchanges. Repetition conveys emotion well; it's a staple of humor, for one thing.

Want to get a laugh? Bring up a funny or unusual phrase that someone has used before, in a completely new context. Suppose your friend Jerry said "Hot dog!" when the waitress brought beers in a bar. Your group laughed at the droll expression. Two pitchers later, when the waitress asks if you want another round, nod your head, adding, "And bring my friend a hot dog." The trick is to keep the phrase in the back of your head until you find an opportunity to use it.

Anger often finds its best expression in repetition; you have seen how it works in making an accusation. Ditto with expressing your love for someone or something.

In deft hands, repeated words can enforce points, get an audience emotionally charged up, or explain something difficult.

Word Repeaters. Any one of a variety of figures that repeat words in the beginning, middle, or end of a group of words.

Repeat Changer. Repetition that changes the meaning.

PART III

WORD ARTIST

You know some of the best tools for creating a

soundtrack in your audience's memory.

Now for the second memory keeper

in the SPA set: pictures. In this section you'll learn

ways to catalog, describe, and transform the

objects of your affection and disdain.

8

DRAW A PICTURE

MR. POTATO HEAD, MAN OF PARTS
Catalogs, Russian Dolls, and Other Ways to Bring Subjects Alive

 A PROFESSOR IN MY COLLEGE liked to tell his students, "When you write, draw a picture." He wasn't urging us to try our hand at graphic novels, which had not been invented yet. Instead, he wanted us to craft details that would form a picture in people's heads. A whole picture; not just lovely hair, but blond hair that cascades down to the shoulders; not just a dank basement, but a basement where the green-gray walls sweat and dark things scurry about. If you ever took a writing class, you already know that the angels are in the details. Instead of telling "about" something you want to describe, show the parts that make a great whole.

Some figures are particularly good at rendering these details in memorable ways, giving striking visual images that stick in people's memories. One of the most effective, the **catalog**, uses a list to draw a picture. The catalog's close relatives also take inventory, using clever ways to put together the pieces of description. The **descriptive label** does that description literally, while the **Mr. Potato Head** turns each part of something into a simile, and the nested figure I call a **Russian doll** wraps a description up in a neat package.

THE CATALOG PARTY

Scientists say that an average thought lasts no more than a minute before we lose it. What's more, most of us find it impossible to learn more than one new concept every ten minutes. But research also shows that people more easily absorb thoughts that have been divided into chunks. Clever chunking can prolong an attention span, turning an explanation or story into a mental movie.

Catalog

One of the easiest ways to chunk a setting, situation, or idea is to convert it into a catalog—a list that describes characteristics or contents. A catalog breaks something down into its constituent parts, letting the mental camera run slowly over them. You see the forest better for the trees, by showing how the trees make up the forest. The genius of this figure lies not only in its simplicity but in the way it allows the coiner to organize the contents. Observe this superb example by Margaret Wise Brown. It comes from one of my favorite poems; not really a poem, actually, but the unforgettable children's book *Goodnight Moon*. In just two sentences, Brown gives a clear impression of a rich little kid (a rabbit in the pictures) who employs stalling tactics to keep from having to go to sleep.

BROWN: In the great, green room there was a telephone, and a red balloon, and a picture of a cow jumping over the moon. And there were three little bears sitting on chairs, and two little kittens, and a pair of mittens, and a comb and a brush and a bowl full of mush, and a quiet old lady who was whispering hush.

I just typed that passage from memory—not because I have a prodigious memory but because the words are so memorable. (My having read them to my two children three thousand forty-two times didn't hurt either.) The book would not have been nearly as memorable if it had followed the usual kid-book format.

UNWRITTEN: "Hush, now," said the Quiet Old Lady as the Rabbit Child said good night to everything in the room. And such a room it was, too!

The written version packs a lot of story into that catalog—antsy kid who isn't hungry, birthday, rich parents who can afford great green nurseries, winter. Think how long it would take to spin out the entire scene; Brown gives the telling details instead, letting the reader or listener fill in the gaps. She organizes these details geographically, wandering around the room before stopping at the old lady. (Note also the sound symbolism in the hushing "brush" and "mush.")

To create your own catalog, follow two easy steps—and I do mean easy:

1. **List the telling details.** If you need to, use the pith method to find the key words. Don't feel obligated to leave in all the minutiae—just the elements that get you where you want to go with your audience. Are you trying to make your audience comfortable and sleepy? Then leave out the stiletto heel kicked off by the drunken mother in the great, green room.

2. **Organize your list.** When you describe a scene, think about a movie camera's panning shot. When a beautiful woman gets out of a cab, we first see her legs, followed by the rest of her, before the camera pulls back to reveal the rest of the scene.

Similarly, when you describe a person in a catalog, you can begin from the ground up, or the top down. Or you can start with the person's most eye-grabbing characteristic, and let the mental camera pan up or down from there before pulling back.

Besides the camera technique, you can arrange your list in a variety of ways.

Chronologically. If you tell a story with a list, chronological order usually works best. This happened, and then this. One way to do a chronology by catalog is to leave out the "ands" or "buts" the way a play-by-play announcer works. You can see how legendary sports announcer Vin Scully used it to build tension.

SCULLY: Sandy backs off, mops his forehead, runs his left index finger along his forehead, dries it off on his left pants leg.

Chronological order works whether you're announcing the last pitch in Sandy Koufax's historic 1965 perfect game, or merely telling an anecdote.

YOU: I packed all the bags, fed the kids, loaded the car, shepherded the kids onboard, stopped for gas . . . and then discovered I'd left my eldest behind.

You'll see more about tension in chapter 13. A catalog of events, told without conjunctions until the end, helps build suspense because it sounds less like an obligatory What I Did for Summer Vacation ("Then I played video games. Then my mother came in and yelled at me. Then I got into the car."), and more like a set of events that build to something.

In order of importance. Speaking of building to something: on the fifth anniversary of the Katrina disaster, President Obama told his audience that he wouldn't "dwell on what you experienced and what the world witnessed," and then he proceeded to dwell on the experience.

> OBAMA: We all remember it keenly: water pouring through broken levees; mothers holding their children above the waterline; people stranded on rooftops begging for help; bodies lying in the streets of a great American city.

While there's some chronology to this list, Obama mainly ordered it for dramatic effect, proceeding from the alarming to the tragic. A broken levee was news; bodies in the streets challenged our identity as a nation. If you want to organize your catalog by importance, start from the least and work to the most. Use this form in political speech to sum up an issue. It also works when you're accusing a loved one of a chain of sins. Begin with showing up late for the party and work your way up to the point where he does embarrassing things with a lampshade.

From the general to the particular. Obama's striking scene might have been even more striking if he had ended his list not with "bodies" but with a single body—maybe someone who had been identified, someone with a name. The technique works on more trivial subjects as well. Think of the movie camera again, starting with the panoramic shot and zeroing in on the main character. Ronald Reagan would often end a list of facts with an anecdote that humanized them. "An example is better than a sermon," he liked to say. He went from the general to the particular, talking about government policy then showing how government policy ruined a small farmer in Chicot County, Arkansas;

or talking about defense and then pointing to a heroic soldier in the balcony. You can do the same when your list consists of facts, including those in a business presentation. Put the finest detail last in a bullet list, going from general trends to the effect on a particular store or branch office.

With rhyme. Margaret Wise Brown didn't just use her catalog of the great, green room's contents geographically; the list also works poetically, using a set of rhymes (kittens-mittens, brush-mush-hush) to create the softest rap song ever written. Rhyming works especially well in an invitation. Compare these two versions.

> UNWRITTEN: I'm throwing a party.
> CATALOGED: I'm throwing a beer-and-Skittles, rhyme-and-riddles party.

Never mind which one you'd actually want to attend. The question is, which invitation would you want to recite to your significant other later? The cataloged version is like Margaret Wise Brown, with beer. As with homonymnastics, you can use the thesaurus and a rhyming dictionary to find the right rhymes. In my case, I'd be willing to alter the party just to get a good rhyme. (I wouldn't have to serve that sickly-fruity Skittles candy, though; the expression originally comes from a British pub-bowling game. "Beer and skittles" referred to the wonderful feeling of hanging out in a pub.)

MEET MR. POTATO HEAD

Another kind of cataloging figure breaks down a person or object into constituent parts and then pretends that those parts came from elsewhere. I call it *Mr. Potato Head*. The journalist William Allen White used this device beautifully in his obituary of publisher Frank Munsey.

> WHITE: . . . the talent of a meat packer, the morals of a money changer and the manners of an undertaker.

> With just three phrases, White gives you a vivid image of the oily crook. You can use it as a form of self-deprecating humor.

> YOU: When I play tennis, I have the agility of a tank, the aim of a mole, and the response time of FEMA.

Mr. Potato Head

The Mr. Potato Head figure comes in handy when you want to call attention to a variety of characteristics by exaggerating them. Say you want to describe a party you went to last Saturday: a chaotic, drunken mess with appalling music, badly dressed guests, and the kind of mayo-drenched snacks that give people food poisoning. Instead of droning on and on about how awful it was, try chunking up a nice Potato Head.

> YOU: A lovely party! The food of a bachelor's fridge, the music playlist of an aging hair-band roadie, and guests straight out of *Dumb and Dumber*, without the witty dialogue.

Creating your own Mr. Potato Head isn't hard. Just take a characteristic or part of the subject you want to describe, and come up with an analog for it. Then take the next characteristic or part, find an analog, and continue until your subject is thoroughly spudded. An analog is something that's analogous—an analogy. We'll get to the metaphorical kinds of analogies later. In the meantime, just look for similarities that create the effect you want. If you intend to make a subject look great, use flattering comparisons. Do the opposite if you want to abuse someone or something.

> YOU: The book had the prose style of the *Congressional Record*, the characterization of a computer manual, and the suspense of a phone book.

An even more fun way to use this figure is to throw in a surprise by offering an unflattering analog at the end of a list of nice ones.

> ME: He had the body of Adonis, the eyes of a hypnotist, and the brains of an aging invertebrate.

Actually, I might have done better by sticking to the same family of analogs, limiting myself entirely to Greek characters or the animal world. Mixing analogies isn't as bad as mixing metaphors—you're not doing any reality bending here—but a Potato Head benefits from consistency. So the guy could have the body of a lion or other preternaturally fit creature, along with the eyes of a deer or eagle. When you're doing a catalog of any sort, make sure your items go together. But they can go together in unexpected ways; the best catalogs contain some sort of surprise.

EXERCISES
---

1. Describe a person in plain language. Now put that description into a Mr. Potato Head.

POTATO HEAD: She has the clothing sense of a cheerleader, the makeup skills of a circus clown, and the hair of a Barbie.

2. Count your blessings. Besides being a proven mood lifter, this exercise lets you practice balancing the expected with the unexpected in a catalog. For every "normal" blessing, give thanks for a blessing that some people would consider a curse. If you really want to get fancy, link these odd pairs with alliteration or rhyming.

YOU: Thank God for my wonderful family and worthy foes, for working play and playful work, for candy and carrots, sunny days and shady ways.

THE RUSSIAN DOLL'S FIGURE

Another way to catalog is to wrap your items up. Winston Churchill, that world-class master of figuring, did this at the beginning of the Second World War, referring to Russia.

CHURCHILL: It is a riddle wrapped in a mystery inside an enigma.

Notice how Churchill uses the Russian nesting doll as a metaphor to illustrate the whole nation. But it works even when you're not playing metaphorically with dolls.

EMILY YOFFE (in Slate.com): Many countries collectively agree . . . that children are a tantrum wrapped in a diaper and not worth the trouble.

Russian Doll Figure

I call this the Russian doll for obvious reasons. To deploy the figure, it helps to have an object with some sort of covering. A diaper serves as a natural covering for babies. But your wrapping doesn't have to be cloth. You might have your victim cover himself.

YOU: The principal is a rulebook wrapped in pomposity inside a whole lot of bad skin.

If you happen to be an actual student, please don't try that particular example; it's for demonstration uses only. But you can see that any object or person with a distinctive outer layer can make for a great Russian doll. Suppose you wanted to say something memorable about the fire hazard of a Christmas tree. You can convert it into a comparable object, cover it with something, wrap it with something else, and deliver a good scare.

YOU: A Christmas tree is an incendiary bomb covered in needles and wrapped in electric bulbs.

UNWRITTEN: A Christmas tree is a terrible fire hazard.

Which one will get you the sound bite on the evening news? The first one, naturally. You just can't beat an incendiary bomb for newsworthiness, and a rhetorical incendiary bomb does the job without harming a soul. Figures don't get better than that.

----------- EXERCISE -----------

Remember that poor friend you described in a Mr. Potato Head? Put that same description into a Russian doll. You may find that the Potato Head can serve as the raw material for your doll.

POTATO HEAD: She has the clothing sense of a cheerleader, the makeup skills of a circus clown, and the hair of a Barbie.

RUSSIAN DOLL: She's a circus clown wrapped in pom-poms and topped with a hair extension.

A CATALOG OF SYNONYMS

Multiple Synonyms

A catalog doesn't simply have to describe a variety of traits and objects. You can catalog a single trait or object by rendering its synonyms. It's an excellent way to exaggerate a particular characteristic. Remember the Monty Python dead parrot sketch?

JOHN CLEESE: It's not pinin'! It's passed on! This parrot is no more! It has ceased to be! It's expired and gone to meet its maker! This is a late parrot. It's a stiff! Bereft of life, it rests in peace! If you hadn't nailed it to the perch it'd be pushing up the daisies! It's run down the curtain and joined the choir invisible!! THIS IS AN EX-PARROT!!

You can see a kind of repetition going on here, except that it's repetition of a concept rather than of words. The image the audience gets is of one extremely dead parrot.

In this same vein of exaggeration, piling on synonyms also helps convey multitudinousness.

YOU: He was big, huge, linebacker huge, refrigerator huge, large. He contained multitudes.

To make your own **multiple synonyms**, boil down your point to just one key word, then return to your favorite thesaurus. I just keyed "dead" into thesaurus.com, and found some additions to John Cleese's parrot eulogy.

ME: This parrot has bought the farm. He has checked out. He's defunct, departed, gone to meet his maker. He is a bygone parrot whose date has expired. He is exsanguinous, spectral, and eternally imperturbable.

Now suppose that at the end of this parrot peroration I said, "But wait. Did it just blink?" Synonyms give you a chance to do a kind of rhetorical head fake, leading the audience in one direction and then ending the sentence in another. The writer Joseph Conrad, in his short story "The Return," uses similar descriptive words—more than he really has to—in order to set up a put-down. The result is a synonymical Potato Head.

JOSEPH CONRAD: She strode like a grenadier, was strong and upright like an obelisk, had a beautiful face, a candid brow, pure eyes, and not a thought of her own in her head.

Multiple synonyms can do the same for you, and not necessarily to deliver an insult. You might want to describe a terrible movie thusly.

YOU: It had color, noise, huge clashing armies, sound and fury, and not a single believable character.

Or you can deliver the opposite emotion by praising a hard adventure.

YOU: The hike was painful, agonizing, arduous, and the most fun thing I've ever done.

EXERCISE

Synonyms are essential to wordplay, as you saw in previous chapters. Whenever you're walking someplace or traveling— free, in other words, to observe a passing scene—find alternative adjectives for everything you see. The day is bright, glimmering, shimmering, sunny, clear, limpid. Now switch to alternative nouns: the sun is an orb, a planetary object, a ball, a fire, an eye, a god. Now verbs. Most of the good writers I know are constantly rewording things in their heads. The exercise makes you better at all kinds of figuring, since synonyms and homonyms lie behind so much wordplay. Plus, when the time comes to level a rapid-fire barrage of multiple synonyms, you'll be prepared, ready, locked and loaded, loaded for bear, eager, poised, and all set.

Multiple synonyms create a rhetorical current that sweeps your audience along until you put your hand up like Moses and make the whole rhetorical river roll back. You saw the element of surprise in the Mr. Potato Head, when I threw in an analog that reversed the tone of the others. This is true of every kind of catalog. Any list offers an opportunity to throw in a ringer. One of the great masters of the catalog was the poet Dylan Thomas, whose short memoir, "A Child's Christmas in Wales," contains all sorts of surprising lists. Here he describes the presents he would get for Christmas.

THOMAS: Bags of moist and many-colored jelly babies and a folded flag and a false nose and a tram-conductor's cap and a machine that punched tickets and rang a bell; never a catapult; once, by mistake that no one could explain, a little hatchet . . .

You can see the order to this list, going from harmless to hazardous. But in the middle of this great wealth of gifts comes one that isn't there—the wished-for catapult (slingshot) that never came. "Never a catapult" interrupts the breathless list to show the unfulfilled wish. It raises a laugh when people listen to it. And it reveals Thomas's deep psychological understanding of small boys. The catalog, in his capable hands, is no mere list. Use it not just for description but also for surprise.

DESCRIPTIVE LABEL: THE ROYAL WAX WORKS

We created a picture by assembling the parts, like a jigsaw puzzle. A trickier tool, the descriptive label, pins a snapshot on a person, thing, or concept. But wait, that's not the tricky part; the snapshot then becomes the thing it depicts, representing the original in people's minds.

We don't usually think of Britain's nonworking stiff Prince Charles as a paragon of wit, but look at what he called the leaders of China in his 1997 journal.

CHARLES: Appalling old wax works.

UNWRITTEN: Old farts.

Ever since Charles's journal leaked into the press some years ago, I have found it difficult to see the Chinese leaders without thinking of Madame Tussauds. The ancient Greeks loved this technique, and clever writers have used it ever since.

Descriptive Label

RUMPOLE OF THE BAILEY [referring to his wife]: She-Who-Must-Be-Obeyed.
HOGWARTS RESIDENTS [referring to Lord Voldemort]: He-Who-Must-Not-Be-Named.

I personally find it satisfying, though admittedly catty, to use a descriptive label when mentioning people I strongly dislike. For example, a guy who works with one of my clients drives me crazy. He is a genially stupid man, with a phony laid-back demeanor, flowing blond hair to match his tanning-parlor bronze skin, and a particularly pleasant way of lying, which he does whenever he gets a chance. Naturally I call him Surfer Boy. It's very unprofessional, and I'm not proud of it. But it keeps my blood pressure down when I call him that instead of his actual name. Besides, I've forgotten his actual name. I only call him Surfer Boy, and now most people call him that. I think he likes it.

What's the difference between a descriptive label and a nickname? One can easily turn into the other. A descriptive label, though, can stand on its own, serving as a description of someone you've never met.

FRIEND: So do you know who drove an ATV through your land?
YOU: I saw him but don't know his name. Fat guy. Orca with legs. At least I think he had legs. He wasn't using them at the time.

What will get quoted among those words? I'm guessing "orca with legs." A good descriptive label attaches an indelible label to someone, becoming not just a substitute for a name but a whole new name in its own right—not as concise as Whatshisname but more memorable. The humorist Tom Bodette told how some Indian tribes have a tradition of naming newborns after a notable event that took place before the birth. He said if he and his wife had followed that custom their kid would have been named Datsun-That-Won't-Start. I rather like that tradition. It attaches a story to every kid, preferably one with a moral; young Datsun presumably would grow up taking the Check Engine light very seriously.

We'll get into other forms of labeling in the chapters to come, but the descriptive label makes a good start. To create one, you can create a catalog of characteristics, then think of something that represents or sums up those traits. You can imagine Prince Charles, consciously or otherwise, remembering the appearance of the Chinese leadership—stiff, and old, with fixed, formal expressions—and think of wax figures. (The alliteration, "wax works," makes a nice finishing touch.)

Your turn: think of a person or group you want to label. I do it all the time in my head; it relieves a lot of frustration on the highway or in the grocery. Think of the traits that annoy you, then think of something else that matches those traits. Or simply make the traits themselves stand for the person.

YOU: That crash dummy in the Lexus just cut me off!

I was thinking "crash" and "stupid," and the guy suddenly turned into one of those bald mannequins with a test symbol. You can as easily call a hectoring vegetarian The Vegan, or a mouth breather the Pink Panter. Yes, it's cruel, and I don't recommend doing it in front of others, except maybe your closest loved ones. Unless they're mouth breathers.

---------- *EXERCISE* ----------

We victimized a friend with a Mr. Potato Head and a Russian doll. Can you take the same description and turn it into a descriptive label?

YOU: The Hair Extension.

A descriptive label need not restrict itself to people, though. A school could become the Brick House or the Smells Lab. A stereotype map of the world posted on i.imgur.com recently applied descriptive labels to every region of the globe. Canada gets the label "Drunks and Nothing." The northeast coast of the United States is "Freaks"; West Coast is "Stoners." In between is "Jesus and Meth." India is "Tech Support," New Zealand is "Hobbits," and everything south of that is "Stupid Penguins." While some people might find it offensive, I think the map says more about attitudes than the regions themselves.

Not all descriptive labels have to be pejorative. Labeling one's abs the Situation can be lucrative as well as self-flattering. But when you substitute a slice of someone for the whole being, that being generally doesn't come out looking great. Even positive characteristics can seem negative in a descriptive label; calling a smart person the Brain, for instance, instantly sticks nerdy glasses and a "kick me" sticker on a victim. The figure dehumanizes enemies and hurts friends. But it sure can sum up some fine bad attitudes.

SLOGAN MOVES

A close cousin to the descriptive label makes it easier to say nice things about people. The **slogan** is like a descriptive label, except that it isn't meant to substitute for the name. Instead, the figure enhances the name.

Slogan

Our second-born, George, got his name from my great-uncle George, a star high school quarterback in suburban Philadelphia and lifelong conservative Republican. Around the First World War, Uncle George's football team refused to play a home game against a rival high school team because one of its members was black. Some seventy years later, he told an interviewer for an oral history project that he still felt bad about going along with the decision, and he gave a moving account of seeing the black boy cry and doing nothing about it. I played the recording in a library after Uncle George died, and decided then and there to try to talk Dorothy into naming our kid after him if we ever had a son. There were more obvious family members to name George after; my uncle Ward shot down three Messerschmitts before dying heroically over the English Channel on Easter Sunday 1944.

Which label would we want applied to our son: Ward the hero, or George the considerer? Heroism makes a simple lesson; on the other hand, I wanted my son's name to attach him to someone who could recognize his own mistakes and learn from them. That's a more complex lesson, and one that most of us find especially difficult to learn. (Though I wouldn't mind if our George became a Word Hero, of course.)

Slogans can make a big difference in someone's posthumous reputation as well. Take Peter the Great, and how much more fondly history remembers the drunken, murdering Russian westernizer than, say, Britain's Edward Lackland (they also called him Edward Softsword) or Ethelred the Unready.

Yes, a slogan can hurt as well as flatter. The late, lamented *Spy* magazine—a triumph of journalistic snark in the late eighties and early nineties—could hardly mention a celebrity without sticking a deprecatory slogan onto him. Socialite Nan Kempner was "Nan Kempner, the knock-kneed socialite"; Henry Kissinger was Kissinger, "the chubby socialite-war criminal"; Sylvester Stallone was "unbearable Play-Doh–faced homunculus–action toy Sylvester Stallone." You can accomplish the same labeling feat by attaching a description to the end—or, sometimes, the beginning—of a person's name.

Bob the incompetent plumber

Plump, frizzy-haired Sharon

Dave the Great Guy

That last one is real. I once worked with a guy named Dave, who was truly a great guy. Salt of the earth. Thoughtful. Also extremely good-looking, in a dreamboat, make-women-go-shy way. Everyone in the office, man or woman, would say at the mention of his name, "He is such a great guy!" As if anyone that good-looking had a God-given right to be otherwise. His being a great guy was a wonderful gift Dave had bestowed on us. So, naturally, the label became a joke, and poor, nice Dave became Dave the Great Guy. Only he really was a great guy. Still is.

DEFINITION: LAWSUITS ON WHEELS

A label comprises a kind of **definition**. If Dave had an entry in the dictionary, it would read: *Dave (n) Nice guy.* When you describe a concept rather than a person, you can label the whole thing with a simple definition. Jon Stewart often does this on the *Daily Show*.

> STEWART: The Internet is just a world passing around notes in a classroom.

Definition

The writer Ambrose Bierce out-Stewarted Stewart more than a century before. In *A Devil's Dictionary*, Bierce defined terms in a way that spelled out a whole dark attitude.

> Befriend: To make an ingrate
>
> Destiny: A tyrant's authority for crime and a fool's excuse for failure
>
> Discussion: A method of confirming others in their errors
>
> Robber: A candid man of affairs
>
> Saint: A dead sinner revised and edited
>
> Truth: An ingenious compound of desirability and appearance

A definition is a kind of alchemy in which a description and a rule are blended together in an attempt to create the truth. When the definer succeeds, the result is memorable. You set your opinion in stone. So if I want to oppose off-road vehicles on my town's roads, I should start with the sentence "Off-road vehicles are . . ." and fill in the blank.

ME: Off-road vehicles are lawsuits on wheels

Not bad. But I don't want to focus too much on lawsuits.

ME: Off-road vehicles are a form of rolling vandalism.

Nah. Too fancy. Remember, my town cares mostly about the cost issue.

ME: Off-road vehicles are toys that burn our money as well as gas.

Well, you get the point. To create your own definition, go through the pith method to get the key words. Now you'll have to narrow those words down to a single word; more than one definition starts looking more like a dictionary than a memorable expression. Then apply a rule to the word. What do ORVs end up in? Vandalism and lawsuits. Then attach wheels to them, reminding your audience of what you're defining. ORVs are very expensive toys, except that most toys don't burn money. Or trigger landowner liability lawsuits, for that matter.

A definition is really a form of description, reinforced with a dictionary-like authority. Or, as Ambrose Bierce might put it:

Definition: Words that turn opinion into truth

THE TOOLS

While this chapter threw a box's worth of tools at you, all of them are variations of the catalog and the definition. Half of these tools list, and the others define.

Catalog. A descriptive list.

Mr. Potato Head. A catalog of analogs.

Russian Doll. A catalog with packaging.

Multiple Synonyms. A catalog of words with similar meaning.

Descriptive Label. A description that stands for the name of someone or something.

Slogan. A description that immediately precedes or follows the name.

Definition. A description that defines.

9

TRANSFORM THINGS

HOMICIDAL ZOMBIE MONETARY INSTRUMENTS
Tools That Shrink and Expand

 EXAGGERATION HAPPENS TO BE a sport in our family. When our kids were little, they couldn't dork skulls without claiming their heads had been split open. The four of us continue to throw around multiples of a billion like Congress. While this kind of reality-inflation produces entertainingly tall tales, it rarely makes for accurate reporting. My friends have learned to discount what they call the "Heinrichs Exaggeration Factor"; years ago, after drinking some thirty beers apiece in a Manhattan bar, two of them came up with an actual number for that factor: six. Divide everything a Heinrichs says by six, they claimed, and you have a reasonably accurate number. For example, if I said they had thirty beers apiece, that would mean they had only five. I got so I would deliberately multiply everything by six when I talked to them, knowing they would discount me.

The Greeks, who were master exaggerators, called this rhetorical inflation *hyperbole* (hie-PER-bo-lee), which means "throw beyond." This tool has ambitions above its station. Its reach exceeds its grasp. It's always getting ahead of itself, biting off more than it can chew and splitting its head open. I love it for that. Hyperbole is the Paul Bunyan, Moby-Dick, and King Kong of rhetoric. It never settles for less, not in a billion years.

Hyperbole

There are those who scorn hyperbole, seeing it as a distortion or even a lie. But exaggeration isn't necessarily lying, any more than calling the moon a balloon is lying. Both hyperbole and metaphor qualify as *tropes*. As you will see in the next chapter, tropes constitute nonliteral language. Metaphors and hyperbole both speak nonliterally; if you use them to mislead and your audience takes them literally, both can become lies.

At its best, the hyperbole lets you apply color to an anecdote or issue. Done artfully, it can also make things look bigger than they are, increasing their prominence in people's memory. While the audience shouldn't be expected to take your exaggeration at face value (or even at one-sixth of face value), throwing the facts higher lets you express a feeling of vastness. But strangely enough, a hyperbole does not only make things hyper. It can also produce the opposite effect, allowing you to shrink objects. In this chapter you'll look at techniques that let you blow up or diminish people, things, and ideas. All of them are related to some extent to hyperbole—nonliteral language that throws beyond.

Among the six billion ways to render hyperbole, four of the most effective include the **last-person-on-earth scenario**, **reductio ad absurdum**, **feigned precision**, and **understatement**. It may surprise you that some of the techniques and variations actually pretend to understate the case. So why did I include them in a chapter on hyperbole? Because more often than not, understatement has a hyperbolic effect—if not exaggerating your case, then inflating your own image.

ABSOLUTE SCENARIO:
USING WHIPPETS AND NAKED ASSISTANTS

But let's start with the most extreme kind of hyperbole, which I call the *last-person-on-earth figure*. Young ladies have traditionally used it to destroy the self-esteem of lads throughout the ages.

YOUNG LADY: I wouldn't go out with you if there was a second worldwide flood and Noah himself invited us on board to propagate the species.

UNWRITTEN: I don't want to go out with you under any circumstances.

You can use the last-person-on-earth technique as a ready-made figure, Mad Libs style.

YOU: I wouldn't [verb], even if [scenario].

Last-Person-on-Earth Figure

While a logician will question whether you can exaggerate an impossibility, most people will tell you (illogically) that anything is possible. So, yes, in the real world, you can exaggerate that case. Instead of merely saying "No way," recruit the last person on earth for dramatic or comical effect. Watch what *Slate* columnist Jack Schafer does in admiring a colleague's reporting.

SCHAFER: Hell, I couldn't write a better piece if given a month, five naked research assistants, and a crate of whippets.

You can see a positive version of the last person on earth here. Use this method to praise someone.

YOU: Nice voice! I couldn't sing that better with another five beers and a goose from Suzie.

Of course, people might take this wrong. They might think you're being sarcastic, which maybe you are. If you are being sarcastic, then make sure you take it over the top.

YOU: Lovely singing voice! I couldn't sing better while gargling ice cubes with my finger in the socket.

EXERCISE

Lavishly compliment a loved one using the last-person-on-earth figure. Use three items for comparison, starting with a fairly reasonable one and working your way up to the truly outrageous.

YOU: Wow, you couldn't look better if you'd taken a Pilates class, gotten your hair done like that secretary on *Mad Men,* and wore a dress with a Frederick's of Hollywood label.

Your loved one may doubt your sincerity; in which case, let her compliment you back for laughs. Can the figure work seriously as well? Of course it can—the last-person makes a memorable addition to a retirement luncheon. ("I doubt that anyone could do better with . . .") And it can make a half-serious reply to a teenager's unreasonable request for the car. ("I don't care if every girl on earth is clamoring for your attention and you're late for an audition with *American Idol.* You're not getting the car.") But for practice, try using the last-person figure humorously. I find it easier than the more straight-faced version.

As you can see, hyperbole can afflict or comfort, depending on whether you set the instrument for stun or kill. Now watch what happens when you direct the ray toward your opponent's own point.

REDUCTIO AD ABSURDUM: WAR IN HIGH HEELS

When security consultant George Friedman wanted to ridicule the notion that America could be made safe from terrorist threat, he used a tried-and-true rhetorical technique, the *reductio ad absurdum*, or "reduction to absurdity." Speaking to a *USA Today* reporter, he used the technique to exaggerate the notion of a secure nation.

> FRIEDMAN: You don't have the resources to childproof the entire country.

You don't get safer than childproofing. While the reductio ad absurdum reduces the logic, it blows up the conclusion, pursuing the argument to an illogical end. Absurdum has a very specific purpose: to exaggerate the weakness in someone else's argument.

Reductio ad Absurdum

To produce one, first look for the weak spot. Suppose you attend a school board meeting in which someone suggests making the sports teams sell raw carrots instead of homemade cookies to raise funds. The proponent points to the epidemic of childhood obesity, and rightly notes that carrots are better for kids than cookies. So what's the weakness in that argument other than the likelihood of young athletes rioting in the parking lot? Well, in order for the carrots to raise money, people have to buy them; and cookies are way easier to sell than carrots.

Having spotted the weakness, you proceed to exploit it. Dream up a scenario in which students are pelted with carrots by homeowners who resent kids lecturing them about their diet. Or the town having to deal with an infestation of rabbits after piles of carrots are dumped all over town. Or the team selling so few they'll have to improvise.

YOU: They'll be stuffing carrots into the buses' gas tanks as an alternative fuel source.

The absurdum can also work in the form of an **if-then clause**: if your opponent's absurd point is true, then this even more absurd point must also be true. Scriptwriters use this method whenever they depict a celebrity meeting regular folk.

KATY PERRY: Hi, I'm Katy Perry.
REGULAR GUY: Yeah, and I'm Ben Stiller.

If-Then Clause

If you're Katy Perry, the logic goes, then I'm equally likely to be Ben Stiller. Russell Crowe used the device when prosecutors in New York State charged him with felony assault. He had thrown a cell phone at a hotel concierge, apparently with better aim than the Yankee pitchers were showing that season.

CROWE: If I'm an international menace like the [prosecuting] attorney is suggesting, then fine. I'll just stay here.

Crowe, who was safe at home in Australia, didn't execute a precise absurdum; he stuck to exaggerating the prosecutor's description of him. I would have preferred a less passive form of rhetorical aggression.

IMPROVED CROWE: If I'm an international menace like the prosecutor is suggesting, then maybe they should send a squad to come get me. Just give me time to grab my breastplate and spear.

The other day, a Saturday, my wife and daughter and I checked into a resort in suburban Philadelphia during a road trip. As someone who has to travel a lot, I have spent more than my share of Saturday nights in hotels where the hallways were filled with late-night revelry. I asked the front desk if they would give us a room on a floor without any wedding parties. The woman at the desk shook her head. "We have three weddings, a bar mitzvah, and a sports team," she said, as if we'd walked into a really bad movie. "People book us because it's a romantic spot," she explained.

My wiseacre daughter stared out the window at an enormous parking lot overlooking an office park on what used to be beautiful farmland.

DOROTHY JR.: If this is romantic, then the Olive Garden must be Eden.

I gazed at her fondly while the manager frantically looked for an isolated room where our sarcasm wouldn't disturb the wedding parties. If a soulless, corporate place like this is romantic, then a chain restaurant must be the ultimate haven.

The figure used to get a lot more use than it does now, perhaps because current society tends to get lost in any kind of logical statement. It's still worth reviving in intelligent company, and in more intelligent ways. Watch *Slate*'s William Saletan at work.

SALETAN: But if this is heart surgery, the wound that made it necessary was inflicted by the surgeons themselves.

Saletan is referring to the BP oil spill of 2010. The unwritten version helps explain what he's talking about.

UNWRITTEN: The ones who caused the problem are now claiming to fix it.

The if-then clause can help you take apart any ridiculous assertion, such as corporate execs declaring themselves heart surgeons. While Saletan's sentence has a certain elegance to it, I like my rhetorical heart surgery delivered in a less sterile fashion.

ME: If this is heart surgery, I'd rather have it done by an auto mechanic.

It would be nice to see more entertaining sarcasm in politics. One does every once in a while. Richard Haass, a former State Department official under George W. Bush, used an if-then clause in response to President Bush calling the war in Afghanistan "an opportunity."

HAASS: If this is an opportunity, what's Iraq? A once-in-a-lifetime chance?

Creating your own if-then clause simply entails provisionally accepting the other person's point by repeating it with an "If" in front ("If this is an opportunity . . ."). This buys you time to think of two things:

1. A comparable—something associated with the subject of your opponent's sentence. (If a, then b.)

2. A possible exaggeration of that comparable. (If a does b, then x does y.)

Imagine a husband coming home and announcing to his wife that he has bought a sports car; he even has the nerve to call it an "investment." This kind of ridiculous claim is ripe for an if-then clause, because the device reduces an opponent's illogical sentence to absurdity. Spotting her chance, the man's wife repeats, "If that car is an investment . . ." while eagerly searching for a comparable and a hyperbole. In this case, a good comparable will come from another luxury purchase. The previous week, the woman has bought herself a sexy pair of Jimmy Choo slingback heels. Now, what would be an absurd exaggeration of "investment"? Think of the synonyms: asset, venture capital, leveraged buyout . . . The phrase "asset management" comes to mind because it sounds stupidly technical.

WIFE: If that car is an investment then my Jimmy Choos count as asset management.

That comeback would work even better if the husband has criticized those shoes as an extravagance. I'd say we're looking at new shoes in the near future.

EXERCISE

The if-then clause makes for a good "top this" game at dinnertime. Ask one person to make an assertion or render an opinion. The next person has to reduce that point to absurdity. Then the next person reduces that absurd point to even more absurd absurdity, and so on.

PERSON 1: Justin Bieber is actually a very good singer.
PERSON 2: If Justin Bieber is a good singer, then my cat should audition for the Met.

> *PERSON 3:* If your cat can sing opera, then I'll let my husband sing in church.
> *PERSON 4:* If Bob sings in church, I'll look for the other horsemen of the Apocalypse.

PRECISION: COLD, HARD, INFLATED NUMBERS

When you speak to your own kind about a rival or enemy, you can use exaggeration as a way of bringing the tribe together. Aristotle called this kind of language "demonstrative"; it deals with absolutes, particularly the values you share. Hyperbole fits right into this kind of speech. When the audience expands to include some who are outside the tribe, though, the results can be laughable. Republicans looked pretty silly, for example, when their attacks on the Federal Reserve got repeated beyond Fox News and right-wing websites. In order to inject some financial Viagra into the flaccid American economy, the Fed bought up some government bonds in a policy it called "quantitative easing." While this isn't the stuff of a Matt Damon thriller—don't ask me how the government can buy its own debt—the Republicans saw it as an opportunity to stir up their own base. One commentator called this bond purchase "injecting high-grade monetary heroin" into the economy. Another warned of an "undead homicidal zombie market." Cool! You can picture tailored Federal Reserve bankers shot-gunning stoned, bloody-mawed zombie quantitative easlings as they stagger down Wall Street. Maybe this is the stuff of a Matt Damon thriller after all.

We won't get to analogies until the next chapter. But while a wild analogy like quantitative zombies has the advantage of being indivisible by six, it seems deranged to anyone but the true believer. Hyperbole shouldn't sound like an LSD flashback. In fact, one of the most effective ways to pull off an exaggeration is to make it sound precise and objective—no zombies, just cold, hard, inflated numbers. The truer, more accurate you can make a hyperbole sound, the better it comes off. Compare these two lines about the weather in New England.

> MARK TWAIN: In the spring I have counted one hundred and thirty-six different kinds of weather inside of four-and-twenty hours.

> UNWRITTEN: In a single day the weather changes a billion times.

Twain's version sounds positively scientific. The unwritten version just sounds like a throwaway exaggeration. The lesson? When you exaggerate, try to make it sound like an understatement.

> SPOUSE: Did I ever tell you about how my great-grandfather patented a false nose for circus clowns?
> YOU: Precisely eighty-two times. Not counting this one.

Exact-sounding numbers lend verisimilitude to exaggeration, and reality is funnier than fiction, even if the "reality" is fictional. My son, George, loved precision when he was little, and he insisted on numbers even when none were at hand. Here's a typical dialogue on one of the family's weekly hikes in the White Mountains of New Hampshire.

> GEORGE: How much farther to the top?
> ME: Oh, I don't know. Not too long.
> GEORGE: How much?
> ME: I don't . . . two miles.

That would satisfy him. After a couple years of this, I learned simply to answer with any reasonable number that popped into my head. I threw in fractions for extra made-up precision.

GEORGE: How tall is that tree, Dad?
ME: That's a big one. Fifty-seven feet three and a half inches.
GEORGE: How do you know?
ME: Instant triangulation. Remind me to teach you when you're old enough.

At twenty-two, George has outgrown both his desire for precision and his gullibility. And for some reason he takes everything I say with skepticism. It could be more than the fabricated numbers. He told me recently that for years he was terrified of bagpipes after I warned him they cause cancer. When he was five, he had proposed buying a bagpipes album for his Scotophile mother, and I informed him of the hazards of listening to bagpipes. I'm guessing that at least three thousand people have died horrible long-term deaths from listening to that album.

UNDERSTATEMENT: NOT QUITE SHOT OR DROWNED

One problem with exaggeration, which feigned precision tries to alleviate, is an audience's tendency to discount your claim—especially if, like me, you favor hyperbole overmuch. But you can actually cause an image to expand in your audience's head if you deliver it as an understatement. In the right circumstances, downplaying your words can make you sound heroic. In other words, understatement can give people an exaggerated picture of you. Watch Winston Churchill at understated work.

CHURCHILL: Nothing in life is so exhilarating as to be shot at without result.

UNWRITTEN: I've been shot at in battle, and the sense of exhilaration of emerging unscathed is indescribable.

Admittedly, you may have to be British and the possessor of an extra-stiff upper lip to get away with the line he used. "Without result" is marvelous because it conveys "Nothing happened" in the lowest of low-key terms while making the audience think of what "result" means. They think, "He could have been killed." War lends itself to understatement, because the horrors speak for themselves. The legendary Admiral William Halsey sent a radio message in October 1944, after the Japanese claimed that the American Third Fleet had been sunk or had "retired."

HALSEY: Our ships have been salvaged and are retiring at high speed toward the Japanese fleet.

UNWRITTEN: Propaganda to the contrary, our ships are in working order. In fact, we're attacking the Japanese.

We live in such a bombastic time that you might wonder whether a heroic understatement like Halsey's might even get noticed. The TV talk mavens get paid for hysteria, not wit. But I like to think that scarcity breeds value. (So does excess, apparently; it depends on the audience.) A rule of thumb in talking about an injury is to downplay the injury in a way that calls attention to it. Instead of acting like my kids and claiming a split-open head, let your audience acquire the gore on their own.

YOU: My collarbone? Tree attack.
ADMIRER: You hit a tree?
YOU: No, the tree attacked my bike. I was just in the way.

You'll get a better response than if you had played up your near-death experience.

I had one of them—a near-death experience, I mean—while trying to canoe rapids on the Mascoma River near my home. The river was in flood, and I had planned to take the safer side at a point where the current forked. But I was so adrenaline pumped and foolish that I decided at the last moment to switch over to the class-four rapids on the other side. Instead I got caught broadside by a "strainer," a submerged tree. My attempt to paddle off only caused the canoe to flip, and I found myself sitting on the dark bottom of the river, blinded by the turbulence and held down by the river's hydraulics.

At this point my story diverges like the river. At times I've stressed my successful escape. Discovering that my hand still held my paddle in a death grip, I poked around for an opening under the tree's branches and trunk and came out on the other side—into class-four rapids. Needless to say, I survived, with skin and ego sorely bruised.

More often, though, I tell the story's other version, in which I spend little time on my escape and focus on the minute I sat on the bottom of the river. The line that gets people's attention, and spurs great conversation, downplays the drama.

ME: As I sat there, I heard a voice inside my head: *You are such an idiot.*

The line gets a chuckle, but it exaggerates my bravery. (I rarely add the fact that I threw up later.) To achieve that effect, I used a common tactic in understatement: focus on something trivial or unscary to show (or feign) insouciance in the face of terror. Fiction writers often use the technique to set off scary moments: the character facing down the gun notices a pigeon soaring in the sky overhead. You use it to exaggerate your character. If you're telling a story about having to speak in front of a large group for the first time, you can describe some funny detail.

> YOU: While I was being introduced and fighting off a panic attack, I noticed a poppy seed stuck in one of my molars. That poppy seed became a kind of talisman.

Or focus on some feeling or memory that has nothing to do with the speech itself.

> YOU: While I was being introduced and fighting off a panic attack, I suddenly thought of Baby Ruth bars. I hadn't had a Baby Ruth bar in years. Now, suddenly, I thought how much nicer eating a candy bar would be than speaking in front of these people.

Another form of understatement, the **litotes** (lie-TOE-tees), exaggerates the opposite while denying it. I'm using the technical name here because you'll find it in increasingly common usage in college and even high school classes. Besides, it's only three syllables, and just two if you mispronounce it and call it a LIE-toats.

Litotes

Watch how the figure works in these examples.

> He didn't exactly set the art world on fire.
>
> Let's say the play wasn't a smash hit.
>
> I'm not defusing bombs for my health, here.

In other words, the art and the play bombed, and working with bombs is extremely unhealthy. Which makes the litotes a kind of understatement, right? Yes, albeit an over-the-top understatement. Then again, not exactly over the top. Maybe a little under the top.

The greatest litotes in history was an often-misquoted cable sent by Mark Twain after newspapers erroneously reported his death.

TWAIN: The report of my death was an exaggeration.

The quote counts as a litotes because it denies a hyperbole. Twain also reveals an important quality of the device: it lets you call attention to a hyperbole in a hyperbolic way. By using a litotes to deny his death, he implies that he's not exactly in the full flower of youth.

Americans as a culture are not very good at being wry. We like too much noise and optimism for wryness. Which is why we should practice it. The figure surprises people who are used to hearing straight hyperbole. The litotes is doubly surprising because it expresses an understatement *through* hyperbole. It works especially well when someone states the obvious. Respond by denying the hyperbolic opposite—the more ridiculous, the better.

LOVED ONE: Looks like rain.
YOU: Yes, it's not exactly a day when the sun does its smiley face in the sky and bluebirds dance on your shoulder.
LOVED ONE: What's gotten into you?

A litotes. Tell him you're just practicing.

——————— *EXERCISE* ———————

The litotes can help you with your story about speaking to a crowd. Suppose you want to convey the size of the crowd—not the precise size, but how big it seemed to you at the time. You could use a simple hyperbole and claim that a billion people were there. Or you can use the more elegant litotes.

YOU: It wasn't like I was speaking at the dinner table.

Or:

YOU: It wasn't exactly an intimate tête-à-tête.

What makes litotes and other figures of understatement re-remarkable is their paradoxical ability to turn up the volume by turning it down. "He didn't exactly set the world on fire" conveys exactly the opposite impression: that his efforts didn't heat up Earth one degree, thank goodness.

THE TOOLS

The English used to call hyperbole "drawing the long bow." I like the analogy; every rhetorical device deserves a worthy target.

Hyperbole. Exaggeration.

Last Person on Earth. Even the most extreme circumstances, this figure alleges, won't produce what your audience wants.

Reductio Ad Absurdum. Reduction of an opponent's point to absurdity.

If-Then Clause. A reductio ad absurdum put in the form of *if* (ridiculous assertion), *then* (absurd conclusion).

Feigned Precision. A form of hyperbole that pretends accuracy.

Understatement. Rhetorical low-balling, often for hyperbolic effect.

Litotes. An understatement that denies an exaggeration.

10

CHANGE REALITY

TROPICAL WORD STORMS
Metaphor, Simile, and the Likable Analogy

LIFE CERTAINLY IS no bowl of cherries, mine little resembles a box of chocolates, and I assure you that no one has ever promised me a rose garden. I did get out of the rat race some years ago and, judging from the speed at which I'm being passed, do not seem to be in the fast lane.

The air we breathe is thick with metaphors (including this sentence). **Metaphors** are the leading tropes, the top nonliteral dogs. The word "metaphor" comes from the Greek for "carry over" or "transfer." But the tool is more mixing bowl than Grecian urn. When the singing nun tells us the hills are alive with the sound of music, we mix those images together in our heads: Alps, Edelweiss, living creatures, music . . . Actually, that metaphor doesn't work terribly well, by my way of thinking, because it's hard to picture hills coming alive without feeling alarm. But you get my point. Air is thick, and hills remain metaphorically alive.

Metaphor

A metaphor makes big claims. It doesn't just say that *a* is like *b*; the trope claims that *a* and *b* are one and the same. The metaphor acts as the incubator of understanding, morphing words where we lack the terms to describe new phenomena, inventions, or discoveries. An old story about the pidgin dialect spoken in the Pacific Islands describes a piano as "black box you hit him in teeth he cries." Funny as that sounds, it's not outlandish to describe the keys as teeth. They look like teeth, cavities and all. Similarly, those scurrying things with tails we use to move the cursor on our computer look like mice, so they became "mice." When things share characteristics, they're ripe for pairing up as metaphors. (Note that "ripe" is a metaphor, in the sense of "just right.") We'll spend some time on this trope as a way of getting used to the tropical world—the world of tropes, I mean. Along the way we'll play with metaphor's more moderate relatives, **simile** and **analogy**.

LICIT METAPHORNICATION

Anything new or unfamiliar offers an opportunity for a metaphor. Have you ever been lost driving and ended up going through someplace that's crushingly dull or empty? Here's your chance to name this area in a way that others in the car will repeat. Time to metaformulate:

1. **Find the pith.** By now you should be pretty good at this and have no need to noodle about with pen and paper. What are the key words here? "Empty" and "boring" come to mind. Next . . .

2. **Think of the comparables**—places or things or even people that share these characteristics. What is the emptiest thing you can think of? How about a vacuum?

Excellent! "The Vacuum" isn't such a bad name. From then on, your loved ones will tell the story about getting lost and going through The Vacuum. You could also play with your other key word. What's the most boring thing you know? How about your uncle Rick? Then you could name the place Rickland, or simply Uncle Rick. It should get a laugh unless Uncle Rick happens to be in the car.

Besides allowing you to make fun of relatives, metaphors also let you explain an opinion or idea. I call the figures and tropes in this book "tools," for example—a metaphor that helps explain what all these weird terms are for. Whenever you have an idea, try to metaformulate a name to make people understand you instantly. If your audience is into sports, don't be shy to come up with a sports metaphor. A shady move by a competitor can be a blind-side tackle. A premature proposal among hockey fans can be "icing." (If they're not all hockey fans who understand the foul of moving the puck past center line without a player to receive it, they might mistake your metaphor for one involving cake.)

Wall Street types have taken to calling their arcane offerings "products," a terrific metaphor that makes people believe they are buying something tangible. You can metaformulate a name that explains your own business or idea by finding the pith's key words, then listing some comparables. Chances are you find an excellent match.

As my examples imply, metaphors make for excellent labels and brands. Suppose you open your own business—a hair salon, say. You want to avoid the usual clichéd names like Shear Beauty, Hairtime, or The Cuttery. (A home-based salon near me disturbingly calls itself "Shear Madness.") To come up with your own brand, think about the characteristics that set your business apart from the competition. Your salon will treat clients as honored guests, making them feel *important* as well as groomed.

That's your pith: clients as VIPs. Now, what comparable institutions treat clients thusly? (We'll skip "Hair Bordello," OK?) Corporate jets certainly make passengers feel important. "G6 Salon" might appeal to the hip-hop crowd, the sort who actually like the horrible song "Like a G6." An exclusive nightclub also makes certain hair-pampered people feel important. Find a defunct club like Studio 54 and name your salon after it (after your lawyer vets it, of course). Or go all the way and make your client feel like the godly elect: The Temple of Perfection or something.

Beware of going to metaphorical extremes, though. Wars make for popular political metaphors because of their very extremity. But that's also why war rarely works as well as its metaphorical users hope. The difference between the two things you combine can't be incredibly far unless you're trying to be funny.

YOU: I'm waging a war on dandelions.

Lyndon Johnson's War on Poverty was mislabeled because it was so easy to see the difference between a human enemy and a social condition. Wars make poverty, not relieve it. Similarly, when Jimmy Carter called the energy crisis the "moral equivalent of war," he didn't get much rhetorical traction.

Some Internet discussion boards automatically expel anyone who uses the word "Hitler." And the best that politicians on the right got when they compared Obama to Hitler was some extreme eye rolling. Obama and Hitler lie too far apart on the totalitarian continuum.

Some people prefer disease to war and dictators as their metaphor of choice.

Terror is a cancer on society.

That's a great metaphor, and even a useful one, until you take it literally. Mistaking terrorism for a medical ailment leads us down curative paths. But then, terrorism isn't war, either, even if it's more like war than cancer is. Americans' first instinct in time of war is to bomb the daylights out of the enemy, then give it billions in restoration funds. This strategy worked great after World War Two. Of course, World War Two happened to have been an actual war and not a metaphorical one. How do we wage war against terrorists when there aren't governments or armies to fight?

But when we take the metaphor seriously, it's hard to resist declaring another country a "terrorist state." That gives us something to bomb and restore—an army to attack and defeat, a dictator to depose, and an economy to prop up. Iraq fit the terrorism-is-war metaphor perfectly. And so, before we finished clearing out the actual nest of terrorists in Afghanistan, we attacked a trope. Or, to put it more mildly: our disagreements over the war tend to be mostly tropical. Iraq was a "terrorist state," the Bush administration said. No, say critics of the war. It's Vietnam. Neither trope helps us understand the best course of action unless we take both of them with a big figurative grain of salt.

Metaphors can help us understand novel events; but when we mistake the events for the metaphors—when we take the tropes literally—we enter dangerous territory.

EXERCISE

Whenever someone uses a metaphor in the media, particularly a political one, think about the ways that the points of comparison *don't* match. Yes, a proposed new tax is like someone planning to rob your house. Taxes are like robbery. But they're also not like robbery. Get into the habit of listing the differences. As you'll see in the next section, that skill can produce a great figure.

SIMILE: MAKING BEDROOMS FLY

The metaphor has a couple of offspring, including the simile and analogy. Easiest and most transparent is the simile.

FORREST GUMP: Life is like a box of chocolates.

Simile

The "like" gives it away as a simile—as in, similar. Life is similar to a box of chocolates. You never know when you're going to bite into something that looks like a caramel and find yourself edited into a scene where you're running across the country. Weird. The simile is a metaphor that gives itself away. "The moon is a balloon": that's a metaphor. "The moon is *like* a balloon": that's a simile.

You come up with a simile the same way you produce a metaphor: by finding the key words—the essential characteristics—and then thinking of the comparables that share those characteristics. One variation of the simile points out one difference between your object and the comparable. This technique lets you make wild comparisons, modifying them a bit so that they seem reasonable. I call it the **like . . . only technique.**

Like . . . Only Technique

You can see a marvelous example of this technique in the movie *Up*, where a little girl explains South America to her young companion.

GIRL: It's like America . . . but South!

Don't you love that sort of wise cluelessness? Here's a more sophisticated example. Congressman Roy Blount once referred to his colleague Nancy Pelosi's jet as a "flying Lincoln bedroom." We'll put it in like . . . only form.

BLOUNT: It's like the Lincoln bedroom, only it flies.

Blount was accusing Pelosi of flying rich donors at taxpayer expense, much the way Bill Clinton rewarded fat cats with a stay in the Lincoln Bedroom when he was president.

To create your own version of a like . . . only, go through the same routine that you would for a metaphor or plain simile. Find the pith and match the comparables. Now think of ways that your comparables *don't* match your object. Sometimes the differences can serve as a source for humor, and not just *Up*-style. In the preface to this book, I used a like . . . only, saying that I was writing something like *Fame* only without the music and dancing. The comparison was ludicrous enough, actually, to compel a like . . . only to keep you from thinking me entirely insane. The comparison itself was easy to come up with. My pith was "words that make you immortal." What part of pop culture talks about living forever? *Fame*. Bingo.

EXERCISE

Have you gone through childbirth or another painful episode? If so, describe it in terms of a like . . . only.

> *YOU:* It's like running a marathon, only with someone biting your nethers and a screaming baby for the goal line.

Not a bad description to offer teen girls before they're sexually active. When my tween-aged children asked me what sex was like, I described it in terms of mutual nose-picking only with the risk of childbirth at the end. Now grown, my kids say that image will haunt them for the rest of their lives. Oh, the power of simile.

ANALOGY: DANDELION WARS

Our box of chocolates counts also as an analogy, a kind of extended simile. An analogy openly points out the comparison—*a is like b*—and then proceeds to show several similarities. Another big difference between simile and analogy is that a simile usually compares things that are like each other, while an analogy often compares things that *act* like each other. A simile is like fraternal twins. The comparables look alike. An analogy is like a substitute teacher. It takes the place of the original, carrying out the same tasks, without pretending to be the original.

Analogy

When someone says, "Afghanistan is like Vietnam," the speaker probably isn't talking about the countries themselves; he's talking about wars. (As you'll see, a trope is going on here as well, swapping the location of an event with the event itself.) The speaker is claiming that one war is analogous to the other. The Afghan war acts like the one in Vietnam, only without napalm and Robert Duvall.

When you want to wax analogical yourself, find comparables that act like the ending to a good mystery novel: it seems both surprising and inevitable. (Nice analogy, right?) This means finding connections between things that your audience hasn't seen. Easy? No, but you can have fun trying. With practice you can come up with pretty good analogies on the fly. Look around you, and you can see all kinds of analogs—figurative substitute teachers. Is your watch (assuming you wear one) an analog watch, turning time into a circle? My computer lets me put "folders" in a "trash can." An iPad shows "pages" on the Internet. They're not metaphors, exactly; the computer's folders and the website's pages don't really pretend to be paper folders or the pages of a book or magazine. You don't even turn the pages.

Keep looking around you. Do you see someone wearing a tie? It's analogous to the neck cloths that men used to wear. While you probably won't find a nuclear submarine near you at the moment, my father, a former marine engineer, once told me that the *ah-OO-ga* sound subs make when they're about to dive comes from old Model T horns that used to be installed on the boats. The recorded sound, imitating a car horn, is analogous to the original sound. Thinking analogically lets you form comparisons to everything in life, making the unfamiliar seem familiar. It's an important skill.

If you really want to achieve immortality by analogy, come up with a Delphic expression that creates a comparable situation to the one you're describing. "Where there's smoke there's fire" counts as an analogy, and the anonymous soul who first thought it up deserves to be in the Immortal Words Hall of Fame. (At least his words were immortal.) The smoke serves as an analog for harbingers in general—or for seemingly trivial signs that might have something significant or dangerous behind them. Many a rumor has been strengthened by the analogy: where there's smoke (wispy unfounded story) there's fire (burning ember of truth). The old adage, "The hen that cackles is the one that laid the egg" works the same way: hen equals friend who complains of a flatulent smell.

Coming at analogies from the opposite direction, what do you say when a reporter on television talks about the salaries oil company executives got after the massive spill in the Gulf of Mexico? First, find the pith: What's this really about? You could say it's about the bad guys winning and the good guys (and Mother Nature) losing. In ocean terms, winning and losing equate to floating and sinking, right? The analogy practically speaks for itself.

YOU: Oil floats; treasure sinks. The slick corporate types win, and the truly valuable resource—nature itself—loses.

You win, rhetorically at least.

EXERCISE

Think up a Confucius-like saying to hold in reserve. Describe something in nature, or typical human behavior. Now think of ways they might be analogous to issues or phenomena you encounter. Look for any excuse to use one in conversation. For example, "Unwashed socks don't get lost in the dryer" could be used to stand for overly fastidious behavior or opinions.

YOU: I'm a slob? I prefer to think of myself as strategically relaxed. It's more efficient to spend less time cleaning. After all [pointing index finger straight in the air], unwashed socks don't get lost in the dryer.

"Kids don't beg for vegetables" might work for the need to ignore public opinion and do what's right.

YOU: We can't expect a good outcome from a referendum on the budget. Taxpayers don't always vote in their best long-term interest, just as kids don't beg for vegetables.

How did I come up with that? The same way you can. First find the pith of your issue or argument. Next, find a comparable ordinary event or truism. Voters don't always vote for what's good for them. Who else doesn't always do what's good for them? Kids. How? By eating junk food. Ergo, kids don't beg for vegetables.

THE TOOLS

"Authors of all races, be they Greeks, Romans, Teutons, or Celts, / Can't seem just to say that anything is the thing it is but have to go out of their way to say that it is like something else." So sayeth Ogden Nash, a towering figure in the art of silly poetry. But then, Nash is guilty of the very sin he condemns; "go out of their way" is metaphorical, after all. Authors of all races don't literally walk out of their way to say something. It's hard to get around the use of tropes.

In the next chapter, you'll meet trickier, less obvious tropes. Meanwhile we'll follow the advice of Aristotle, who was friend-lier with metaphor than Ogden Nash was. Aristotle called the use of metaphor the most important skill of style.

Metaphor. A trope that claims *a* is *b*.

Simile. A comparison, *a* is like *b*.

Like . . . Only Technique. A simile, with exceptions.

Analogy. A kind of extended simile: *a* acts like *b*.

PART IV

WORD WIZARD

Now that you know how to make

indelible word sounds and pictures, it's time for

the third leg of the SPA stool: associations.

Here you'll learn the most powerful tools of all—

tropes that do their work invisibly.

11

PRACTICE MAGIC

THE BELONGING TROPE
Rhetoric's Sneakiest Trick

A SWEET PAIR OF GAMS sashayed into my office. Legs, I mean. The kind that go on forever.

"Mr. Heinrichs, I presume?" she said, leveling her baby blues at me.

The chair squeaked as I put my Guccis up on the desk and stared back. "Who's asking?"

The dame gave a little snort, like a greyhound before it catches the mechanical rabbit. "Your name's on the door. I'm told you help people with their persuasion problems. But you look like a private eye."

"Not private eye, private *are*," I said.

"'R' for 'rhetorician.' Hilarious." She wasn't laughing, though. "So are you available?"

"Depends on what you mean by 'available.'" I leered at the feat of gravity that lay beneath the unbuttoned top of her blouse.

"Keep your eyes to yourself. I'm married." She sighed. "To a husband who won't do any chores around the house."

"A pig." I nodded. "I got ways for dealing with his type."

"I can pay."

I grabbed a pint of rye from under the desk. "Care for a toot?" I was beginning to like this broad.

This isn't some rhetorical fantasy of mine. OK, it *is* a rhetorical fantasy, but I wrote it for your edification. The passage comes packed with those make-believe devices we call *tropes*. The word comes from the Greek, *tropos*, meaning "turn." Whereas figures are a "turn of phrase," tropes can turn your whole mind. They spin better than the finest spin doctors. You met the number one trope, metaphor—the tropical head honcho, to put it metaphorically—in the last chapter. But there's a lot more to tropes than metaphors. They're the most powerful word tools in all of rhetoric, because they happen to be the hardest for audiences to spot. The best tricks hide themselves, and many tropes paint themselves in rhetorical camo. It's worth your while to understand what makes tropes work, so you can make them work for you.

ETERNAL LEGS AND MARITAL PORK

So what, exactly, is a trope? Just about any kind of nonliteral language—words that aren't literally true but aren't outright lies, either—can qualify as a trope. A metaphor counts as one kind of trope, neither literal nor a lie. In our story, the woman's husband is not literally a pig. He brings home the bacon, but not in the form of his own body. Hubby merely acts like a pig, wallowing around the house without doing the dishes or taking out the garbage. This makes him a metaphorical pig: a trope.

But my "private are" story used a number of other tropes as well. While a metaphor pretends that something (husband) is something similar (pig), the majority of tropes in this list don't quite do that. Try to get a feel for what the tropes in this list have in common.

1. I make a woman's legs stand for the whole woman, having her "gams" walk into the room. Sexist, yes, but it's also a kind of trope in which a part of something (legs) stands for the whole (woman). The legs are not literally a woman. Just a part of one. A trope.

2. "Baby blues" stand for the woman's eyes. In this case, the trope has to do with making a characteristic of something (color) stand for the thing itself (eyes).

3. Instead of merely noting that her legs are long, I say they "go on forever." The statement is not literally true; her legs do not extend infinitely. But I'm not lying, either. I'm just exaggerating. Not literally true, not a lie. Therefore, a trope: hyperbole. You saw it two chapters ago.

4. I put my Guccis on the desk, meaning my feet. By naming the shoes instead of my feet, I unload another trope—one in which the container (shoes) stands in for what it contains (feet).

5. The woman snorts like a greyhound. You should recognize this one as a simile: *a* is like *b*. A simile is a close relative of a metaphor. Her snort would not literally be mistaken for that of a racing dog, except perhaps by a deaf cat.

6. The woman says my name is on the door. Is my name literally on the door? No; a name*plate* hangs on the door. A nice brass one, with letters that spell my name and title, "Private Rhetorician." Swapping nameplate and name constitutes a kind of trope.

7. The same dame says my Private Are title is "hilarious," but she clearly does not really find it funny. She waxes ironic—saying one thing while meaning another. Is she lying? Nope. Her sour expression tells me she doesn't literally mean what she says. Irony: another trope.

8. Continuing my sexist ways, I leer at the woman's cleavage while calling it a "feat of gravity." What the object does (defying gravity) swaps in for the object itself (pair of breasts). By the way: I am not literally a sexist, but do sexism for the sake of my art. The assumption of a sexist role qualifies as—you guessed it—another trope. Two tropes in one! What a pair!

9. She tells me to keep my eyes to myself. Yet my eyes have not literally left their sockets, rolled across the desk, and slithered into her cleavage. Her command has a tropical nature: things (eyes) represent their purpose (looking).

10. To offer her a drink, I grab a "pint"—a pint-sized bottle, that is—of "rye"—whiskey. Two more tropes. A measurement (pint) stands in for the thing measured (bottle), and an ingredient (rye) pretends to be the whole thing (whiskey). If a drop of confusion remains, think of it this way. One cannot literally drink rye, a grain related to barley and wheat, eaten in unprocessed form by livestock.

11. I ask if she wants a "toot," meaning a gulp of whiskey straight out of the bottle. Here we swap a sound (toot) for the action that makes the sound (blowing on a horn), then swap an imitative motion (like tooting a horn) for the action itself (drinking from a bottle). Whoa, this stuff is starting to go to my head.

ONWARD, BILLIONAIRE SOLDIERS!

All this plain-sounding language turns out to be dripping with rhetoric—particularly the association memory keepers that swap things around, quietly baiting and switching in the audience's brain. Tropes aren't just rhetorical tricks; they help us understand the world around us, by making connections between things. The world doesn't function as well without them. Psychologists say that one of the distinguishing symptoms of autism is difficulty in recognizing tropes. A 2004 ad for the National Autistic Society in Britain summed up how tropes look to someone with the syndrome.

> "All thumbs, two left feet . . . every cloud has a silver lining, eyes in the back of your head." How can someone with autism trust people when all they do is lie?

In one of the best novels written in the past decade, *The Curious Incident of the Dog in the Night-Time*, author Mark Haddon writes through the eyes of an autistic boy.

> These are examples of metaphors
>   . . . He was the apple of her eye.
>   They had a skeleton in the cupboard.
>   We had a real pig of a day.
>   . . . I think it should be called a lie because a pig is not like a day and people do not have skeletons in their cupboards. And when I try to make a picture of the phrase in my head it just confuses me because imagining an apple in someone's eye doesn't have anything to do with liking someone a lot and it makes you forget what the person was talking about.

In a sense, we could diagnose our entire culture as mildly autistic. We celebrate untricky language; but an inability to interpret may be a dysfunction, not a sign of complete honesty. By tying concepts and things together, tropes can tie us together. We wear red, white, and blue on the Fourth of July, associating ourselves with the flag like good tropes. We convey symbols that we belong to certain groups, wearing expensive shoes to show our membership in the upper middle class, or thongs (the foot kind) to show we're dudes and dudettes. Barack Obama wore thongs (again, the foot kind) on vacation in Hawaii, and while aging voters condemned his unpresidential attire, younger bloggers praised it. How's this a trope? Because, as a rhetorician put it long ago, style makes the man. Clothing style represents the man, at least; and when you represent a man with a pair of flip-flops, that representation counts as a trope. One that's pretty easy to spot, because it stands as a symbol.

It's when we fail to recognize tropes that we get ourselves in trouble. For instance, when we refer to undocumented immigrants as "illegals," we're using a trope. Calling undocumented immigrants "illegals" implies that their very existence is against the law. Which may be the point, but it's a silly one. (The term also makes a dumb trope, frankly, since a stronger word already exists for people who live outside the law: outlaws.) In any case, when someone else uses a trope, you should ask yourself what kind of baggage accompanies it. Is a three-year-old girl smuggled over the border from Mexico an "illegal"? Here the term schleps some heavy rhetorical baggage for such a little kid: an illegal is illegal. Yet it's not illegal to play with an illegal, or even to educate one (though that may be changing, thanks in part to the trope).

Back when Barack Obama made a deal with the Republicans

over tax cuts, Senator Bernie Sanders of Vermont made a speech that quickly went viral among the American left. Referring to the vast shift of wealth over the past two decades to the richest one-tenth of 1 percent, Sanders metaphorically declared that a "war" was being waged against the middle class. I criticized Sanders in my blog, saying that war metaphors rarely worked under such circumstances. (Sanders didn't say that the rich were waging something "like" a war; his trope crossed the enemy lines from analogy right into metaphor.)

"I'm not a writer," one critic responded to me on Facebook. "To me the war isn't a metaphor. It's real." But it's not real. No armed forces were invading his middle-class neighborhood. The guy was just angry, and his anger made the metaphor seem real.

Why don't we follow the example of autistic people and consider all tropes lies? Shouldn't we speak the simple truth the way scientists do? Sounds nice, but the scientific method itself constitutes a kind of trope. Science doesn't create reality; it can only represent reality, through a core sample or a lab experiment. Those are tropes of sorts, aren't they?

In your own life, you speak tropically all the time. You saw analogies all around you in the last chapter. Now really go to town (I meant that in a tropical way). Try to describe your surroundings. Take your time. I'll wait.

Now let's determine whether your description used any tropes, intentional or otherwise. Maybe you pretended that one thing was something else—that something similar was the object itself. You called the children playing outside "munchkins." That's a metaphor which makes your audience think differently about those kids. In the audience's mind, the kids take on some of the characteristics of the little people in Oz.

Suppose you described a ratty old chair, unwillingly inherited from your in-laws, as "picturesque." This counts as an ironic euphemism; irony forms one of the basic tropes.

Outside the window you see a flag waving in the breeze. If you want to get literal about it, though, the flag isn't waving itself; it's being waved. That colorful, symbolic cloth isn't responsible for its own actions. Therefore you have another trope, personification, in which we pretend that something nonhuman has the characteristics of a human.

If the room contains "healthy" snacks and a "warm" afghan, then you're on tropical soil. The snacks aren't alive, so they can't be healthy themselves. The afghan isn't called warm because its own temperature is toasty; it's called warm because it warms you.

What other tropes did you find yourself using? Did you make a part of something stand for the whole thing? A container for what it contains? The purpose for something stand for the thing itself? You can see why tropes are the most secretive, sneaky part of rhetoric. They can sound like unadorned language even while they form unconscious associations in their audience's heads. And they surround us with a tropical web, filling our conversations without our even knowing it. Some rhetoricians even argue that all language is tropical, since words stand for something other than the words themselves.

"What's that?" you ask a toddler, pointing to a picture of a cow.

"Cow!" she answers.

But the picture isn't a cow, it's a picture.

We're starting to have the kind of philosophical conversation people used to have over a shared pipe of cannabis back in the seventies. I'm sure no young folks do that sort of thing today.

Hey, count the tropes in those last two sentences. I found four: "conversation" (you talking to me?); "cannabis" (dried marijuana); "seventies" (1970s, back when social networking often entailed actual physical contact); and "I'm sure" (irony). Each phrase refers to some other meaning from the literal one.

The tropes you've seen so far fall into four basic categories:

> HYPERBOLE
> METAPHOR
> BELONGING
> ROLE PLAYING

You saw hyperbole in chapter 9. We'll get to role playing in the next chapter. And you're already familiar with metaphor and its offspring. Right now, let's talk about belonging.

Remember, when you put two things next to each other and call them alike, you make a simile or—if you're comparing more than one trait—an analogy.

YOU: My uncle Bob is like a sturdy pine tree. He never goes anywhere and sighs when it's windy.

When you show me one thing and claim it's something else, you probably make a metaphor. Unless you're simply lying.

YOU: All humanity lives on a beautiful blue marble.

So what do you get when you show a lock of blue-rinsed hair and declare it a whole elderly woman?

ALL EYEBALLS ON DECK

Imagine you're a marketer trying to sell junk food that enhances bowel motility.

YOU: Our new convenience food product will go way beyond the traditional bluehair market.

"Bluehair" means "old lady." It goes like this: the blue hair belongs to the old lady—or, rather, to a type of person imagined by sexist and ageist marketers. This fictional senior citizen carries the flag for what I call the **belonging trope.**

Belonging Trope

This trope takes an ingredient, representative sample, container, trait, or overlap of some sort and makes it represent the thing it belongs to. The belonging trope occasionally does the opposite as well, making the owner represent what it owns. Here are other examples of this blue-haired tropical wonder.

All hands on deck.

Wiser heads prevailed.

They speak many tongues in India.

My blog attracts a lot of eyeballs.

In addition, my "private are" story contained a number of belonging tropes.

Sashaying gams (the legs belong to the woman)

Baby blues (the color belongs to the eyes)

Guccis (the brand belongs to the shoes—or vice versa—and the shoes to my feet)

Name on the door (my name belongs to the nameplate, or vice versa)

Feat of gravity (the trait belongs to the breasts)

Eyes to yourself (my vision belongs to my eyes)

Pint of rye (pint being a measure that belongs to the whiskey, and rye being an ingredient of it)

Broad (the trait belongs to the woman)

Keep your eyes peeled (!) for belonging tropes in your own life, and you will find them everywhere you look. Say you're watching the classic movie *Groundhog Day* when Bill Murray's weatherman character snaps at the local news anchor.

MURRAY: For your information, Hairdo, there's a major network interested in me.

The hairdo belongs to the news anchor. Murray makes the hairdo *stand* for the news anchor. He focuses all our attention on a trivial aspect of the woman, implying that there's nothing else to her. Never mind the journalism degree, the years battling sexist producers, the hours standing in the rain waiting for some politician to emerge from his car; while Murray looks like an obnoxious jerk saying it, the "hairdo" label would be hard to shake. Like the Cheshire Cat who reduces himself to nothing but his smile, the news anchor gets reduced to a do.

The belonging trope also acts as the stem cell of tropes. Extract the rhetorical DNA from a thatch of dyed hair, and ZAP! A whole gang of senior women! When a speaker has the floor, he stands on a belonging trope. The White House can't talk, but it issues press statements constantly in its role of belonging trope, the building representing the entire presidency. Similarly, the Crown or Throne stands for royal heads (another belonger!) of kingdoms.

Rhetoricians divide the belonging trope into two subspecies with difficult-to-spell names, *synecdoche* (sin-ECK-doe-kee) and *metonymy* (meh-TON-ih-mee). The division is useful for understanding how the belonging trope works; besides, those terms show up in the Advanced Placement English Exam, which means that years from now, show-offs will be sneaking them into conversation. So let's spend a little time on each and begin using them for your own purposes.

PUTTING THE SIN IN SYNECDOCHE

The synecdoche swaps a part for the whole—blue hair standing for the whole blue-haired woman. It also makes an individual stand for the group—blue-haired woman standing for elderly people—or a group stand for the individual. If I say, "Canada won the Olympic tournament," I'm making the country stand for a few athletes. When an admiring boy says, "She's a Betty," he's doing a kind of double synecdoche. "Betty" is the pretty, blond, good-girl character in the Archie comics. She stands for a type of pretty, seemingly nice girls. Calling a single nice girl a "Betty," then, puts her in the Betty group.

Yes, that sort of leap constitutes a generalization, and generalizing can be hurtful. Calling a black man a "Tom" slots him into a category named after the obsequious Uncle Tom in *Uncle Tom's Cabin*. Remember the Welfare Queen in the early days of welfare reform? A single bad example—not necessarily a real one either—ended up representing all mothers on public assistance. But if you want your words to be memorable, and you want to change people's reality, the belonging trope can work that magic; whether it's black magic or white is up to you. Say you want to describe an obnoxious teenager.

UNWRITTEN: His loud talking only worsens the impression his horrible complexion gives.

BELONGING VERSION: He's a zit with a mouth.

Get used to thinking belonging, and you can truly astonish people. The Rolling Stones' Keith Richards once told a reporter that he had, in effect, belonging troped his dad.

RICHARDS: The strangest thing I've tried to snort? My father. I snorted my father.

The ancient rocker, bored with blowing his mind, claimed he had indulged in a hit of old man by mixing some of the deceased father's ashes with cocaine. He didn't snort all of Dad; just enough to represent him. Thus he turned his father into a synecdoche. Or claimed to. Richards later woke from his reverie and said he was just kidding. Meanwhile, the online magazine *Slate* quipped, "So 'Sister Morphine' isn't a metaphor?" (Actually she's more of a metonymy, as you'll see in a bit.)

That's the difference between our culture and that of the ancient Greeks. The old rhetoricians agreed that tropes and figures can act like drugs, changing people's perception of reality. But, unlike us, they usually took their rhetoric without the drugs.

The belonging trope's synecdoche has entered politics big-time as our political conversation becomes more divisive. If you want to generalize, labeling whole groups of people, then belonging is the trope for you. The bizarre journey of Joe the Plumber provides a perfect illustration. Joe Wurzelbacher, who worked for a plumbing contractor, met Obama when the candidate was campaigning in his Ohio neighborhood and asked tough questions about his tax plan. "Joe the Plumber"—a belonging trope standing for regular Joes everywhere—became a mantra for John McCain and Sarah Palin. The Joe the Plumber trope gained traction during the presidential debates, to the point where Obama felt compelled to retort that McCain was fighting not for Joe the Plumber but for "Joe the Hedge Fund Manager." As for the real, actual Joe, he technically wasn't a plumber, and he proved an unreliable McCain supporter, calling the candidate the "lesser of two evils." Which shows how tricky a synecdoche can be.

I once did a story on the death of Smokey Bear, the cartoon character used by the U.S. Forest Service to discourage forest fires. Bright minds in the agency decided to take a real bear cub rescued from a real forest fire and ensconce him in the National Zoo in Washington, D.C. When this real-life Smokey eventually died, no one knew quite what to do with him. What do you do with a dead cartoon character? I mean, what if Mickey Mouse succumbed to cancer? (Smokey went to his eternal rest in his home state of New Mexico.)

More effective uses of the belonging trope have to do with place names instead of people's names. During that same presidential campaign, we began hearing a great deal about "Wall Street" and "Main Street." Wall Street: bad. Main Street: good. Sarah Palin proudly called herself a "Main Streeter." The term conjured up a distaff sheriff of Mayberry strolling past the sweet shop and the good ol' barbershop where the boys hung out, past the savings and loan—the one Jimmy Stewart took over for his pop, not the evil Fannie Mae. The reality is a bit harsher. Your average American Main Street looks nothing like Mayberry or Jimmy Stewart's Bedford Falls. Try strolling down one and you'll get run over. Main Street isn't very pedestrian friendly, for the most part.

The real-life Wall Street, on the other hand, happens to be more pedestrian friendly than Main Street. Besides, many of the evils perpetrated by financial wizards took place not on Wall

Street but far away in places like Washington, D.C., and Charlotte, North Carolina. Which makes "Main Street" and "Wall Street" great belonging tropes: they refocus our loyalty and ire on targets that benefit the tropes' coiners. And they evoke exactly the kinds of emotions politicians want.

Even Supreme Court justices get into synecdoches. Try to find a court opinion on any issue dealing with privacy that doesn't include the word "bedroom." The bedroom belonging trope counts as a kind of judicial porn. What happens in the bedroom should stay in the bedroom, even if the issue has nothing to do with any literal bedroom.

Why does this matter to you? Because when we don't know about belonging, we tend to take this stuff literally. On the other hand, the trope isn't entirely manipulative. It can help us explain complex concepts. Suppose one wishes to equate marriage with monogamy—a concept that tends to escape the less subtle sex. Simply turn marriage into a gold band.

BEYONCÉ KNOWLES: If you liked it, then you shoulda put a ring on it.

The trope also lets us say things quickly and entertainingly.

BELONGED: Pillow talk revealed her husband's ambitions.

UNWRITTEN: Only during those moments before sleep, when a mate shares his most intimate desires, did she discover her husband's ambitions.

In short, when your audience has difficulty seeing the forest for the trees, pick a tree and make it represent the forest. The famed biologist Louis Agassiz once said he could understand nature with sufficient study of his backyard. Henry David Thoreau wrote that he had traveled far in his hometown of Concord, Massachusetts. Both great men were great belongers, taking a core sample to understand the universe.

METONYMY: A BIG OL' BOTTLE OF MEANING

While the synecdoche switches between individual and group, part and whole, the metonymy performs a more complicated belonging function, performing magical sleights of tongue such as these:

Container for the stuff it contains (*I drank a bottle.*)

Cause for effect (*He was flooded with e-mails.*)

Sign for the thing signified (*Your name's on the door.*)

Material for the thing made (*He won five golds in the Olympics.*)

Object used for the user (*The first violin took sick.*)

Part observed for the observation (*He gave me serious face time.*)

Something different is happening here from the tropes we have seen so far. The metaphor goes after similarity—the earth is like a marble, so I'll call the earth a marble. The synecdoche works on scale, making little things stand for big things or vice versa. The metonymy is all about sharing. Red is a color, and it's the color of your hair, so I'll call you Red. Whiskey is held in bottles, and I've been drinking a lot of whiskey, so my friend notices I've been hitting the bottle. What I'm hitting—drinking, actually—is not the glass itself but the contents. Rhetoricians say that what's going on here is "contiguity"—the state of things bordering each other. If two things share a border, if they press up against each other, or if they share a single trait, then you probably have a trope-making opportunity in the form of a metonymy.

The original proprietors of one of the nation's most thriving tourist traps, South of the Border, showed good tropical sense in naming the place. The sprawling establishment in Dillon, South Carolina, has a heavily Mexican theme. Its logo bears a sombrero. You can get a decent burrito there and buy genuine Mexican jumping beans. But it lies hundreds of miles from Mexico, next to South Carolina's border with Georgia. South of the Border and the sovereign nation of Mexico share that trait of southern contiguity, permitting the tropical leap in geographical imagination.

If you're still not grasping the difference between the two branches of belonging—the synecdoche and the metonymy—I don't blame you. It can be hard to tell them apart. Just keep in mind that, while the synecdoche swaps parts and wholes, the metonymy focuses on things that flow into one another, either literally (bottle and whiskey) or in the mind (color red and red-colored hair, national and state borders). Then, unless you're about to take the AP English exam, call both metonymy and synecdoche the belonging trope.

NOW YOU

Having learned the ins and outs of the belonging trope, you're ready to use it on your own. Say you want to describe the vast inequality of wealth in South Africa. You could choose among several ways of telling the story.

You could state the facts, starting with South Africa's status as the most unequal country in the world. This would be the straightforward, untropical approach.

You could tell a fairy tale about a prince who lives high on the hog and treats his poor subjects like pigs, concluding with a moral: "That's like South Africa today." The tale would qualify as an analogy.

Or you could focus on an actual single young mother and how she struggles to provide for her children on tiny wages paid by her rich employer. You often find this kind of treatment in the news media, but it's not just journalism. It's pure belonging trope, the synecdoche. You focus on a single person to make her represent all of the exploited masses in South Africa.

Which reminds me of a woman named Julie Beasley, a thirty-one-year-old traveler forced by airport security to toss her Chanel lip gloss and lipstick into a trash barrel at the Phoenix airport.

BEASLEY: I'm throwing away my whole face.

Try taking that expression literally, and you get a pretty scary picture. But Beasley is throwing away the stuff she puts on her face, not the face itself.

Back to South Africa: another way to use the story is to focus on some aspect of the poor mother's situation. She cleans her employer's pool but struggles to provide clean water to her own children. At the end of the tale, label the phenomenon with a belonging trope: "the water gap."

Look at the tools we just used to describe the income gap in South Africa: metaphor, synecdoche, and metonymy. The metaphor tells a good story, while the two aspects of the belonging trope label give the issue a human label. Get used to employing the belonging, and you might find yourself coming up with striking phrases when you most want them. Whoever first thought of "boots on the ground," a belonging trope that means "soldiers in the field," deserves a Word Hero medal. Ditto for the clever bureaucrat who came up with "shovel ready" for "needs funding to begin." Both examples let you picture individual, understandable objects in place of abstractions like tactical maneuvers and engineering plans.

So let's see if we can do something almost as touch-ready. Take an abstraction and try to find an object, a person, a place, or an institution to represent it. You know, something eyebrow raising. (Yes, that's a belonging trope, a physical gesture representing an abstract emotion.)

We'll start with politics—the Supreme Court decision to allow corporations to buy unlimited advertising in election campaigns. Boil the issue down to a single company "buying" a candidate. Apple? No, that's a hard company to demonize politically. It raises visions of Steve Jobs inventing a beautiful, svelte iCandidate everyone loves but who drops their calls. McDonald's and Walmart might work better. The McCandidate. Feeds you junk but comes cheap. Or the United States of Walmart. In each case, you belong the issue by making one power-grabbing company represent the whole notion of corporate dollars buying elections.

If this seems unfair—just the sort of language that's bollixing our politics today—consider that Justice Antonin Scalia's consenting opinion in the *Citizens United* case called the very idea that corporations weren't people "sophistry." If Scalia meant that corporations are indeed people in the First Amendment's eyes, then the justice pulled off one of the biggest tropes in court history. (It's interesting that the people who first invented tropes three thousand years ago called themselves Sophists.)

Take another abstraction, children's lack of outdoor exercise. The average American kid plays outside half an hour a week.

This issue is rhetorically tricky because the causes are manifold: neighborhoods without sidewalks, two-income families unable to supervise play, suburban streets where kids used to ride their bikes now filled with speeding SUVs, budget cutbacks closing parks and playgrounds, twenty-four-hour news keeping parents permanently terrorized, America's zero tolerance for underage risk. We need to imagine one little microcosm hitting just one of these factors; say, Empty Playground Syndrome. Or the No Sidewalk Childhood. Chicken Little Parenting. Can you see the belonging here? Take a single childless playground, a sidewalkless street, or a representative cartoon character and convert it into a handy stick-on political label.

The belonging trope can work closer to home as well. Say your significant other wants to vacation in Vegas this year, while you might prefer to rent a cabin on a lake in Maine. Your partner extols Vegas's many virtues: the food, the nightlife, Cirque du Soleil, the Bellagio fountains—even a possible day trip to hike in nearby Red Rocks to get your outdoor fix. But you're not playing fair; instead, you decide to label the issue with an entertainingly sarcastic belonging trope.

First, think of a person who most represents the cheesiest aspect of Vegas to you. Are you over forty? Then Liberace might come to mind. The glittery, oily pianist was a fixture of old Vegas. So every time your loved one brings up the proposal, you label it the Liberace vacation.

Vegas being a gambling destination, how about "the gambling vacation," implying a waste of your hard-earned family income? Not specific enough. Besides, most people have accepted the industry's tropical name change to "gaming," a metonymy that converts a destructive vice into a pleasurable pastime. So we'll stick to the vice. The "slots vacation" comes closer. But an effective belonging trope zeroes in on something instantly recognizable—not "slots" but a single entity. How about the "Danny Ocean vacation"? Uh-uh. *Ocean's Eleven* makes me want to go to Vegas and rob a casino. Still, we're on the right track. Aim your belonging at the smallest possible target—one your audience dislikes in this case. Ideally, you know someone who lost his shirt (holy belonging!) in Vegas. Then you can simply name the vacation after him: the Ricky vacation would be perfect, assuming Ricky lost everything on his vacation and now buses tables on the wrong side of town.

If this technique seems sleazy to you, by the way, it sure can be. In all fairness, you should teach it to your victims so they can do the same thing. In my family, we use the belonging trope all the time. If one of us proposed Vegas instead of Maine, another would counter my "Liberace vacation" with, "So you're proposing a black fly vacation instead?" In our family, we appreciate that kind of back and forth. You may choose to adjust for local circumstances.

THE TOOLS

Belonging Trope. Takes an aspect of something and makes it represent the whole. The synecdoche uses a part or member, while the metonymy uses a characteristic, container, or purpose.

12

PUMP IRONIC

ADORABLE PET ROCKS

Irony, Personification, and Other Role Players

ALL TROPES PLAY PRETEND. Hyperbole pretends that something is way more or less, bigger or smaller, than its literal reality. Metaphor pretends that one thing is something else. The belonging trope pretends that a trait or possession is the entire owner, or vice versa. What's left in our tropical exploration? More pretense.

A group of devices I call *role-playing tropes* claim one thing while meaning the opposite, or make believe an object or animal is a person, or pretend to be foolish or authoritative when they're anything but. In short, role-playing tropes let you play roles. When you want to focus the attention on yourself as well as your words, portraying pretend characters can strangely make you more memorable. Like all of rhetoric, though, this tricky stuff can get, well, tricky. Will the real Stephen Colbert please stand up? And if he doesn't, how can we tell? The secret lies with who's in on the joke. Role-playing tropes speak to an inside audience and an outside one—those who get the double meanings and those who don't.

If this fails to make sense to you, look at **irony**, the favorite trope of fake newscasters.

BUT I PLAY IRONY ON TV

While irony seems familiar to most of us, many people mistake it for mere coincidence. The following is not ironic.

> TWELVE-YEAR-OLD GIRL: You were at the Justin Bieber concert too? That's so ironic!

Two sixth-grade girls from the same town showing up at the same Justin Bieber concert? What are the odds? (That last sentence *was* ironic.) The gods can certainly create irony on their own: a firefighting boat catching fire, for instance. The boat's central purpose—its meaning—gets flipped. That's irony: a trope that contains another, opposite, meaning.

But what makes it a trope? How is irony like the metaphor and the belonging trope? I'm glad you asked that question. (Since you didn't really ask it, I suppose I'm being ironic; but I really am glad.) Like its cousin tropes, irony qualifies as nonliteral language. Its meaning isn't the literal one. All three of these statements are nonliteral:

> He's a tattoo with a foul mouth in the middle.

> We've painted ourselves into a ditch on this business.

> Nice mixed metaphor, dude.

The mouth and tattoo stand for the whole person. Since the guy presumably possesses other attributes, the statement isn't literally true. You might have guessed that it's a belonging trope.

In the second case, there's no actual ditch—just a mixed metaphorical one.

The third sentence makes fun of the second one by ironically pretending to praise it.

I love irony with unironic ardor. Irony is especially cool when you and your posse are in a crowd of people who don't get it. Only you few have the secret trope decoder ring!

Irony

But what if your group ignores the decoder? Jon Stewart's TV show ranks first in sources of news for Americans under twenty-five. Yet Stewart is a comedian posing as a journalist. He's on the Comedy Channel, for crying out loud. So the rising generation of citizens keeps current with a daily dose of irony. I for one am just *thrilled* with what that portends for our republic.

Nonetheless, irony can serve your fondest purposes, offering words that are especially memorable because they cleverly say two things at once. One of my favorite uses of irony relieves my boredom in conversation with the pretentious or cliché-prone. Take a cliché, any cliché, and respond to it seriously. The result can be pretty funny.

> FRIEND: There's nothing new under the sun.
> YOU (nodding profoundly): Including the sun.

Irony can also help you tolerate the clichés you hear on television all the time. The next time some big-headed lawyer says she's "humbled" by her nomination to the Supreme Court, talk back to the TV.

> YOU: Oh, I don't blame you. A justice makes less than your average litigator in Fargo.

--- *EXERCISE* ---

Take your least favorite cliché and manhandle it. How would you respond to "The early bird catches the worm"? One way is to respond to it with ironic literalism.

YOU: Gee, I'd hate to see a rival worm lover beat me to the juiciest night crawler.

More important, the trope can serve to bring you closer to your audience, making everyone feel part of a group that's led by you. Irony constitutes a kind of code shared by the group. The fact that others don't get it—that they might take the irony at face value—makes the tribe feel that much closer. The result can be snobbishness on the one hand and hurt feelings on the other; but some forms of irony are so gentle that the victims emerge unscathed. And even professional ironists like Jon Stewart don't leave many bodies in their wake. Stewart doesn't attack. He just gently deflates.

People who like and trust you are more inclined to listen to you. Irony helps make people like and trust you. So let's get at it.

THE LADY WAS A REAL GENTLEMAN

There is irony of language, and then there is irony of character. Stephen Colbert is this second kind: a guy who only pretends to be a right-winger. You don't have to make an ironic ass of yourself to use character irony for your own purposes. Hipsters practice it all the time to let other hipsters know they're hipsters. They dress in ironic clothing—suits from the fifties, or feminine clothes, or more difficult-to-decipher ironic press-on tattoos or real ironic piercings. They play pretend, tropically, while letting their fake uniform serve as the uniform of their ironic tribe. I happen to own an old T-shirt that announces an even older affiliation with Dartmouth College. The shirt, colored green, has big white letters that spell GREEN. I ran into a hipster friend once while wearing it.

"My respect for you just went up," he said, smiling at my shirt. "I didn't think you were capable of that sort of irony."

I wasn't sure quite what to say. The shirt was sort of ironic, I suppose, saying "green" in letters that weren't. And from the hipster's perspective, any type pointing out that the shirt was green constituted a kind of irony, since the label pretended to be helpful but really wasn't. What my friend didn't seem to realize was that green is Dartmouth's color. In fact, its athletic program calls itself the Big Green, even though the school likes to think of itself as a small college. Calling a school by its color constitutes a belonging trope (metonymy, to be specific), while the little big school is an unintended irony.

Pretty ironic all around. Here I was, unironically playing somebody ironically ironic. Still, my friend's point was interesting: he respected me for showing I could be one of his tribe.

Irony can help you present a surprising side of yourself or, even better, set your words in a surprising context. I once spent the day with Gary Kelly, the CEO of Southwest Airlines. We were judging an annual corporate Halloween competition in which departments performed skits. Kelly himself was dressed as Edna in *Hairspray.* At six feet six, with size 16 feet stuffed into high heels, the former college quarterback made a stunningly ironic teenage girl. Just before the marketing department performed a beautifully choreographed imitation of the Bellagio fountains, with thirty employees spitting water to classical music, Gary turned to me. I gazed at his enormous bouffant wig, false eyelashes, and generous layer of rouge. His lips, which had been painted into a scarlet moue, stretched into a smile. Then he spoke in the deep voice of a man who skippered a profitable company and its thirty-five thousand employees: "Thank you for coming."

It was one of the strangest things anyone had ever said to me. "Thank you for coming." Don't see any figure or trope there, do you? Oh, but it was there. The man talked as if unaware that he was done up like a drag queen. While the words themselves were plain vanilla, the getup drenched them in caramel and put a cherry on top. My career has led me to meet plenty of prominent people; I can't remember what most of them said to me. Gary Kelly's "Thank you for coming" will stick with me forever.

I'm not saying you should dress in drag, necessarily; instead, the anecdote shows the power of the ironic gesture. In rhetoric, facial expressions and body language count as gestures, adding to or changing the meaning of your words. The way you dress also qualifies as a gesture. Picture a job interview. You show up in torn jeans and a dirty T-shirt and say, "I really want this job." Unless you're interviewing for a part in a touring show of *Rent*, your words will come off as ironic. It's the same as if you slouched in your chair and said, "I really really want this job—not!" Similarly, the medium of your message can get pretty tropical. A colleague recently told me about a friend who found himself smitten by a waitress. The young man, an architect by training, was too shy to speak to her. Instead he took a knife and carved his phone number into a large french fry. While he probably wanted to convey a certain artistic wit, the message probably would have come off as obsessive micrographia—not perfectly ironic, but enough to turn off all but the most susceptible waitress, I suspect. We'll never know; as the waitress approached, the man took his love-fry in hand and ate it.

But that was unintentional irony. Deliberately gestured

irony does the same thing as irony of words, bringing insiders together. Many years ago, I had to attend a karaoke party, an activity that I rank right up there with team-building exercises and colonoscopies. Unfortunately, some people at the party were well aware of my karaokaphobia and were all too eager to take advantage of it. I heard the MC speaking to me over the loudspeaker: "Jay, get on up here!" Hilarious.

"Choose your song," the MC said when I got up onto the little stage. He pointed at a list on a computer screen.

"Won't need that," I said. "I'm singing a cappella."

"What?"

"Without music."

The MC frowned. "I know what a cappella is. I majored in music. But you can't sing a cappella karaoke!"

"Watch me." I stepped up to the mike and suddenly realized what a horrible idea this was. In a wavering voice, I sang an unaccompanied song about a boy who goes to prison, where his mother brings him peanut butter sandwiches. A hundred people stared up at me in confusion. My friends looked away, clearly embarrassed. I got through the song somehow and headed straight for the bar.

While I was downing a restorative beer, several people came up to me. "That was great!" one said. "I hate karaoke too!" said another. We had a fine time that night. I had made new friends. One of them friended me recently on Facebook with the message, "Let's catch up. A cappella." My awful ironic time onstage turned out to be memorable after all.

Think of ironic gestures when you want to bring a few people together in hostile circumstances. Have you ever had a boss make an impossible demand on you and your team at work? An ironic response can sometimes make everyone happy. Respond with an over-the-top solution requiring a maximum amount of work on the boss's behalf. Thank him for the opportunity to execute new ideas. Just be ready to step up if he calls your bluff. Meanwhile, continue to be obnoxiously positive with those around you. Don't admit to any irony. It's not ironic if you admit to it. I've used this technique myself over the years, and it's worked every time.

EUPHEMISM: THIS GIFT MAKES ME SEE YOU IN A NEW LIGHT

Irony can also let you sound tactful without being entirely dishonest. You can see a gentle irony when someone receives a special commemorative plate celebrating Abba's musical oeuvre. The standard response—"Oh, you shouldn't have," or "You went to far too much trouble"—carries the kindest of tropes. Irony can hurt people's feelings, but it can also spare them. The technique depends on a straight face and a gullible audience; otherwise, when you say, "I will waste no time in getting to your proposal," you have to look sincere to stay out of trouble.

You can gain some temporary parental sanity by employing this sort of "Oh, you shouldn't have" irony with your children. For all his many talents, our son, George, didn't set the art world on fire with his kindergarten paintings. I learned early on not to guess what the painting was trying to depict, because his beautiful cow would inevitably turn out to be a tank or his mother. (A very unrealistic mother, I hasten to add.) Asking "What's that?" would provoke a tearful "Can't you tell?" And his mother's diplomatic "Ooh, tell me about this" came off a little bland and insincere when I said it. So I took to ambiguous statements like, "I'll bet no one else in your class made a picture like this!," or "This really says a lot about your talent!" His mother would shoot me a satisfying cautionary look while George beamed. We kept up this little joke year after year until George was twelve and his painting of a frog was sold in a Santa Fe gallery. Thus ended my ironic art-critic period.

Nonetheless, such tactful irony counts as a kind of **euphemism**, the sugarcoating we apply to unpleasant things.

Euphemism

Euphemisms have genteelly gilded awkward lilies for as long as humanity has had manners. Some of them have gotten out of hand—or leg, as the case may be. During Victorian times, the gentility never referred to "legs" in mixed company. Even a table was held up by "limbs." "Dandelion" is a euphemism for its original name, *pissenlit*, which means "wet the bed." (The tea from its leaves encourages that sort of thing.) Military leaders traditionally use euphemisms to make killing sound more palatable— "Terminate with extreme prejudice" in *Apocalypse Now* being the most famous example.

But under the right circumstances, a good euphemism becomes the best of tropes: nonliteral, reality bending, utterly convincing, and, ultimately, immortal. Shakespeare was a euphemistic master who could apply doublespeak to make something sound even more obscene. In the play *Antony and Cleopatra*, a character describes how Julius Caesar got the Egyptian queen pregnant.

> AGRIPPA: Royal wench!
> She made great Caesar lay his sword
> to bed;
> He plough'd her, and she cropp'd.

Readers of my last book might have noticed that what I'm calling euphemism also qualifies as innuendo. And in fact an innuendo is an ironic form of euphemism—a circumlocution that calls attention to what it's supposed to be hiding. That's my favorite kind. You don't have to limit the device to sex, either. Say you want to make fun of a friend's obese dog. You can describe it as "Rubenesque," after the ample-fleshed maidens in Peter Paul Rubens's paintings. Or you can refer to its "low hound-to-pound ratio." If that sounds cruel, think of how much blunter an instrument the unadorned truth would be.

YOU: Holy cow, your dog is fat.

Shame on you. Your unironic, unhyperbolic approach has the poor mutt hiding behind a tree. A very wide-trunked tree.

To convey a gently ironic euphemism, take your unpleasant subject and pith it down to the key words. Now hunt for the pleasantest synonyms you can find. Feel free to use words that connote a contrasting quality to your original key words. You usually don't think of a dog in the context of Peter Paul Rubens's Baroque paintings. Similarly, you can describe a close-lipped dullard as "contemplative," or a slob as "informal" or "Bohemian." The gentility in this form of humor may not appeal to everyone; but a word-loving audience will quote you. You will stand out heroically in our foulmouthed, angry culture. Or, rather, our *frank*, *passionate* culture.

EXERCISE

Among the most playful euphemisms are the ones that put "challenged" at the end of deficiencies ("directionally challenged" for someone who often loses his way) or create fine-sounding alternative titles to jobs ("sanitation engineer" for garbage collector). Years ago my daughter and I came up with a list of outrageously euphemistic job titles, including "biological artifacts collector" for headhunter.

Have your own fun. Describe one of your failings as "challenged" in a way you've never heard before. Now create a new job title for yourself or a friend.

PERSONIFICATION: DOG IS MY COPILOT

You can see why I call irony a role-playing trope. You *play* irony. It's a form of acting. So what do we have when we address a dog as if it's an actual person, or make a pet out of a rock? Another kind of acting—and also of nonliteral language: a trope.

If you're old enough to remember the Pet Rock craze, then you have had an important lesson in the literal value of a trope. Pet Rocks were the brain, um, child of a California ad exec named Gary Dahl who came up with the idea in 1975. Each rock sold for $3.95, complete with a box (it had air holes so the rock could breathe), straw, and a thirty-two-page manual with instructions on teaching the rock such tricks as "stay," "sit," and, with an assist by the owner, "attack." The fad lasted half a year; Santa brought me one for Christmas and I set it free in the backyard. Dahl used his profits to open a bar, which he ironically named after the antialcohol crusader Carrie Nation. Leave it to an advertising man to make a fortune out of tropes.

Personification

You will find this make-believe tool, called **personification**, anywhere Hollywood has sprinkled its fairy dust: Tom Hanks talking to a volleyball named Wilson in *Cast Away*. Jimmy Stewart palling it up with an imaginary rabbit in *Harvey*, Charlton Heston schmoozing with a burning bush in *The Ten Commandments*, and nearly every animated film made by Disney. As with the other tropes, personification makes the world a richer place, where hermit crabs sing, dogs fly airplanes, brooms dance, and candles affect French accents. When I was younger, my friend Jesse would distract me in chess by tilting his pawns back and forth while chanting, "We will not be beaten, because we are united!" And what big-bellied uncle hadn't been tempted to make his belly button talk to his appalled nieces and nephews? Never mind their discomfort; a bit of tropical vaudeville never harmed a kid. In fact, one of the best ways to soothe a toddler who has tripped and hurt herself is to punish whatever tripped her: "Bad rug!"

Adults fall for the same thing—tropically, that is. Formal occasions often call for personification. (Catch the personification in the previous sentence?) Lincoln used it in the Gettysburg address when he talked about a nation "conceived in liberty" as if it were a newborn. Talkmeister Glenn Beck speaks of the Constitution as if it's a Victorian Christian maiden whose chastity is in danger. Beck has mastered the subtlest form of personification, in which the speaker uses humanlike traits to convey a character without pretending the character can speak. Enjoyable as it might be to watch the man speak sympathetically about a sepia-colored document and interpret its oracle-like, special-effects mutterings, he is speaking tropically.

You often hear members of Congress describe a bill as being on life support. The phrase has become a cliché. Your own proposals at work or in your community might be healthier. You could have them taking baby steps or going through an awkward adolescence. A proposal might be the wise uncle among other proposals—not excluding those other ideas but informing them, making them better. If your constituency or audience has a sense of humor, you might take your personification in a less subtle direction and give the thing a human name. Your idea for a new bike path in your neighborhood could have the friendly moniker of Bonnie, from the acronym BON, Bike Our Neighborhood. Get an artistic resident to draw an anthropomorphic bicycle with fluttering eyelashes. Some people may find the image too cute, but it's a lot harder to kill Bonnie than it would be to kill the Sustainable Pedal-Powered Transportation Plan.

To personify your own abstraction, start with an acronym. Ordinarily, I find acronyms annoying. Often the work of lazy labelers, they can lead to unintended consequences. Officials at the federal Bureau of Outdoor Recreation, or BOR, found themselves saddled with the label "Bore." The agency got a name change with a more complex acronym, Heritage Conservation and Recreation Service, only to be called "Hookers." Recreation indeed. But an acronym can help you with personification, as long as the letters loosely spell the name of a person.

Suppose you invent a new luggage fastener that attaches handbags and briefcases to rollerboard bags. Your patent calls it the Hook-and-Eye Fastener System for Secondary Carry-on Bag Stability—not quite sexy enough for the marketplace. You could name it after what it does and call it the Grip. But I'm guessing that products already exist with that name. Time to try personification. While this may not seem like an occasion to use the pith method, key words could come in handy here. List the words that best describe your invention's function, and mix up their first letters until you come up with something namelike. *Baggage, luggage, carry-on, accessory, attach, stabilize, and stick* come immediately to mind. So we have *B, L, C,* a pair of *A*'s, and two *S*'s. That yields names like LASS, CASS, LAC, and SAL. Now turn them into friendly sounding names: Lassie, Cassie, Lacy, and, um, Sal. Since we're personifying something that carries your bags, we probably should avoid women's names. ("Cassie! Carry my bag, and be snappy!") Besides, men tend to avoid buying products with feminine names, while women aren't bothered by gender-bending accessories. So Cassie and Lacy are out. Sal is a reasonably common man's name, while Lassie, being a dog, is too perfect a creature to be human. We will go with Sal, the Stabilizing Accessory for Luggage. OK, the brand may not make you and me rich, but you see how personification can help you label or brand a product or idea: pith, key words, acronym, then name.

While you might find it useful to brand products with human names, I'm not a fan of naming possessions. It's just not pleasant to watch a car owner cursing an automobile to whom she has given a name. And I believe it's a bad idea to humanize computers; that could lead to fantasies of demonic possession. Those suckers have minds of . . . I mean, the operating systems are prone to glitches. Better stick to personifying things that don't become strange members of the family.

I NEED YOU TO PAY ATTENTION NOW

Another cousin of personification performs one of the greatest feats of legerdemain: it channels the character of someone else (or occasionally some*thing* else). Students in ancient Rome practiced the technique as an exercise in oratory. The idea was that the kids would not just learn how to think like the great leaders of old; by speaking like them, students would absorb some moral character as well.

Kids continue to do that today, only less gracefully.

"This is you. Ga ga goo goo . . ."

"This is you. Eep eep eep . . ."

Imitating a distorted version of an opponent is immature, unfair, and often effective. Better to do it with public figures and celebrities. *Saturday Night Live* has based many of its best skits on this sort of imitation. Witness Tina Fey as Sarah Palin, or Chevy Chase as Gerald Ford, or Will Ferrell as George W. Bush. The trick is to imitate your victim's speech to make the words you put in his mouth sound credible. This doesn't mean you have to do a brilliant job of mimickry; Chevy Chase never even attempted to sound like the thirty-eighth president. Instead, take a favorite expression or attitude and work it into a caricature—with words, not necessarily the accent or speech impediment.

I once had a genial boss whose favorite expression was "I'm with you, brother." The expression hid a brutally competitive streak in the man. So I would get laughs in meetings by saying, "I'm with you, brother. Now hold my briefcase while I beat you with this stick!" I rarely did this routine behind his back, and to his lasting credit, he laughed when I did it in front of him.

A less cruel way to channel has you imitating the voice of someone in authority—not any particular person but an authoritative-sounding figure. Have you noticed that flight attendants and kindergarten teachers often sweeten their commands by expressing them in terms of their own need?

I channeled this authoritative tone after I had a seventy-five-pound backpack stolen in the Wind River Range. While hiking with the family, I had taken the pack off to visit a waterfall by the trail, and when we came back the thing was gone. I ran several miles down to the trailhead, where bystanders told me they had seen a young woman put it in the trunk of her car. They pointed to the car, where she was sitting behind the wheel—waiting for her mother, as it turned out. I asked the woman to open her trunk, and she did. (She may have been intimidated by the Wyomingites in the parking lot who were saying things like "Oughta hang her for that.") Next thing I knew, her mother showed up—a woman whom we had met earlier on the trail; she had asked us a lot of questions in an English accent. Now, with an American accent, she asked what was going on.

"Who are you?" I asked.

"Her mother."

"Her *mother*? What kind of mother are you, helping young women steal backpacks?" At that point I ran out of things to say. So I blurted out something coplike: "Ma'am, I'm going to need to see some ID."

And, lo and behold, the woman produced her driver's license. I pocketed it, shouldered my pack, and camped in a high meadow away from the tent where my family slept, so I could keep an eye on it. Next morning I turned the license in at the Lander, Wyoming, police station.

"Where'd you find it?" the receptionist asked.

"I didn't find it, exactly. I took it from the mother of the woman who stole my backpack."

The receptionist gave me a look, and a pair of detectives showed up immediately.

"What did you do to her?" one asked.

"I didn't do anything to her. I just asked to see some ID."

The cops thanked me and let me go. Turns out mother and daughter were part of a gang of western pack rustlers. But I didn't just ask to see some ID. I told the woman I was *going to need to* see some ID.

Kindergarten Imperative

The technique was first coined by the wit and word expert Ben Yagoda, who called it the **kindergarten imperative**. Instead of issuing a command, you state your own need.

TEACHER: Billy, I need you to put down that hammer and pay attention.

You will find the kindergarten imperative used far from kindergarten, as any frequent flier knows. ("I need all seat backs and tray tables upright and in locked position.") While Yagoda, the term's inventor, dislikes it—he thinks it shows the decline of the more straightforward imperative mood—the kindergarten imperative allows you to issue a command in more words than you need, so you look more controlled than angry. And I even think I sounded kind of western when I requested the woman's ID.

YOGISM: THE PROPER WAY TO HOLD THE FORK IN THE ROAD

If you want to sound wise without boring people or making them resent you, act like that ageless baseball manager and guru of contradictory wisdom, Yogi Berra. Every baseball writer can recite half a dozen **Yogisms**:

"Nobody goes there anymore. It's too crowded."

"If you come to a fork in the road, take it."

"You can observe a lot just by watching."

"It's déjà vu all over again."

"If you don't know where you are going,
you will wind up someplace else."

"Baseball is 90 percent mental. The other half is physical."

Yogism

The Yogism throws a baseball at the head of logic, deliberately (or otherwise) committing a fallacy. At the same time, it makes a higher-wisdom kind of sense. You saw Warren Buffett early in this book telling us to "rise above principles" occasionally. While this defies logic—you don't get higher than principles—the quote does tell us something, doesn't it? Sometimes principles fail to apply to a particular situation. Remember the scene in *Huckleberry Finn* when the boy decides to go to Hell rather than report an escaped slave? Huckleberry had been taught never to steal, and here he is helping to hide stolen property.

This figure works best when you encounter an exception to the rules. Take the parental rule of positive reinforcement—that you should always praise a child's earnest work. When the child shows zero aptitude for something he thinks might make a pretty good career, praise may actually do more harm than good. How would we put that in a Yogism? By expressing it in self-contradictory terms. In this case, you could just imitate Warren Buffett.

YOU: Sometimes you need to rise above good parenting.

Or you could work out a perfect Yogism by starting with the rule or principle and then enforcing it with the exact opposite.

YOU: The best way to praise a kid may be to insult him.

See what we did? We started with the rule—"The best way to praise a kid"—and then stated its opposite. The Yogism makes an especially effective form of irony because it pretends to be more idiot than savant, saying something silly with a serious underlying purpose. That's the opposite of what most ironists, including

Jon Stewart, do; they pretend to be serious while trying to make us laugh.

My own ironic purpose was perfectly serious. I had too much respect for my own kids' many talents to praise their weaker efforts. Admittedly, I wasn't the best father in the world; I probably shouldn't have said "Don't quit your day job" when they brought especially bad artwork home from school. But I may have saved the world from especially bad art.

THE TOOLS

Role playing makes the most fun let's-pretend tropes. How else can you make a dog talk or turn it into a Rubens model without getting yourself committed? All of the tools in this chapter fall under the rubric of irony, that most acting-out of tropes.

Irony. A role-playing trope that says one thing while meaning the opposite.

Euphemism. A form of irony that makes bad things sound good—or at least not as bad.

Personification. Pretending things are human: another role-playing trope.

Kindergarten Imperative. Issues a command in terms of a personal need.

Yogism. A foolishly wise expression.

13

PULL WORDS TAUT

THE JUMBO SHRIMP PARADOX
Ways to Build Creative Tension

IF YOU EVER TRIED to create telephones out of tin cans and string, you can understand the theory of tension in communication. Kids might find the can-telephone confusing ("How do I update my Facebook on this thing?"), but the concept is simple: attach string to two cans, pull tight, talk. The tighter you hold the string, the more the sound carries. Theoretically. It never seemed to work for my little brother and me. Fortunately, rhetorical tension works much better.

I'm not talking about tension in the stressful sense, or necessarily in the political or argumentative sense. Instead I mean the mental tautness between two concepts pulling at each other. You can create tension by tightening the rhetorical string on these pillars:

1. **Between paired unalike things.**

2. **Between what you deliver and what your audience expects.**

Tension lies behind great storytelling, humor, sex, and persuasion. This chapter focuses on devices geared specifically to

tighten things up. We'll cover that magnet of positive and negative forces, the **paradox**, along with its snub-nosed version, the
oxymoron. Then we'll look at the **contraster**, a figure of relativity
that uses contrasts to make things look better or worse, bigger or
smaller. And we'll finish with my favorite figure of all, the **mirror
image**, which runs a thought backward to show its flip side.

Charles Dickens was a genius at tension, whether he was
suspending the reader between a holiday tale and a spooky ghost
story, or describing a minor character.

> DICKENS: . . . with affection beaming in one eye, and calcu-
> lation shining out of the other.

Affection and calculation. Sort of describes the sentimental
master storyteller himself, doesn't it? Dickens treated his writing
as a vast tightrope tugged between good and evil. In this instance,
he forces opposites to live together in the same face: a paradox.

PARADOXOLOGY

When you want to describe any person memorably, toss in bad
and good ingredients of their personality and let them have at it.
This is especially true of someone you dislike. Watch the difference between a 100 percent evil description and one that's a little
more ambiguous.

> EVIL: She had a thin, quick, mean look about her—scary-
> looking even when she smiled, which was rare.
> AMBIGUOUS: She was lithe and smart and quick as a whip-
> pet, with the rare smile that a whippet makes just before it
> bites.

The evil version is conversational, descriptive, and blandly unmemorable. The second version condemns the victim to an infamous eternity by starting out pleasantly—creating tension.

Frederic William Henry Myers used paradox to describe Saint Paul.

MYERS: Coldly sublime, intolerably just.

The line makes me shiver. Whether you think Myers is playing fair or not, the technique is flawless: bad paired with good in each balanced phrase. You don't have to be nearly as literary to be memorable. Just think of a way to balance the good and bad side of every trait.

Paradox

The term comes from the Greek, *para*, meaning "opposite" or "contrary to"; and *doxa*, meaning "belief." You see *doxa* in "orthodoxy," which literally means "correct belief." A paradox takes a pair of truths and mashes them together like positive and negative ions in a nuclear experiment. The opposites can be attractive, helping your audience understand complexity while holding their attention.

Contradictions come up a lot when we describe people. Just look at reasonable key words for famous people. The terms frequently contradict all on their own.

Lindsay Lohan: Beautiful, funny, screw-loose drunken nutcase

Sarah Palin: Fit, savvy, tough, funny, vicious

George Clooney: Handsome, suave, monotonal

Mel Gibson: Handsome, funny, racist drunken nutcase

You don't have to describe a person to find a good paradox.

JONATHAN SAFRAN FOER: Christians chop down trees to make houses to put trees in.

Most Christians don't chop down trees, and the primary purpose of houses isn't to hold Christmas trees, but Foer found a funny, paradoxical way to accuse Christians of environmental hypocrisy. Here's the same way to do what Foer did.

ME: Developers destroy fox habitat to build developments called "Fox Fields."

The tension here should be obvious. People often mistakenly call this sort of activity "ironic," but it's really a paradox—a set of conflicting notions. The development's sign, on the other hand, is unintentionally ironic. It says one thing (a field for foxes) while standing for something else (doomed foxes).

The reigning favorite kind of paradox takes self-contradictory rules and turns them into catch-22s. The original catch-22, in Joseph Heller's book of the same name, summed up the insanity of war. Anyone attempting to get discharged for insanity, according to the fictional rule, would be declared sane because only the insane would want to be in the war. Years ago, I lived in an isolated, signal-free part of northern New England where broadband was considered to be a type of stretch pant. I maintained my website by dial-up, over a phone line that had a fainting spell during every storm. After one long interruption, I finally reached the phone company over a crackling voice connection. "Your phone has been out for two days?" the company representative said, paradoxically. "Why didn't you call before?" A perfect catch-22.

You can find an even more extreme example on National Public Radio's show *This American Life*, which ran a story by Jon

Ronson about a seventeen-year-old Brit who tried to get out of an assault charge by feigning insanity. The boy recited lines of every lunatic he had seen in movies and found himself permanently locked up in Broadmoor, an infamous London asylum for the criminally insane. When he behaved himself, the shrinks reported that institutionalization was good for him. When he acted out, the shrinks said he was a psychopath. The only way to get out was to prove himself sane, but every attempt to prove himself sane proved himself insane. Catch-22: the ultimate tension between the sane world and the insane.

In most cases, a catch-22 takes a certain amount of exaggeration, stretching your description of a rule to make it contradict itself. My phone company probably considered its representative's question a legitimate one. After all, didn't everyone have a cell phone? (Not in my case.) But some rules take very little hyperbole to show them as paradoxical, as many a recent college grad knows. To get a job, you need experience. To gain experience, you need a job. The IRS cracks down on companies that use unpaid interns without credit. So in order to have a job after school, you need to have a job during school—a job for which you fail to qualify because you're still in school.

To create a paradox of your own, look for a contradiction in a person, subject, or issue. It can come from hypocrisy, as Jonathan Safran Foer's Christmas trees did. Take so-called social conservatives' stand on gay marriage. An advocate for gay marriage might point out that the high divorce rate threatens the institution of marriage more than licensing stable gay relationships would. Part of that argument could be expressed in a paradox.

YOU: They're protecting marriage by opposing it.

The line may remind you of the apocryphal quote during the Vietnam War, "We had to destroy the village in order to save it." While no one actually seems to have said it, the sentence captured the paradoxical nature of the war itself, which wreaked havoc on the populace in order to save it from the ravages of Communism. Those words became a rallying point for antiwar protesters.

Sometimes, though, you want to describe a complexity—or not just describe it but convey it as well, making the complex sound even more complex. Time to employ the pith method, narrowing down to the key words. Then choose the most extreme of those words and pair them. Let's try it with one of the most complex topics of all: dieting. The problem with diets is that your body tends to adjust to its own food intake. Rapidly reduce the number of calories, and the body slows down its metabolism and frugally stores all the energy it can into fat. This paradox constitutes the single biggest reason diets fail. People want instant results. The faster the results, the bigger the rebound effect.

Put that pithily, using words and phrases to summarize the problem.

COUNTING CALORIES

FAT

STARVE

LOSE WEIGHT

GAIN WEIGHT

The extremes here are "fat" and "starve." Can you put them together in a paradox? Sure you can.

YOU: The best way to get fat is to starve.

You'll need to explain this proposition to your audience, but I guarantee it will get their attention. A paradox works whenever you speak to an audience that believes the difficult is easy, or the complex is simple; your average audience, in other words.

Another way to work up a satisfying paradox is to flip stereotypes.

John F. Kennedy combined two regional stereotypes to describe Washington as a city of "southern efficiency and northern charm." Try it with any standard stereotypes, taking care to try it out among highly tolerant audiences.

> YOU: He boogied with a grandfather's legs and an Irish dancer's arms.

The world is full of flippable stereotypes. Suppose you want to describe someone as fat and lazy. Can you think of a busy animal that's plump, along with a lazy creature not known for its obesity? Beavers are industrious and well rounded. Snakes are skinny and not known to be particularly hardworking, but they carry too much symbolic baggage for us to think of them as simply slim and lazy. Sloths aren't slim, but they might do the job lazily.

> YOU: Fat and lazy? She has the shape of a beaver and the work ethic of a sloth.

EXERCISE

Tension is an essential narrative device. If you want to tell a story—or lend your expressions and proposals a storytelling quality—master this creative suspension. Do you keep a diary? Go back and see how many ways you can insert tension in an entry. If you don't keep a diary, just jot down a short account of yesterday's events. Then tensify it with paradox and contrasts. Is the result more readable? It should be.

When I was in ninth grade, a teacher told me that good writers always keep a diary. That sounded like a fine idea, except that as an unexceptional ninth grader I made a terrible subject to write about. Every day I would come home from school and sit there with absolutely nothing to say. It was my first experience with writer's block. Finally it occurred to me to take literally the old adage, "You are what you eat." I began recording what I had for lunch that day. The physical act of writing loosened me up, and I would go off from there to record all my adolescent thoughts and stories. As I learned some of the techniques of storytelling, I actually wrote tension-filled pages about food: the raging argument in my hometown over the best cheese steaks, the arm-wrestling contests in the cafeteria, with blocks of ice cream placed where the loser's arm would descend; I eventually even calculated the energy costs of walking versus taking the bus and decided that the extra food I ate to replace the burned calories made riding the best environmental choice. Lunch, it turned out, supplied the scratch ingredients of a writing career. And I owe it all to the storytelling quality of tension.

ADDING OXY TO MORONIC

A particular kind of figure combines a paradox in the shortest possible space, as a contradiction in terms. You've probably heard its name: oxymoron (ox-ee-MOR-on).

Oxymoron

The ancient Greeks, those witty chaps, made their term for an oxymoron . . . an oxymoron! The word means "sharp dullness"—referring to "cleverly stupid," not "old knife that can give you tetanus."

That etymology helps us understand why bipartisanship fails in Congress these days. In a democracy, "partisanship" means "along party lines." As in, "I'm voting for this even though it doesn't make any sense, simply because I'm a (circle one) Democrat/Republican." "Bi," when not used by adolescent males, means "two." Put them together and the meaning becomes, "People who detest each other singing 'Kumbaya' for the cameras." When people go beyond party lines and actually accomplish something—I'm old enough to remember when that actually happened in Washington—the effort is not bipartisan but *non*partisan. The oxymoron makes for a nice parlor game, the winner being the person who comes up with the most apt one.

Airline food

Military intelligence (Groucho Marx first pointed out this one, of course)

Open secret

Microsoft Works

Free love

Jumbo shrimp

Pretty ugly

Undeclared voter

Continental breakfast (hardly continent sized)

Compassionate conservative

Pragmatic idealist

You may see some stereotype flipping here: Microsoft is infamous for its klugey software. To consider "free love" an oxymoron, you have to think of love in typically cynical terms. The oxymoron often flips stereotypes. You can, too, by listening for terms that contradict commonly accepted notions of a subject.

Another way to pick up an oxymoron is to think homonymnastically: look for puns that make ordinary expressions seem paradoxical. Try to ignore the sexism of this next example. I'm just making a point.

ME: She was a skinny broad, and that wasn't the only part of her that was oxymoronic.

"Broad" simply denotes "woman." The sexism lies in the belonging trope, which stares at the broad part of her otherwise skinny flesh. "Jumbo shrimp" does the same thing, as does "pretty ugly." By thinking of puns, and constantly pithing in your head, you can come up with oxymorons to label ideas or movements you oppose. Imagine that you dislike the Democrats' health-care plan because you believe that it spends a lot of money to buy very little. Write down your key words or list them in your head: liberal, health, helping, expensive . . .

Being a pun-oriented type myself, I see "liberal helping" as a pun.

ME: Only the Democrats could make "liberal helping" an oxymoron.

Oxymorons lie all around you. You just have to look for hypocrites, ridiculous rules, and puns, while keeping your piths and homonymnastics at the ready.

CONTRASTS: USING MERLOT AND SEX

While paradoxes shackle opposites to create tension, you can achieve the same tightening effect with figures that show the differences between things. Figures of contrast let you leverage the world, using one thing to make another thing seem larger or smaller, less or more important.

It's mind control, man. Look what happens in the classic 1950 film *Sunset Boulevard*.

> JOE: You're Norma Desmond. You used to be in silent pictures. You used to be big.
> NORMA: I *am* big. It's the *pictures* that got small.

In just two lines you get the theme of the movie: has-been film prima donna lamenting a Golden Age of moving pictures. We need to spend a little time on this gem of a quote, because it illustrates a powerful tool for memorability—one that sets up a contrast in order to change the perspective on an object. Picture short-statured Tom Cruise. Put him next to even shorter-statured Drew Barrymore, and he looks tall. Cast him with six-foot-tall Uma Thurman and he'll insist on some computer magic to shrink the woman. Poor old Norma Desmond works the same magic figuratively. Rude young Joe says she used to be big, which implies that she (or her reputation) has shrunk. Norma rebuts that assertion by setting up a contrast. By pulling in the movies that had been made since her prime, and shrinking *them*, she refocuses her own reputation. Result: one of the best-remembered lines in movie history.

A logician might point out that her line makes no rational sense. If pictures have gotten smaller, wouldn't that have made Norma look bigger? Or is she saying that the diminished state of film shrank everyone associated with it? Ah, here you find the true beauty—and manipulative evil—of figures and tropes, which appeal to right-brain, intuitive, emotional responses. They have to do with magic; and even a Muggle knows that magic gets a bye from the rules of logic. Or, to put it metaphorically, figures and tropes are perpetual motion machines. They chug away on their own volition into eternity as people repeat them through the generations. Every logician or physicist will tell you that perpetual motion machines are impossible. They're magic. Therefore, this trope is magic. Let's make some.

Start with the exact same expand-by-shrinking-something-else technique that Norma used. Only we'll do it in reverse. Suppose someone insulted your shape.

> JERK: Sure you ought to eat that? Your spare tire has gone from economy to full size.
>
> YOU: My stomach isn't bigger. It's the shirt that got smaller.

Nah, too easy. Besides, the American clothing industry has you covered, literally. My own size has gone from large to medium on most clothing, and I certainly haven't shrunk. We need to be more clever, and in the process see just how this particular figure can help you and your figure. We should "privilege" the object under question, as a modern rhetorician would say. Bring in comparables to place next to your object and make it look better in contrast. Now think of things that would privilege your underappreciated, overestimated stomach.

Contraster

Remember, logic need not be an element here. We want to show some wit and take attention away from your gut, not win a debating prize. Look at other things to place beside you; the room, for instance.

YOU: My stomach hasn't grown. The plates are smaller.

Ooh, better not. Your interlocutor could reply that the plates aren't small enough in your case. So try the jerk's petty mind.

YOU: That minuscule brain of yours makes everything look big.

All right. That works, in a crude way. To do it yourself, find a contrasting object or person, then blame it. You can even be logical. For example, the United States is losing its first-place status among developed nations on a whole variety of fronts, from productivity to health to education. A contraster helps to calm anxious Americans: we're not deteriorating; they're improving.

Now we will move up from things to whole concepts. The contraster uses one thing to make another seem different. It can also work with ideas or events. To change a concept, put another concept next to it to make it seem better or worse. This next quote—by *Slate*'s Jacob Weisberg—may seem a bit dated, but this sharp piece of political figuring shows how well the contraster works.

WEISBERG: In 1994, Gingrich had the Contract with America. In 2006, Democrats will have another glass of merlot.

Oh, how awful, a Democrat says. Besides, the party won back Congress that year. So either the Democrats got their act together or a little imbibing did the body politic good.

UNWRITTEN: The Democrats aren't doing much to win the next election.

The unwritten version is perfectly adequate, but if Weisberg had used it, I wouldn't be quoting him years later. Here it's not a matter of looking big or small, or fat or skinny. You use something weaker to make your focus look stronger, or you bring in a strong ringer to make your focus look weaker. The Dems were being lazy. Instead of merely describing them as lazy, show an example of high-energy politics as a contrast.

You can use this technique to fend off attacks on your waistline.

JERK: Sure you ought to eat that? Your spare tire has gone from economy to full-size.

YOU: Compared to your average American, I'm size svelte.

The contraster puts two concepts on a scale and lets it tip. We'll do it again, with slightly more subtlety. This time we'll use a great Billy Crystal line from the 1991 movie *City Slickers*.

CRYSTAL: Women need a reason to have sex. Men just need a place.

UNWRITTEN: Men don't need a reason for sex. Just give them a place to do it.

The unwritten version goes straight at the point: men want sex all the time. By bringing in women, Billy Crystal sets up a funny, wise line.

Sometimes a good comparison will come to you naturally. My father-in-law entered family legend during his honeymoon, when he and his wife stopped to eat at a roadside rest stop. They met a woman in a beautiful fur coat. The woman looked vastly relieved; she confided to my mother-in-law that her husband refused to stop whenever she needed to. It had been a long time between rest stops.

"I'll never be able to afford a fur coat," Bob said when the woman had left. "But I can promise that I'll always stop for the bathroom."

Bob and Anna Jane are no longer living, but the story still gets repeated on family occasions. The anecdote seems quaintly dated, coming from a time when men bought the coats and did the driving; but I still consider it one of the great family lines of all time. With just a few words, Bob demonstrated his wit, solidified his two-day-old marriage, and saved thousands of dollars.

MIRROR IMAGE: FOULING FAIRLY

My favorite figure of all brings together opposites by taking a phrase or clause and playing it backward. It must have been among Shakespeare's favorites as well; he certainly used it a lot. Take the famous line in *Macbeth*.

SHAKESPEARE: Fair is foul, and foul is fair . . .

Or this equally famous line in *Measure for Measure*.

SHAKESPEARE: What's mine is yours and what is yours is mine.

Mirror Image

The name the ancient Greeks gave this figure, *chiasmus*, shows how the mirror image works. *Chiasmus* describes the letter x in Greek. Crisscross. Take an expression, then flop it as if you were seeing it in a mirror. While it isn't the easiest figure in the rhetorical toolkit, it displays a show-stopping amount of wit.

The mirror image works best when you're talking about some sort of action—or, in grammatical terms, a subject doing something to an object: a achieving b. If you can reverse the formula, then you have an appropriate—and powerful—mirror image.

YOU: Some say a achieves b. I say, b achieves a!

The figure is useful in writing and in speaking in front of a group. If you're in a more intimate setting, on the other hand, it can sound a little fancy.

YOU: It's not that I love you for the sex; I sex you out of love.

That wouldn't win the speaker any more love, but the mirror image can achieve several other important purposes, including:

1. **Showing an event reversing itself.**

2. **Contradicting a statement.**

3. **Drawing a contrast between groups of people.**

The first purpose can prove the wisdom that what goes around, comes around. I worked on a story recently about a man exonerated of a rape charge after spending fourteen years in prison. The state ended up paying him three million dollars in restitution. In writing a blurb for the piece, I thought of a chiasmus.

ME: They punished the wrong man. Then his innocence punished them.

What went around, came around. Sometimes that can cause a perpetual motion, as during the Cold War. President John Kennedy captured the arms race with a chiasmus.

KENNEDY: Each increase of tension has produced an increase of arms: each increase of arms has produced an increase of tension.

To make the mirror image work in describing a chain of events, look for the kind of story in which celestial justice is served. If a misdeed leads to its own punishment, then you may have a mirror opportunity.

YOU: She looked for trouble, and trouble found her.

Take Bernie Madoff, who ran an infamous pyramid investment scheme and went to prison for it. State simply what he did: Madoff cheated investors out of millions. Then think of what happened to him, besides going to prison. His life was ruined, for one thing, with his own sons turning him in and one son later committing suicide—the kind of cosmic, cruel outcome that implies a chiasmus.

YOU: In cheating others, he ended up cheating himself.

That doesn't quite make the point, does it? You used the right process: state what he did, and the consequence; then try to rewrite the consequence to mirror what he did. Don't give up. Did he merely cheat others? Or did he ruin people's lives?

YOU: Madoff ruined people's lives, and they ruined him.

Besides showing causes and cosmic effects, the figure also lets you hold a fun-house mirror up to an idea or argument. Newt Gingrich, the former Speaker of the US House of Representatives, neatly contrasted his party with the opposing Democrats.

GINGRICH: We're prepared to place our trust in the people to reshape the government. Our liberal friends place their trust in the government to reshape the people.

There's a form you can imitate. Some do x to achieve y; others do y to achieve x. People reshape the government, or the government reshapes people. You can often distinguish groups of people by reversing their actions and their goals (or, in Gingrich's case, their beliefs and their actions). How might a Democrat respond, mirror-wise? Think of a good x and y pairing that sums up the difference between the parties. How about the many and the few?

DEMOCRAT: We believe that the efforts of a few can enrich the lives of many. Our friends on the right believe that the efforts of the many should enrich the few.

There's a bit of a cheat here—the two clauses don't exactly match—but it works. Why? Because of the pun in "enrich." In the first instance, it means to fulfill, make meaningful; in the second, it means making money. Puns can help create memorable, if not hilarious, mirror images. Shakespeare loved this kind of chiasmus. "Your means are very slender, and your waste is great," says one character. "I [wish] my means were greater and my waist slenderer," the other replies.

In most cases, though, you can keep your mirror image simple. "What's Hecuba to him or he to Hecuba, that he should weep for her?" Hamlet asks. A couple centuries later, Henry David Thoreau goofed on that line in *Walden*: "What am I to learn of beans or beans of me?" he asked. Many a relationship can be described this way.

YOU: What is he to her, or her to him?

Get used to an easy mirror image like that, and you can work your way up to more sophisticated versions.

YOU: He's romantic for the sex. She has sex for the romance.

There's a big generalization, and an even bigger, humanity-sized mirror, to that expression. Tension at its best.

THE TOOLS

"Yet a man may love a paradox, without either losing his wit or his honesty," said Ralph Waldo Emerson. I would take Mr. E. a step further: paradox lies behind a whole strange alternative world of wit. The essential nature of this trope—the mating of things that don't ordinarily combine—also constitutes the core of creative tension.

Paradox. A trope that claims the truth of a contradictory statement.

Oxymoron. A paradox expressed in one two-sided phrase.

Contraster. Uses a contrasting example to make something look larger or smaller, better or worse.

Mirror Image. Runs a clause and its reverse in one reflective sentence.

PART V

WORD HERO

Welcome to the pantheon,

where you use your newly acquired tools

to tell stories, get your way,

and achieve immortality.

14

TELL A STORY

THE LAZARUS COKE
Figuring a Great Yarn

WHAT MAKES A STORY A STORY? You probably learned in school that a story consists of characters, a setting, and a plot—essential ingredients, sure, but you can have all those things without actually having a story. Suppose you're telling your spouse about a trip a friend made.

YOU: He flew to London and stayed with a cousin, who took him to the British Museum. Then he flew to Rome and stayed at a great hotel. He was there three days before flying to Athens. . . .

This is news, and well worth telling, assuming your spouse is as interested in your friend as you are. But can you imagine if a Hollywood screenwriter used those same words to pitch a movie? He shouldn't hold his breath about getting the film made. It's just not a story. News and story are two different things, even if they both contain character, setting, and plot. Now, if your friend has flown to Europe to find love, without knowing that the love of his life has been pining for him back in his hometown—that's a story. Or suppose he has gone to find peace from his shallow, partying life, only to fall into a wild European crowd . . . these are two very different stories, but they share the element you saw in the last chapter: tension.

Whether you're inserting a narrative into a business presentation or recounting your disastrous vacation, tension is the catalyst that turns characters, setting, and plot into a tale. We'll start out with the tropical underpinnings of tension, and use figures to enrich the setting, characters, and action. And then we'll look at a few figurative ways to end a story. This is one chapter that will have you at the edge of your seat.

Well, wait. Isn't this book supposed to be about short, memorable expressions? Yes, but this section also shows how you can use figures to help you organize your thoughts, discover the tension in a narrative, and light up a story along the way. We've played with dozens of figures in the earlier chapters. Here you can see their power put to the highest use—not just in snappy one-liners but in telling our essential stories.

TENSION: WINNING JULIA ROBERTS

The playwright Tennessee Williams was one of the great storytellers of the twentieth century. *A Streetcar Named Desire*, *Glass Menagerie*, and *Cat on a Hot Tin Roof* are masterpieces of creative tension. The man almost couldn't help seeing a story in everything. He once got advice on the draft of a new play from the famous movie director Elia Kazan. Add a speech praising misfits, Kazan told him, suggesting a whole catalog of representative samples: "romantics, eccentrics, rebels, Bohemians, freaks . . ." Tennessee Williams took that advice and wrote an eloquent prayer into *Camino Real*. But the resulting catalog in the play is much more than a catalog.

WILLIAMS: God bless all con men and hustlers and pitchmen who hawk their hearts on the street . . . the courtesan who made the mistake of love, the greatest of lovers crowned with the longest horns, the poet who wandered far from his heart's green country and possibly will and possibly won't be able to find his way back . . .

Every part of that list contains a miniature story that could serve as the germ of a play all its own. The liars and cheats underdone by their own sincerity. A woman who sells her body to a man she loves. A superb lover who becomes a cuckold. A poet who leaves the very home that turned him into a poet. You and I may not intend to write any plays, but we can learn a lot about the particular kind of tension Williams employs here. They all come from irony, paradox, or a combination of both.

The single most effective way to create tension in a story is to base its theme on two elements that don't ordinarily go together. We're in tropical territory again, convincing our audience that we can marry opposites. Ask yourself which story you would rather hear.

(a) A con man robs a rich casino owner.
(b) A con man discovers an honest streak, despite his worst intentions.

(a) A prostitute sells her body on the street.
(b) A prostitute falls in love with her client.

(a) A great lover thrills his wife with his romantic attentions and his skill in bed.
(b) A great lover loses his wife to an ugly, selfish jerk.

(a) A poet travels abroad and finds wonderful new lands to write about.

(b) A poet travels for inspiration and finds he has left it at home, with no means of returning.

Of course, Hollywood might make a lot of money out of a con man robbing a casino owner. He could gather ten guys, hatch the perfect crime, and win Julia Roberts in the end. But what makes *Ocean's Eleven* a story isn't the plot about robbing casinos. It's that this cool, shallow man is actually trying to win his wife back—hawking his heart on the street if you will. Two things that don't seem to belong together: heartless openheartedness, or a con man conning for love.

When you're planning to tell a story of your own, use the pith method to boil down to the key words. Now look for any irony or paradox—for the oppositely charged poles that create magnetism. Here's an example:

Several years ago my mother-in-law, Anna Jane, developed congestive heart failure. The prognosis was grim, and Anna Jane didn't want the doctors to take any extraordinary measures. A strong-willed woman who liked to do the right things at the right moment, she figured it was time to join her beloved husband, who had passed on a couple years before. Anna Jane's four grown children gathered at her bedside and sang hymns all night.

Let me pause here to point out that, while you might find the scene moving, the tension is limited to morbid curiosity about whether Anna Jane actually died that night. (She didn't, or I wouldn't be telling this story.) It becomes a story when Anna Jane raises her finger.

Back to the story: around three in the morning, Anna Jane lifted a weak finger and pointed to my wife's Coke. "Sip o' that?" she whispered. So they propped her up and give her a sip. She downed half the Coke, despite an oxymoronic nurse's protest that caffeine was bad for the dying woman. Three hours later

Anna Jane was sitting up on her own; two days later she checked out of the hospital, furious that she failed to die on schedule. Being a purposeful woman, Anna Jane soon set her sight on the next presidential election two years off; she lived long enough to vote for Barack Obama in the primary. And then she joined her husband at last.

Now, if you were to write the figurative or tropical pith of that anecdote, how would you put it? Here's my take.

The doctors couldn't save her, but a Coke could.

This simple trope of things that don't belong together—helpless doctors, salubrious junk drink—make the story. The tension adds humor and becomes the tale's climactic moment as well as the central point. The pith itself could even serve as an ending, as we'll see in a bit.

Speaking of family, my sister, Sherry, is a natural storyteller, thanks to her instinct for irony and paradox. She recently married a terrific guy named Mike, and they went on a honeymoon in Florida. So far we're still in news territory. But anyone who knows Sherry can't wait to hear about her latest travels, because something always goes horribly wrong. Keep in mind that Sherry is a veteran traveler who doesn't fall apart easily; her tone is more eye rolling than aghast.

Let me start with a summary. The pith: Sherry and Mike got stopped at the airport when Mike tried to take his large bottle of suntan lotion through security. Mike resisted, and Sherry pretended to cry in order to deflect the officers' attention from Mike. He in turn backed down, surrendering the lotion, and they continued on their honeymoon.

Now let's choose a tension-filled pith that would turn this into a great story. Sherry piths her stories instinctively, while less gifted storytellers like me have to think about it consciously. The trick is to look for things that don't ordinarily belong together.

> They had thought of everything for their vacation—including a bottle of sunscreen that almost ended it.

> She married a strong, independent man. And that almost ruined everything.

> She didn't cry at their wedding. Good thing she cried at her honeymoon.

> It would have been the ideal honeymoon, if only they were speaking.

EXERCISE

This kind of pith finding, putting the essence of a story in terms of a paradoxical or ironic statement, makes for great practice. Next time you want to tell a story to family or friends, tell the pith first as a teaser: "I want to tell you what happened on my honeymoon. We'd thought of everything for it—including a bottle of sunscreen that almost ruined it." You're bound to get your audience's full attention, even if you sound a bit like an announcer in movie trailers.

While any one of the piths above might work, my sister knows that the best stories focus on their characters. So when she tells her honeymoon tale, she works to maximize the crying part.

SHERRY: TSA calls for backup and it looks like they're going to arrest Mike. The line behind us just keeps growing. So [she asks any woman in the audience], what would you do in my shoes? I did what any woman would do: I made myself cry. "We're on our honeymoon! Mike, you're going to ruin the whole thing!"

The way Sherry tells this part, she sighs just before saying "I made myself cry." Yes, it was childish and manipulative, the sigh says. But the situation was desperate. The TSA officers backed off, by the way. This was a family affair, and no one wanted to be responsible for ruining a woman's honeymoon. Sherry quietly threatened to go on the honeymoon without her recalcitrant husband, and he gave up the lotion. A day or so later, he and Sherry were speaking again, and they had a great time—until they got home and discovered that the thermostat had been turned up all the way, blistering the paint on the walls. But that's a different story. Sherry is about to leave with Mike on another vacation, by the way. I can't wait to hear about it.

The Vacation Gone Bad is a classic theme for a story, because of its ironic nature (the pursuit of relaxation causes huge stress), or a central paradox (the most memorable vacations are often the worst ones). Veteran hikers have an old expression: it's not an adventure if everything goes right. Which is just another way to say it isn't a story, either. When you tell your own story, think of what people expect to hear, and then decide how to undermine those expectations. There's your irony or paradox.

These tropes aren't the only ways to create tension in a story, of course. You can build a story around other tropes, such as a metaphor or its figurative offspring, the analogy or simile. Sherry could retell her story by imaging it as a real-life movie tale, asking her audience to suggest actors for the main characters. (Julia Roberts for Sherry, of course; Robert De Niro for Mike.)

The belonging trope can also help focus the story. Start with a detail and make it represent the whole theme. Suntan lotion makes a nice belonging trope. It's a safety item—SPF-50 prevents skin cancer. But what happens when the concern for safety becomes obsessive, even ridiculous? I mean, what if you're willing to wreck a whole travel experience for the sake of safety? What if the focus on suntan lotion makes you miss the real dangers, such as a furious bride? Now the suntan lotion starts to stand for bigger themes, such as creepily named Homeland Security.

Tropes make great story themes, because stories often have meaning beyond their literal sense. A planet full of blue people serves as a metaphorical stand-in for an overly exploited Earth. A girl traveling alone to the big city stands in for leaving home to find love and scary independence. Stories are big old trope envelopes. Why, after all, do people get upset when an actor portraying a gay person does a limp wrist routine in a movie? Or when every black person in a film is a welfare mother or a drug-using thug? After all, they're just pretending! The anger comes from characters serving as tropes, representing types as well as individuals.

SETTING: THE CURIOUS INCIDENT OF THE DOG IN THE COFFEE SHOP

Once you have developed your pith, you can employ a variety of figures to help you tell it. Just about every figure can aid a story, and the ones you find yourself most comfortable with will probably serve you best. But if you're willing to experiment beyond your figurative comfort zone, then consider a few tools that work especially well in setting the scene:

Sound symbolism

Catalog

Venereal language

Special effects can help you set the scene. If you're telling a story about a coffee shop, for instance, don't shy from an onomatopoeia.

YOU: It was hard to hear over the CCCCHHHHHHAAAA of lattes in the making, but I could swear I heard a young woman say her dog wasn't wearing any pants.

Subtler kinds of sound symbolism can help as well. Spoons in the coffee shop can *click* and *slop*, the R&B coming out of the sound system can *woo-woo*, the dog chained to a metal chair outside can *yip* or *woof*, depending on its size. Customers can be *I'll-having* and *That's-me-ing*. Sound symbolism sets the background soundtrack that makes your audience feel as if it's there.

For the visuals, you can create a movielike effect with a catalog. Don't forget to think about which way the camera is panning; list the details in some sort of natural order.

YOU: It was your typical downtown, Fair Trade kind of coffee shop, with a dog chained out front, students inside chained to their laptops, and a long line of hipster types waiting for their coffee. That's when I saw this woman talking earnestly to the nose-ringed barista.

A catalog can also help you introduce tension with a list of items that don't ordinarily go together. The technique works best if your character bears a whole slew of traits or experiences.

YOU: I later learned that she was training for a marathon while launching a new company and traveling constantly, and for some reason even she can't explain, had acquired a mutt named Skye from the SPCA.

In any scene with a lot of people, venereal language can help you make some shortcuts, giving your audience some vivid visuals without making your story too long. Let's venerealize that coffee line.

YOU: . . . and a slouch of hipsters waiting for their coffee.

More than one group might be worth your venereal attention. You could have a clutch of nervous ladies from the suburbs. A woosh of baristas. A pitter of e-mailing laptoppers. A yearning of leashed dogs. Though that might just possibly be overdoing it in the venereal department.

CHARACTERS: THE POPEYE-KARDASHIAN GRAFT

Different figures work best in portraying individual people, depending on whether you're dealing with minor characters or the protagonist. The length of your story makes a difference as well. In a longer yarn, it helps to attach labels to characters to distinguish them from one another. These figures all provide great labels:

Descriptive label

Slogan

Belonging trope (metonymy)

Whether you're telling a joke or describing something you witnessed today, the descriptive label helps your audience track a character through his description. For instance, the barista talking to the young woman can be Barista with the Nose Ring throughout the story. This works far better than the way we usually tell a story, with pronouns whose antecedents got lost an eon ago.

WRONG: So he listens to her while serving him, and he doesn't want what he gave him . . .

Your audience is left retracing your steps like a detective looking for a perp. A descriptive label, on the other hand, works even better than a name. People forget names. They remember descriptions like "Barista with the Nose Ring." If you do have a name, simply attach a description to it, and you have a handy slogan: Jorge, the barista with the nose ring

But why go to all that trouble when you can use a belonging trope? Name the guy after a characteristic: Nose Ring.

YOU: So Nose Ring listens to the woman while serving this hipster who's wearing an ironic T-Shirt, and T-Shirt says he didn't order an iced macchiato.

See what we're doing here? Think of these character labels literally, as if your audience can picture them as type hanging in the air with arrows pointing to the appropriate people.

Nose Ring ⇨

T-Shirt ⇨

Slouch of Hipsters ⇨

Simply take a characteristic or description of each minor character, and let the audience imagine the arrows. Can you think of scenes where strangers interacted in your own life earlier today? How would you describe those characters in just a couple of words? Now create labels for them as you would in telling a story.

But first we need to do something about the woman. We can't just leave her there, undescribed. For the main character in your anecdote, you might want to linger on her a bit. If her appearance is extraordinary, a little exaggeration might be in order. Time for Mr. Potato Head to make its appearance.

> YOU: She was a real beauty—the cascading hair of a Kardashian sister, the eyes of a fawn, and the forearms of Popeye. I figured her for a baker.

When you're telling a story, Mr. Potato Head works best if it contains a bit of tension—a part that seems out of place. Remember those awful multiple-choice tests you took as a kid, when you were supposed to pick out the item that doesn't belong? I was terrible at that kind of question.

> Which does *not* belong with the others?
> (a) Fawn   (b) Kardashian sister   (c) Real beauty   (d) Popeye

Whenever I saw a question like that, I would start imagining a scenario in which all the elements made perfect sense. I *wanted* them all to belong. And that's what great tropes and figures do. They welcome the black sheep into one big tense family, figuratively speaking. Come on in, Popeye! Love your forearms; they look great on that Kardashian girl. Of course, I'm not saying you have to deploy a Potato Head every time you tell a story. Sometimes a detailed, un-analogous description will do, or maybe your character needs no introduction.

ACTION: ENTER DOG, DRAGGING A CHAIR

We already talked about the usefulness of sound symbolism in describing a scene. Same goes for action.

> YOU: Suddenly, the woman snatches the cup and slings the iced macchiato at T-Shirt. It slishes down his front onto his low-rider jeans.

The icy sibilance is a nice touch there, beginning the sound effects even before things get really slishy. Besides sound symbolism, an informal story might call for some tropical aid. T-Shirt guy can stand there with a frozen expression, or he can wear a contemplative mien, like a man unexpectedly invited to a macchiato-tasting party; or he might have a mysterious expression—Whistler's Mother after Whistler has thrown an iced macchiato in her face. But nothing ramps up the action more than **hyperbole** and its nephew, **feigned precision**. You might start out with a bit of an understatement to set up the exaggeration.

> YOU: After that, things started to get interesting. T-shirt grabs a double-espresso latte and makes like he's going to throw it at the girl, when suddenly Nose Ring throws himself over the counter at T-Shirt, sending up a cascade of coffee products. Forty-seven hipsters are screaming about coffee on their ironic clothing, when I hear the sound of a pack of dogs barking. I turn around and a sheepdog the size of an actual sheep is tearing through the door. The woman sees it and screams, "Skye!" Everybody looks up toward the ceiling before realizing she means the dog.

Assuming you're not doing a newscast for CNN or writing a Hemingwayesque short story, your exaggeration—turning half a dozen hipsters into a false-precise forty-seven, making coffee products cascade, expanding the dog—heightens the scene's entertainment value.

We have left out one other trope: personification. Humanizing the nonhuman can lend surreality to your story—a boost when you describe something surreal.

> YOU: So put yourself in the dog's, um, shoes. You see your owner in the middle of this fracas, with two wet humans going at each other. You don't see great to start with, what with all that hair hanging over your eyes. Besides, you don't have a lot of time to contemplate the situation and take in all its ramifications. You're a dog of action. So you charge into the place, dragging the chair on the leash after you and scattering hipsters like tenpins. You head right into the middle of the fight and sink your teeth into Nose Ring. Who happens to be your owner's husband. Which, come to think of it, you probably knew.

Admittedly, you won't want to use personification every day; it's one of those tropes that lie in the background, like the really specialized kitchen tool that dwells patiently in a drawer just waiting for that moment of glory when it finally gets to make pasta. Just knowing it's there—personification, I mean—makes you feel more competent. You know that, any time you want, you can teleport your audience into the brain of a dog in a shaggy-dog story.

ENDING: TAKE A BOW, OR A WOW

Have you ever told a terrific yarn only to have it peter out at the end? Some of the best stories end up as shaggy-dog tales, with no discernible point. A well-rendered figure can fix that problem by creating a tagline, summarizing the story or serving up the theme as a kind of moral. Look again at the instances of irony and paradox I listed for themes in my sister Sherry's honeymoon story.

> They had thought of everything for their vacation—including a bottle of sunscreen that almost ended it.

> She married a good, strong, independent man. And that almost ruined everything.

Each one of them could serve as a moral or summary.

YOU: So, in short, they'd thought of everything—including that bottle of sunscreen that almost ruined everything.

Or

YOU: Now, I don't want to give you the wrong impression of Mike. He's a strong, independent man. Which, when it comes to honeymoons, can be the last thing you want.

In other words, if you discover the tension that makes your story work, you can put it to use in the story itself. Your tension can help you achieve a higher wisdom (or bigger laugh, as the case may be), and deliver a memorable line.

Several specific tools can also serve to deliver a bang-up story ending.

Catalog

Pun, particularly the Feghoot

Yogism

If you don't want to use your story's tension as its ending, consider a catalog ending.

YOU: Grabbing the one remaining intact latte, I picked my way out of that coffee shop, leaving behind a pool of coffee, a legion of screaming hipsters, some strange love triangle, and a dog—who was lapping up the foam like some sleep-deprived undergrad in finals period.

Creating your own catalog ending is like making a curtain call, having the major elements of your story all take a bow. Your audience gets reminded of the good parts, and you wrap things up neatly without petering out. Cue the applause.

If you're skilled at punning, and have had time to prepare in advance, you can try the ambitious Feghoot ending—the elaborate pun that concludes a shaggy-dog story.

YOU: And the moral of that story? Well, to coin an espresso, young Skye walker, may divorce be with you.

OK, I set you up for that. A more doable Feghoot arises from a cliché that matches your theme, serving as an Aesop's-like moral. What standard theme would appropriately conclude our shaggy-dog tale? It sometimes pays to get into a lovers' quarrel? Or you can find excitement everywhere? Or that you found stimulation in a coffee shop before you drank a drop?

EXERCISES

1. Come up with your own Feghoot. Think of a moral to the story, then go through homonymnastics to find the appropriate synonyms. Last, try to find an old saying or cliché to pun off. You may not find this exercise worth it, given that the groans you elicit from your audience might be those of real pain. But I love trying to think up puns for the stupidest reasons. I have this theory that such mental exercise will prevent dementia when I'm older; in any case, my puns already make me sound demented, so any real deterioration in my faculties won't be noticed as much. So here's what I can get out of our coffee-shop morals.

ME: The moral of this story? When the Skye isn't the limit, reach for the Starbucks.

Or

ME: Only because I outran the dog and its crazy leash, I got to lap up a free coffee. Which goes to show: he who laps last, laps the leash.

But you need not get quite so elaborate with your ending. If you can pull off a Yogism, achieving a higher wisdom through a foolish-sounding expression, you will impress your audience all the more. A Yogism is a moral on its own, and the story can serve to prepare the audience for it. Yogi Berra himself remarked that you can observe a lot by watching—a moral that happens to suit our coffee-shop tale to a . . . I almost said "tea." A great Yogism is a kind of paradox, with two parts that don't belong together.

YOU: So if there's a lesson to be learned from this, it's that boring places are the most exciting.

Nice ending.

2. Write or tell a What I Did Over Vacation story without planning it in advance. Now plan to retell it, marshaling figures to help. Start with a paradoxical pith, containing two elements that don't ordinarily go together. Set the scene with a catalog. Try to describe the main character by using a Mr. Potato Head. Think of at least one instance of sound symbolism for the action. Now dream up a Yogism ending. If you're up to it, memorize those figures or jot them down on a small piece of paper. Try to tell the story to a sympathetic listener. Then ask yourself: Was it better for the figuring? I bet it was.

15

SPEAK TO A GROUP

BATTLE YOGA

Applying Your Figurative Knowledge for Public Glory

As SOMEONE WHO SPEAKS frequently in front of groups large and small, I'm all too familiar with performance anxiety. Speech coaches tell you to gain courage by focusing on the friendly faces in the audience, the ones who smile. That advice makes me instinctively look for the frowners and scowlers, the ones who shake their heads whenever I make a point. The feeling is exactly that of a timid rock climber who looks down.

Fortunately, I have a few tricks to get through even the worst moments of terror. Figures can help you focus your thoughts, outline your talk, and give your audience some words to remember. This chapter will show you how to do all that.

Even better, I find that a few memorable expressions—or, in a short talk, just one—can serve as a talisman. If I can memorize one to three sentences, and be prepared to deliver them at the appropriate times, then I won't worry as much about the rest of it. If those sentences are good enough, they're all the audience will remember. Your most memorable words—and very few words at that—will serve as the takeaway. Does anyone remember

Winston Churchill's speech in Fulton, Missouri, where he used the paradoxical phrase "iron curtain" for the first time? Perhaps a few; but most people remember only "iron curtain." It became the central metaphor for the Cold War.

So, rather than worrying about delivering a perfect talk, I concentrate on delivering a perfect sentence. Just one perfect sentence, well delivered, can make a whole speech.

Let's sketch out a speech and see how we do.

THE "KIDS THESE DAYS" SPEECH

Congratulations, I think. Your old high school has bestowed on you the great honor of giving the commencement address at the June graduation. You accept graciously and call your spouse.

> YOU: Can you believe they chose me over my rival, the guy who became the billionaire bond trader?
> SPOUSE: What makes you think your rival wasn't asked first? Maybe he turned it down.
> YOU: Wow, thanks for the buzz kill. Who would turn down an honor like that?
> SPOUSE: Maybe he didn't want to stand up in front of hundreds of hot, bored students.

You realize that your spouse could be right. What's worse than trying to make yourself heard above a horde of celebrating students packed into a high school gym? You're an alien to them—an alien whose every word delays the moment when they can shuck their stupid robes and mortarboards and party with their friends.

Feeling stoked now? Sorry, but I wanted to give you a

realistic, have-to-prepare-a-speech feeling. The actual preparation won't feel nearly as bad.

The first thing we need to do, obviously, is to find a theme for our speech. If we were giving a business presentation instead of a commencement address, we'd already have a theme; but even then we'd need some central rhetorical focus. Are we going to dwell on the product exclusively, or compare it with the competition? Will we talk about the idea or theory or just stick to the concrete facts? A commencement address is even more of a blank slate, assuming you don't plan simply to do the standard "follow your dream" theme. When in doubt, flatter your audience. Tell them that the naysayers are wrong about them. Then come up with a word repeater that will bring the kids out of their seats.

So we go through the pith method, writing down key words to repeat. Then we base our speech on what we come up with. We get out a notebook and scribble some phrases or sentences.

The critics are wrong.

Kids are no better or worse than before.

You have to prove yourself.

Don't let them stop you.

Just from those lines, I see a couple of juicy words that might make a word repeater: "wrong" and "prove." "Wrong" is a great word to say loudly, because it's very sound symbolic—"wrong" rhymes with "strong," sounding strong. "Prove" is something an ambitious young person wants to do with herself. Can we use both words in a sentence? Sure we can

YOU: Prove them wrong.

Love it. Here's the anchor for your whole speech: the old farts say kids these days are ruining civilization. *Prove them wrong.* That could be the title of your speech, in fact. And the phrase can inform your outline. Start by saying how honored you are to speak to the generation who will run things someday. Then talk about the world they'll be inheriting. Jon Stewart did this in a famous 2004 speech to graduating college seniors at his alma mater, William & Mary. After talking about the real world, he tossed them a metaphor, making our planet sound like an expensive gadget.

STEWART: I don't really know to put this, so I'll be blunt. We broke it. Please don't be mad.

The metaphor works well in speeches because it allows you to talk about big, complicated, abstract things as if they were concrete. Environmentalists do this with Planet Earth, turning it into a mother, a spaceship, or a fragile organism. Conservatives do it with the economy, making it into a machine or a miracle from God. Liberals do it with cities, pretending they're villages or families. Nearly every speaker these days, unfortunately, turns life into tourism by calling it a "journey." (A word of advice: don't make life a journey. It has been used often enough to qualify as a road-weary cliché.)

Once you describe the world the graduates will inherit someday, you can talk briefly about how different their lives have been from those of their elders: born with the Internet, able to write with their thumbs on tiny keyboards, and so on.

Now you come to the fulcrum of your speech. I like having a speech with a fulcrum—a climactic moment that tips the balance of your thoughts. Up till now you have openly agreed with the adult's perspective on kids. Now tilt things. In this case, talk about how many adults feel that kids these days haven't been brought up right. That they don't have the right stuff to grow into leaders. Then you can ask your young audience: "Are they right?" Some kids or even adults may shout, "NO!" Whether they do or not, you can add, "I don't know if they're right or wrong." Pause. "That's up to you." Now's the time for your big word repeater. You glance down at a simple list of words:

VIDEO GAMES

CODDLED

SPOILED

LACK DISCIPLINE

LAZY

SELFISH

Now gazing at the graduates, you fire away with your word repeaters, which we've placed at both the beginning and the end of each line.

YOU: They say that video games are ruining your ability to think. Are they right? Prove them wrong. They say your parents coddled you—worried too much about your self esteem. Are these critics right? Prove them wrong. They say you're spoiled, given everything, don't know how to work hard. Are they right? Prove them wrong! They say you're selfish, self-centered, that you'll grow up thinking only of yourself and not of your community or your country. Are they right? Prove them wrong!

When you use word repeaters in front of a sizable audience, consider using a different tone for each one. In this case, you can gradually turn up the volume on "prove them wrong" until you're practically shouting that last line. Or, even better: pronounce that last sentence slowly.

YOU: Prove . . . them . . . wrong!

Your audience should be plenty stirred up by this. Look studiously down at your notes while they applaud and try not to smile. You *did* it—you delivered your figurative payload, giving the graduates something they will remember. Having delivered it, let it sink in. Take your time. In performing memorable words, think about the tone of voice, and give your audience a rest for brief periods, especially if they have responded well to a line.

When the applause dies down, you ask: "How can you prove them wrong?" Then feel free to repeat the Prove Them Wrong line a few more times, this time at the beginning of consecutive sentences. To prepare this part of the speech, you go through the same process you did for your climactic lines, writing a list of simple phrases.

Commit to learn

Stay fit

Volunteer-Vote

Learn to lead

YOU: Prove them wrong by committing to learn. Learn all you can—not just on the Web but through good books. Prove them wrong by staying fit and eating right. Prove them wrong by volunteering in your community, serving your country, and voting in every single election. And prove them wrong by learning what it takes to lead!

Yeah, some of that sounds a bit clichéd. Next thing you know you'll be talking about your journey. But I hope you found the process helpful. Start with the pith method. Write detailed notes for when you need them, and simple lists for when you don't. Use word repeaters to hammer in your key memorable line and make your audience feel like participants. Remember: what seems like crushingly dull repetition on paper can sound positively thrilling in person. I've sat through many terrific speeches thinking, *I should publish that in my magazine.* Then, when I read the text, I realize you had to have been there. Word repeaters, and metaphors that turn your audience into warriors or saints, bring up the emotion in the room and make you look eloquent.

Word repeaters can also help you create your ending. Let's finish the commencement address.

YOU: Prove them wrong, and you, my friends—you—will become the Greatest Generation.

And the crowd goes wild! The part of the crowd that's not checking text messages, I mean. Or maybe those bowed heads mean they're immortalizing your words on Twitter.

EXERCISE

Create the core of your own imaginary commencement address: the words you would repeat at its fulcrum. Find the pith of your speech. Come up with a phrase that urges your students to do something. Then see if you can describe the results in terms of that same phrase. "Prove them wrong, and you will become . . ." What's your version of "Prove them wrong"?

TERRIFIC US, TERRIBLE THEM

Word repeaters get more use in speechmaking than any other figures, for several good reasons: they make your words easier to follow, cause the audience to unconsciously complete your sentences, and make it easier to speak without notes. But they work best for sizable audiences, and not so well for more intimate groups, such as a presentation in a boardroom. ("Rumor has it that you're going to choose our rival. Prove them wrong!" . . . . better not.)

Besides, word repeaters alone aren't always the best figures for pointing out differences between people or ideas—one major reason people give talks in the first place. Sure, our commencement example pointed out differences, but only by repeating a flat contradiction. You now have other figures to choose from if you want to point out differences. One device that works in small or large settings is the mirror image. Use it whenever you're inclined to say, "The reverse could be true." Because that's what the mirror image does: it gives you the opposing argument, in reverse. In fact, you could use the figure for the fulcrum of your high school address.

YOU: Right or wrong, that is what they teach you. Now it's time to teach them.

The mirror image works just as well in the boardroom.

YOU: In their model, customers have to come to them. In ours, we come to the customers.

Or

YOU: We have the human advantage. While our competitors say they run superior technology, I say their technology runs them.

A mirror image can serve as more than just a mental take-away for the audience. It can serve as a literal takeaway as well, serving as a slogan on the "leave-behind" literature and on your website. It's a tricky figure, I'll admit, but worth trying for.

An easier figure, the contraster, also works well for righting wrongs and bringing up stark differences between you and the other team or ideas. Imagine you're a coach firing up a team for a big game.

YOU: We practiced, we sweated, we ran the drills. They hired a yoga instructor.

Use the contraster when you want to use a foil to make your audience feel bigger or smaller. Why do we look so noble? Because they're so ignoble. Or, more civilly: they're not as bad as they look; we're just better.

While we're comparing sides here, consider what you can do with a contrasting metaphor or analogy. You, the coach, want your players to picture themselves as warriors. Warriors don't do yoga poses! So you add that to your locker-room speech.

YOU: And why didn't I have you do poses? Because you're warriors. And warriors don't do poses!

The implication here is that the opponents are the exact opposite of warriors. Peaceniks. Appeasers. They'll roll over if you look at them mean. Now, assuming you don't happen to be a coach, think of the mirror image, contraster, and metaphor as ways to compare one group, person, or idea against another. Which do you use when?

Remember, the mirror image works best when you're talking about some sort of action. The contraster lets you grow or shrink your subject by measuring it against something else. In fact, politicians often use it in speeches to slam an opponent without sounding nasty.

> POLITICIAN: It's not that I'm perfect. It's just that my opponent makes me look great in comparison.

The metaphor, like tropes in general, can sound poetic, or overly fancy; but it can also come off as plain and simple. It depends on the metaphor. Sports players are used to seeing themselves as warriors, but the term can sound overblown when you're firing up a sales team to go hawk Internet advertising. Use a metaphor when you have a perfectly suitable match, where you and an opposing idea or person make perfectly contrasting images.

We'll talk more about contrasting tools in the next chapter, on argument. The mirror image, contraster, and contrasting metaphor work especially well when you're speaking to a group, because they weigh things side by side simply, lend themselves to repetition, and make groups feel they're part of something better than their individual selves. They're members of a tribe. Your tribe.

FILLING OUT YOUR ORATORICAL WHEELHOUSE

We give talks for a variety of reasons. The commencement speech expresses the feelings of a group, or gets kids charged up about their future, or offers an excuse to pick up an honorary degree "without putting in any effort," as Jon Stewart phrased it.

Public speech can also help you label your competition or opponents, through a descriptive label ("Robots with name tags")—or, to be wittier, with venereal language, the group-names technique ("A fluxion of engineers").

When you're explaining a process—or want to make an outcome sound inevitable—the "for-want-of-a-shoe" figure sounds terrific out loud in front of an audience.

YOU: Burning carbon traps the sun: the sun turns polar ice to water; the water floods the cities; and our cities become unlivable.

You might not think that "fancy" figuring could help you simplify a process for someone. But it can. Research shows that people understand complicated matters more easily when the concepts get linked up with multiple parts of the brain. The more you can associate a process with your audience's existing knowledge, beliefs, and expectations, the better they absorb the new stuff. That's what makes the simile and analogy such great teaching tools. The enormously complex national debt makes an excellent example, being alarming, hard to understand, and boring. Quick, link it to something familiar.

YOU: The debt is like a battery. Budget surpluses charge it up, and deficits draw it down.

You still have a lot of work to do to explain where tax revenues, Social Security, Medicaid, the military, and interest on the debt factor in. But you can do that with chunking, breaking each sector down into a piece of the analogy.

YOU: Take tax cuts. Advocates say they cut the debt by stimulating the economy. But economists say that isn't true. It's like claiming you'll lose less power by driving your electric car faster. You get there sooner, right? Wouldn't that save energy? No, tax cuts and driving faster just drain the battery more.

If you have pithed an issue and discovered a paradox, see if you can render it as a play on words. In a speech before a sizable audience, emotions tend to get exaggerated. So even the barest flicker of wit can get a big response. How do you convert a paradox to wordplay? Look for a possible repeat changer. For instance, suppose you're giving an Earth Day speech. You decide that the pith of your talk has to do with humans' natural tendencies to destroy the environment. It's nature (human) versus nature (everything else). That's a paradox ripe for repeat changing.

YOU: If we keep doing what comes naturally, we'll destroy nature.

But maybe wordplay doesn't evoke the emotion you want. Instead, you hope to stiffen the environmental backbone of your audience. When you want to sound never-say-die determined, try the getting medieval figure.

YOU: I will take no more "we can'ts." From now on, it's about "we will."

And, of course, all the storytelling tools you saw in action in the last chapter can work in a speech as well. The Greeks invented figures for their oratory. And they were first-rate storytellers. The combination, in your hands, can be positively epic.

--------- *EXERCISE* ---------

When's the last time you gave a talk? What emotions were you trying to evoke in the audience? Now list the figures that might have helped your audience get emotional. You may be thinking, "My talk was informative. I didn't want the audience sobbing and clinging to one another." OK, but what about a little humor? Would wordplay have helped you? What about a humorous paradox?

16

WIN AN ARGUMENT

CONSENSUAL SOCKS
Comebacks, Brands, and Labels

THE FIRST ARGUMENTS we have as kids tend to spoil us for argument. They start with logical claims like, "Mine!" and progress to witticisms like, "I know you are, but what am I?" These arguments aren't much fun, and without the confidence and tools we need for the job, disagreements can be nothing but misery. This chapter won't teach you all the tricks for argument (I covered argument in a previous book), but it will give you opportunities to create a memorable line, seemingly spontaneously. After all, you don't have to win an argument to make people love you and your wit. Focus on getting off a good line and you will feel better about losing; plus, your audience will feel better about you.

One thing to keep in mind, though: you first need an audience. If you argue with just one person without any observers, you might want to focus on calmness instead of memorability. Generally, when you face an impatient or angry client, a memorable, figured line is not a good idea.

YOU: You express the logic of a hamster in the dulcet tone of a schnauzer.

Don't expect the victim of a Potato Head to repeat it later. Still, figures can help you in a one-to-one argument. Use sound symbolism to render soft tones—avoid words with *p* or *t*, or any vowels that make you open your mouth wide. *V*, *w*, and *l* sounds soften things up, with *s* making soothing sounds.

BAD: I'm absolutely happy to take care of you, ma'am.
GOOD: Let's work through this.

Listen carefully, repeat the customer's words unironically, and prove you're listening. When you prepare an answer in your head, try to avoid words that make you open your mouth wide ("Calm down!"). Use sound symbols to sound reassuring. Doesn't "reassuring" sound reassuring? That's because your mouth need not open threateningly large.

In many cases, simple subservience won't work. Assert yourself a bit with the kindergarten imperative, giving your client an action item upon which you shall act with vigor.

While we're calming our customer down, a trickier figure can work wonders to tamp down emotions—if you use it right. The understatement can show that you recognize the problem while putting it in perspective. The kind of understatement I'm talking about, though, doesn't deflate the customer's claim; in fact, it denies the exaggeration of its opposite. Yes, that's complicated, but this example will demonstrate what I mean.

CUSTOMER: Waiter, this soup is cold!
YOU (nodding): You're certainly in no danger of burning your tongue with this. I'm sorry. I'll get you a replacement right away.

We ran into this kind of understatement that denies an exaggeration of the opposite in chapter 9. Called a *litotes*, it can make for great sarcasm. But you don't have to employ it entirely ironically; in fact, you can use it quite agreeably. *Boy, are you ever right, sir. This soup isn't what you'd call boiling!* You're taking the other person's side enthusiastically. At the same time, you're planting the opposite idea in your interlocutor's head: he complains of cold, you talk of heat. Try it sometime. If it doesn't work—well, to put it litotily, I didn't claim it was a miracle cure. While it may not get you the world's largest tip, it should lower the temperature of the accusation.

IF-THEN CLAUSE: UNNATURAL SOCKS

But enough with humbling ourselves. Let's give as good as we get, flashing snappy answers at an opponent's challenge. Then we will engage in some argumentative labeling and branding. While some people might object to such an elbows-out use of figures, argument does not have to get ugly. An ongoing, years-long debate over socks by my son, George, and me would be thoroughly enjoyable if it didn't involve the loss of my socks. George and I banter constantly; some people would call it bickering, except that it qualifies more as a rhetorical contest than as mutual complaints.

One of our favorite bantering figures is the reductio ad absurdum and its associated tool, the if-then clause. You may recall that the if-then accepts the opposing line as a hypothesis and then takes it to a logical extreme. If *a* is true, then a ridiculous *b* must be true as well.

ME: I had twelve pairs of socks in that drawer. Now there are two pairs and they don't match.
GEORGE: Twelve pairs? If you had twelve pairs of socks, then your two pairs had babies that grew up and left the nest.
ME: And moved to your room?

George and I love the ad absurdum because it reduces the opponent's argument—shrinks the other's tool, as it were. Maybe that's just a guy thing, but the technique works. One of the problems we all have with effective argument is coming up with something great off the cuff. The pressure of argument can tie the tongues of the best of us. The if-then version of the ad absurdum makes a good under-pressure tool, because you can pull it off spontaneously, especially with practice. Simply listen for an unreasonable point; your odds of hearing one in the average argument are quite high. Then stretch it out like taffy. In addition, the if-then can buy you some time to think of a retort. Notice what George did. He repeated my point twice before he began the stretching.

GEORGE: Twelve pairs? If you had twelve pairs . . .

Meanwhile, I picture his brain furiously pulling my logic to some absurd point. He thought that my claim of twelve pairs greatly exaggerated the number I actually started with. (This, of course, is a shocking lie, but I'll leave it there.) If in fact my few socks suddenly turned into twenty-four, then they must have multiplied. Not much of a leap to imagine a few pairs making woolly whoopee in my sock drawer.

You don't always have to fabricate your own absurdity. Often your opponent will provide you with one—for example, by expressing piety toward an entity that has done something ridiculous on its own. Take the evergreen concept of the "will of the people."

JON STEWART: You have to remember one thing about the will of the people: it wasn't that long ago that we were swept away by the Macarena.

While I'd rather not imagine the geeky Stewart doing the Macarena, you can see the if-then clause at work. The argument reduces the notion of the wisdom of the crowd to absurdity; you could actually express it as an if-then clause.

> If we should trust the will of the people, then why aren't we still doing the Macarena?

You could steal from Stewart by inserting your own stupid fad of days gone by whenever people talk about public opinion or the wisdom of the crowd.

> YOU: Wisdom of the crowd? The same crowd behind the success of Farmville?

Stewart shows the infinite variety you can get out of figures. Once you get used to a particular tool like the if-then, you can express it different ways. Or you can combine it with another figure or trope. For instance, the if-then clause can express an analogy. If *a* is true, then isn't that like *b*? Stephen Colbert did just that on the *Colbert Report* with a guest.

> COLBERT: So you're the fashion editor at the *Washington Post*. Isn't that like being the dance critic at the Southern Baptist Convention?

Colbert is thinking, "Washington is an infamously fashion-backward town. So that's like being a dance critic at a place where people can't dance." Let us try.

> ME: I'm a consulting rhetorician for NASA.
> YOU [stalling for time]: A rhetorician for NASA. Isn't that like being . . .

What? NASA is full of engineers, the sort of people who don't naturally take to figures of speech and manipulative tropes. (That's exactly why they hired me.) So let's conjure an analogy.

YOU: Isn't that like being an elocutionist for the SPCA?

NASA may not appreciate the canine analogy, but it works for me. You could also say it's like a fashion designer hiring a camouflage expert. Or is camo fashionable? In any case, the if-then analogy works like any other ad absurdum: look for the silliness, then stretch it to its extreme.

EXERCISE

Take a quote by a politician you especially dislike, and reduce it to an if-then clause. Now, if you're feeling ambitious, do something harder: reduce to an ad absurdum something you personally believe in. Making fun of your own beliefs is good for you. It keeps you humble, and also nimble.

REPEAT CHANGER: A GOOD USE FOR HITLER

The single easiest thing to do in any argument is to repeat what the other person said, while looking for a way to use those very words to your own advantage. It solves that problem of lacking something to say; your opponent *gives* you something to say. The harder part is using it to your advantage. You need to pay close attention to what your interlocutor has just said. A comeback is a response, not a non sequitur. Take this line from *Casablanca*, spoken by a German officer, and pretend you're the morally ambiguous Captain Renault. Strasser is talking about an American nightclub owner played by Humphrey Bogart.

MAJOR STRASSER: You give him credit for too much cleverness. My impression was that he's just another blundering American.

If you were a typical American and not a morally ambiguous French officer, you might respond something like this.

TYPICAL AMERICAN: Oh, yeah? Well, you're a Nazi #@*%-er.

Instead, Renault calmly quotes the German back at him.

RENAULT: We mustn't underestimate "American blundering." I was with them when they "blundered" into Berlin in 1918.

The Frenchman introduces a good rule to follow when you're throwing someone's words back at him. Instead of saying, "You're making a mistake," say, "We're making a mistake." Share the error so your opponent can save face. The second-person plural may sound annoying when nurses use it ("How are we feeling this morning?"). But in a debate it's best to sound as though you're reminding yourself rather than correcting your opponent. This is especially important if your opponent happens to be a well-armed Nazi. Renault uses tact as a survival strategy. You and I—we—should use it as a persuasive tactic.

FANATIC: Obama planned all along to have government take over everything, just like Hitler.
YOU [looking interested]: Just like Hitler?

This alone could be enough to make the fanatic retreat in mumbling qualifications. But let's say this guy happens to have been hermetically sealed in a rhetorical jar of right-wing talk shows and conspiracy blogs. He's used to having people endorse his astonishing political insight. If no audience happens to be present, you might just quietly walk away. But if others are present, and you want to pull off a good one, you might try this repeat changer.

YOU: Just like Hitler? Do you like Hitler? You make paranoid claims about legitimate governments just as he did.

If you like to pun, as I do, then the repeat changer gives you the opportunity to wing those words right back at your interlocutor. Let's move from Hitler back to socks.

GEORGE: The socks grew up and moved to my room? That would be an impressive feat, even for your socks.
ME: "Impressive feet" is right. The smell of yours makes any sock unwearable.

The repeat changer takes careful listening and a predator's patience. Assuming you love wordplay, I urge you to drive your family insane by practicing the repeat changer as much as possible. In any conversation, listen for any words that could have a double meaning.

LOVED ONE: I think we should get behind the school board on this one.
YOU: If that board were on a ledge, I'd get behind it and push.

It's like a game of catch where you hurl the baseball as hard as you can at the other player, the loser being the one who drops it. That, too, may be a guy thing. If you don't feel that quick, take your time. Repeat your opponent's line with a skeptical tone.

OPPONENT: We think the tax cuts should apply to everybody.
YOU: The tax cuts should apply to *everybody*?

Often a witty reply will occur to you then and there. In this case, the word "cut" offers the opportunity to use a punning form of the repeat changer.

> YOU: All I hear about from my opponent is tax cuts. He never talks about what the tax cuts are cutting. They're cutting my children's education. They're cutting my bus service on the way to work. They're cutting back on my husband's unemployment checks. And meanwhile, the people who most want tax cuts are cutting jobs!

Talk about cutting remarks. The repeat changer depends on your staying alert to the meanings of words. You don't need an amazingly witty line every time; just one memorable sentence in an argument would vault you to the pantheon of arguers. That's what others will quote; so that even if you lose the main argument, you win over your audience's memory.

Your opponent's words can give you multiple opportunities for repetition. For instance, the repeat changer offers a mirror-image reply to our tax-cutting friend.

> OPPONENT: We think the tax cuts should apply to everybody.
> YOU: Tax cuts apply to everybody? Maybe, but the working class need not apply.

While it's all well and good to craft a beautiful line and deliver it in a speech or presentation, your greatest opportunities for immortality will come on the fly. True wit is spontaneous wit, which also happens to be the hardest wit to conjure. But don't despair. Even the faintest spark of wit seems brilliant when it comes ad lib. Just take your time. What seems like a delay of eons to you may be just a second's delay. When I view a videotape of one of my rhetoric lectures, I'm often amazed that my awkward pauses during the Q&A aren't as lengthy as I thought. You can gain more time by repeating what the person just said.

> SPOUSE: I don't see how that explains your behavior.
> YOU: You don't see how? Really?

Hmm. Repeating your opponent can make you sound pretty guilty, can't it? Well, it all depends on your attitude and demeanor. Whatever you do, say it with confidence.

> YOU: You don't see *how*? Really? Then let me put it in the simplest terms.

Meanwhile, you're frantically going through your mental database to make witty connections and put them together with words.

> SPOUSE: No, *I* will. You stood with your beer next to the moose head and. staring at our hostess s chest, you said, "Nice rack!"

Whoa. Your spouse's interruption is the equivalent in chess of making two consecutive moves without giving you a turn. You might feel compelled to cheat. Fortunately, you are primed for puns and near puns.

> YOU: Nice rack? You misheard me. I said, "Nice rock." And I was staring at her, um, necklace.
> SPOUSE: She was wearing pearls, and you were clearly staring at her chest—her surgically enhanced chest, by the way. And comparing stuffed objects.
> YOU: Stuffed objects?

OK, maybe you shouldn't lie. Besides. her reference to stuffed objects reminds you of taxidermy. Which contains the word "tax," which in turn reminds you of the Ben Franklin quote that nothing is certain but death and taxes.

> YOU: I was about to say something profound about nothing being certain in this life but death and taxidermy. I always bow my head when I'm saying something profound.

This sort of mental process only works if you prime yourself for puns. But if you listen for every possible pun, you will come up with lines like that, I promise. Which, by the way, is not always a good idea. A line like "death and taxidermy" would make my wife smile. Another spouse might not appreciate the humor.

IRONY: A VICIOUS, WELL-AIMED "YES"

The use of other people's words has several advantages: it turns their own weapons against them (assuming weapons are involved), proves that you are listening, and buys you time to get your own thoughts together. But you don't have to use the other person's words to cause self-inflicted wounds. You can use their thoughts. And the greatest mind-reading technique ever? Ironic agreement. This will take some explaining.

When someone expects you to disagree, she often assumes that you don't really understand her logic or her feelings. That's one reason she keeps talking. When you seem to agree with her, you short-circuit her thoughts. It's as though you got inside her head and took over for a while. The short circuit often lasts just a second or two until you make it clear that you're really disagreeing.

Jon Stewart, a master of ironic agreement, practices his art on victims who usually aren't present. He'll play a video and then reply agreeably to it. The following is a comment on a clip that Stewart ran when George W. Bush was still president.

> BUSH: America needs to conduct this debate on immigration in a reasoned and respectful tone. . . . We cannot build a unified country by inciting people to anger or playing on anyone's fears.
>
> STEWART [agreeably]: That's what terrorism and gay people are for.

Stewart wasn't being fair. Bush was proposing an even-handed, practical way of dealing with the millions of undocumented workers in this country. But Stewart, who makes his living off politicians' hypocrisy, used the occasion to his own advantage.

The great thing about irony is that it lets you walk right through the huge rhetorical openings people create when they talk. Enjoyably vicious *Glee* villain Sue Sylvester doesn't just walk through these openings. She performs nasty aerobic routines in them. Remember these lines from the introduction?

> WILL: Who's to say everything I do is one hundred percent on the ball?
>
> SUE: No one would say that.

Again, it takes careful listening to find the openings. You need the observation skills of a football halfback in a running play. Find the openings and then use them. Instead, most of us run away from the openings.

> OPPONENT: You know what your problem is? You don't listen.
>
> USUAL ANSWER: Go to hell.

Which proves our opponent's point. Better to rebut her point with your own good behavior.

YOU: You're right. I've never learned how to stand listening to people like you.

On the other hand, you might want to calm things down, improve the tone a little. There may be someone else there, and you can gain points by appearing the more reasonable person. So throw in some self-deprecating humor.

YOU: That's my only problem? You flatter me.

Or maybe you'd want to try something in between a slam and self-deprecation.

YOU: I have worse problems than not listening to you.

Though clearly you have been listening. And that's not a problem after all. Let's get back into people's heads, starting again with *Glee*. Will, Sue's curly-haired nemesis, has come in peace. He offers to "bury the hatchet."

SUE: I won't be burying any hatchets, William, unless I get a clear shot at your groin.

This line is more subtle than it may look. OK, it isn't subtle. But let's unwrite it ever so slightly.

UNWRITTEN: I won't bury the hatchet, William, except in your groin.

Sue's version seems more threatening, because it implies that she's waiting for the opportunity at every moment. Instead of going straight for the action, Sue describes the condition in which the action would take place. The unwritten version implies that someday she might just take that hatchet to Will's groin. If she chooses to. The original version, Sue's version, makes it sound pretty definite whenever Will has an unguarded moment.

Remember another Sue-ism mentioned earlier.

WILL: Hold on a second, Sue.
SUE: I resent being told to hold on to anything.

Even less subtle. Sue manages to make half of what Will says sound like sexual harassment. She's the figurist from hell, and I love her. In each case, Sue takes her opponent to the logical—or figurative—extreme, whether it's a trope (hatchet) or pun (hold on). If you have ever secretly enjoyed a "That's what she said" joke, you understand the enjoyably crude humor.

SKEPTICAL WOMAN: I find that hard to swallow.
SOON-TO-REGRET-IT MAN: That's what she said.

The secret is to wait for every open-legged, unguarded opportunity—to be ready to bury the rhetorical hatchet, as it were.

NEMESIS: That which doesn't kill you makes you stronger.
YOU: Interesting experiment. Let's start with you.

Well, buried, sir or madam!

LABELING: WEARABLE SMELL BAGS

Sometimes, agreement does not make the ideal way to disagree. Instead of simply repeating your opponent's words, or pretending to agree with them, or getting behind them and pushing, you might want to issue an immediate denial. The contraster lets you go beyond denial by changing the focus of the argument, making an object or action look bigger or smaller.

GEORGE: I'm not stealing your socks. You've been donating them.

Admittedly, this won't get George off the hook, but it may buy him time to think up what he means by "donating."

GEORGE: I mean, you leave your dirty socks all over the place. And as you like to say, anything out of its place is up for grabs.

This particular use of the contraster does something besides simply contrasting arguments. It relabels the accusation, changing theft into charity. You can use this kind of relabeling in a variety of arguments, including those of the nonspontaneous type. To use the contraster in relabeling an issue, look for the key term in your opponent's sentence. It's not hard for George to spot "stealing" as the salient point of my argument. He can either create a contrasting definition, or distract me altogether with another instance of stealing that makes his own theft seem trivial.

GEORGE: That's not stealing. Your putting up my baby pictures on Facebook—that's stealing.

Again, George is just throwing rhetorical sand in my eyes here. He knows this argument is ridiculous, but he's buying more time to put his defense together. A better relabeling defense might be to use a descriptive label to make the theft seem less important.

GEORGE: No, I didn't steal those holes with wool around them.

I tell you, this guy is good. This past Christmas, my wife resorted to buying me more socks. I've hidden them carefully.

The descriptive label lets you belittle the object by refusing to dignify it with a name. Socks can turn into "smell bags," or "your unwashed minions"—anything to make it sound as if theft might actually be doing me a favor. You can relabel political as well as personal issues this way, calling progressives "big-government types" or "tax-and-spenders." More usefully, descriptive labels can help people see beyond the usual terms. Years ago, while we were house hunting, my wife fell in love with an 1810 farmhouse in rural New Hampshire. The asking price was more than we could afford, and the charm-to-comfort ratio—the austere beauty—was a good deal higher than I would have liked. The house had just one bathroom, and nothing a modern American would call a kitchen. So while our Realtor referred to the house by its address, my wife started calling the place "the meadow with the house below Cardigan Mountain," knowing I'm a sucker for meadows and mountains—especially mountains. We ended up buying it, meadow and all.

The portmanteau also makes for terrific labeling. In politics, you'll hear opponents label each other by combining portmanteaus and eponyms. Hence "Billary" for Bill and Hillary Clinton and "Rudy McRomney" for Republican presidential candidates Rudy Giuliani, John McCain, and Mitt Romney. I call the technique a *portmanym;* the term itself is a portmanteau of "portmanteau" and "eponym." You can use the device to make a list of people sound alike.

Remember that you can also add a standardized syllable to the beginning or end of our key word. Suppose you want to label those awful political talk jocks who make a buck ensuring us that our freedoms are being taken away through government conspiracies. Shocktrons? Conspiraholics? No! The bitterati!

Why include a section on labeling in a chapter on argument?

Because logic alone doesn't win arguments. Changing the focus of the argument can be more effective; that's what often has happened when you find yourself gasping for air during a disagreement. You think you're arguing about one thing, then you're suddenly defending yourself for something you hadn't anticipated. It's not the logic that's getting you. It's the label.

17

BE THE HERO

THE JIMMY KIMMEL DEVICE
A Well-Figured Life

ONE OF THE PLEASURES of adulthood is the opportunity to shock our juniors. I found myself with an especially good opportunity years ago, when my daughter, Dorothy Jr., was five. My wife and kids had joined me for dinner at Dartmouth College's Moosilauke Ravine Lodge, a giant log cabin where incoming freshmen were given a feast. Dorothy Jr. sat next to me on a long bench, and a freshman sat on her other side. The boy looked really hungry, and for good reason: he had spent two nights camping in the woods and eating badly cooked food as part of his college orientation. Starvation must have made him clumsy or greedy; when he tried to raise a large drumstick of barbecued chicken to his mouth, the thing slipped from his hand and dropped onto his lap. Exclaiming the F-word, he picked the chicken off his sauce-covered pants and then glanced guiltily over at Dorothy Jr. My little blond, pigtailed girl was watching his face with interest.

"Oh," the boy said to me. "Sorry."

"That's all right," I said. "Dorothy, explain to the gentleman what you know about that word."

"It was originally a term that meant plowing," Dorothy Jr. said.

"Oh." He held his chicken uncertainly.

"I know a lot of words," she explained. "Would you like to hear about some others?" She listed several more four-letter words and offered to give the etymology of each one.

By now most of the table was staring at Dorothy Jr. The freshman looked across her at me. "Dude!" he laughed nervously.

Even better than shocking our juniors is using our own children to shock our juniors. "She's interested in words," I shrugged. "All kinds."

I didn't explain that Dorothy Jr.'s erudition was part of an experiment of mine to see whether knowledge of taboo words could erase their black magic and make them merely enjoyable. If my kids learned the story of individual "foul" words, would they seem so foul when it came time to use them? I had assured my skeptical wife that the words would probably lose their charm; without magic, why cuss? It's the taboo that makes blue language work. But my secret hope was that my kids would grow up into imaginative employers of four-letter words.

And boy, did they. Not to brag or anything, but at twenty-six my daughter talks like a sailor—a very articulate sailor. I love that she appreciates "bad" words for what they can do to add spice or shock or express rage. Oh, she can be offended; she hates four-letter words when they're used for no real purpose, or when they're hurled at people simply to upset them. I like to think that she speaks a lighter shade of blue.

THE LION, THE CANDIDATE, AND THE WARDROBE

It's not that I wanted potty-mouthed offspring. On the contrary, I wanted my kids to rise above foulness. Rather than be shocked or victimized by the crude language that permeates our culture, I wanted them to become connoisseurs of language. Besides "bad" words, I taught them figures of speech as I learned them myself. I did it partly out of selfishness: sophisticated children are interesting children. And it's no accident that the very word "sophisticated" came from the Sophists, the Greek itinerant scholars who invented figures in the first place. Figures of speech make a person sophisticated.

I hope you find yourself endowed with a dollop of added sophistication from this book. For one thing, you should be able to read and listen differently. When you come across something clever, you have a way of parsing that wit and using it as your own.

First, you unwrite it, putting the expression into plain English and comparing the difference.

Then you give that difference the SPA treatment, looking for sounds, pictures, and associations.

Next you pick out your favorite figures—your mirror image and word repeaters, your catalog and Mr. Potato Head, your belonging trope and contraster and if-then clause. At this point, you may have achieved that degree of English acumen where you have to bite your tongue. Otherwise you'll constantly startle people with, "That's a repeat changer!" or "You just used some nice feigned precision." It's best to keep quiet about these terms—and to keep quieter about their technical equivalents. I have been known to say, "That's an anadiplosis" when someone uses the for-want-of-a-shoe figure. And I once got shushed during a Harry Potter movie for blurting the Greek term for descriptive label, *periphrasis*, when a wizard mentioned "He-Who-Must-Not-Be-Named." My bad. Sophistication is not about mere labels.

Nor is it about memorizing tools. While I tried to give you specific tools to use, my chief intent was to offer ways to discover new tools for yourself. Good thing, too; hundreds of figures named by Greeks and Romans ended up on this book's cutting-room floor. I was forced to omit countless official figures, along with many that have never been given formal names. But the point isn't to name every one of them; it's to learn how they work, what makes them tick. I'd rather show the why and how of figuring so that you can make discoveries on your own. Figures are like insects in the rain forest: an infinite variety of undiscovered species.

For instance, a friend recently sent me a joke he heard on late-night television and asked what figure it represented. Jimmy Kimmel was talking about Christine O'Donnell, an unsuccessful candidate for the U.S. Senate who had once declared herself a witch. "Apparently," Kimmel said, "voters said they'd rather vote for the lion or the wardrobe."

"Is this kind of maneuver a figure of some kind?" my friend asked.

Of course it is. Any unusual use of words for a purpose counts as a figure. In this case it doesn't have a technical name. So, like a scientist discovering a nondescript species in the rain forest, you have naming rights. First, though, you have to dissect the thing. Having had some practice by now, you can tell at a glance that the expression has to do with pictures of some kind. By saying "lion" and "wardrobe," Kimmel makes you think of a third word, "witch." OK, but where did "witch" come from? It came from a book and movie title, *The Lion, the Witch and the Wardrobe*. But the trick would work with any set of words that go together, such as a cliché, or song lyrics. Take these associated words, leave one out, and let the audience fill in the blank. Since I just described the process, I get to name the figure: call it the fill-in-the-blank figure. (My wife teases me for my reluctance to give fancy names to things. My boats are called the Red Canoe, the Green Canoe, and the Kayak. My cat does have a name, but I call it The Cat. Sometimes, unexpected bluntness becomes a kind of cleverness all its own.)

The final step in our examination of Jimmy Kimmel's technique is to find how to steal it. Our dissection shows us a way: take a common expression—words that people associate together—and leave a word out. In Kimmel's case, he or his joke writer was trying to come up with a gag about O'Donnell being a witch and running for election. A synonym for election is "choice." So voters are choosing between a witch and . . . lion and wardrobe!

Yes, a lot of cleverness lies behind that connection. Can we be that clever? Maybe not, but we can try. The other day I didn't receive my mail because of a blizzard that hit the East Coast. Could we use our newly defined fill-in-the-blank figure to comment? The key word here is "snow," of course. Which just happens to be contained in the words engraved on a post office building: "Neither snow nor rain nor heat nor gloom of night stays these couriers from the swift completion of their appointed rounds."

YOU: Apparently, they met their quota with rain and heat and gloom of night.

Not bad. At any rate, part of the fun is in your skill to analyze a witty expression and then play with it. The point is not to steal other people's words; in publishing they call that plagiarism (and, in academia, "research"). Instead, steal the technique behind the words. That's not plagiarism. It's an essential act of creation.

PLATO'S CAVEMEN

As with my children and their study of foul language, a knowledge of figures can immunize you from the tools' more nefarious
effects. When you hear a "plain"-spoken politician use manipulative tropes, you should be able to point out exactly which tropes
and what might have worked better. Your grasp of the tools less-
ens their emotional effects and keeps them from twisting your
view of reality. You see the magician's sleight of hand, and that
removes the black magic.

Each sentence offers a splendid variety of words in a myriad
of arrangements; depending on our choices, we affect our audiences differently. Even if we make our choices unconsciously,
the words have their effect. Words inspire, excite, hurt, bore,
create desire or disgust. We don't just use them to convey facts.
We're not robots.

LOVER: I want you to be aware of my desire to mate with you.

Yet the biggest criticism I get of my work in rhetoric is that
I don't seem to be ashamed of the tools' ability to manipulate
people. And what's with the techniques I offer to insult and parry
and exaggerate? Not to mention my proclivity toward raising
young citizens who can talk blue and hurl clever insults at their
loving father.

Mea culpa. The truth is, if I'm going to be insulted, I want it
done well. If you're going to abuse me, at least make me laugh.
Don't tell me my writing stinks. Hurl an analogy at me.

YOU: You sound like a carnival barker with Greek Tourette's.

Or do it in the form of a Mr. Potato Head.

YOU: Your writing has the grace of a telegram and the brevity of a legal brief.

Or maybe fire off an if-then clause.

YOU: If that's good writing, then I'm going to read more closely the messages my cat leaves me in her litter box.

Our family goes by survival of the wittiest. The more clever members tend to win the arguments. We spend so much time trying to think of something witty that we forget to be angry. An insult without wit is merely offensive. A witty insult, on the other hand, is *wittily* offensive. It's like having an Ultimate Fighting match with our family and appreciating our opponents' form as they throw us to the mat.

Sure, others might hurt my feelings. But at least they put some effort into it. Thoughtless insults are the worst of all. I'm hoping the tools in this book let you put some style in your worst-intentioned language. I'll respect you the more for it.

More important, any names you call me will come in two forms: literal and meta. I'll hear what you say and understand your intention; but I'll also examine the style you used. Once a person gains awareness of figures, every sentence seems to come in a package—the choice and order of the words the person hears or reads. Both the words and the package reveal themselves. The study of rhetoric lets you step outside Plato's famous cave—a cavern where chained prisoners can see nothing from outside but shadows on the walls. Only if you get outside that cave can you see what produced those shadows. Figures release you from your figurative chains, letting you see communication from a new and larger perspective. Our belief systems can either inform us or trap us. We can live within our prejudices, or rise above them by understanding the language that formed them. The Greeks called this meta-awareness "cosmopolitanism." The cosmopolitan belongs to no single group. He has the sophistication to rise above tribes. We need more cosmopolitans today.

Having been introduced to forty-three tools for making your words memorable, you may have discovered that the techniques do more than just show specific ways to coin an expression; they help you become a cosmopolitan. Language no longer controls you. You control the language.

Now take the forms you discover, and fill them with your words. Through your conversation, through your writing and speaking, turn the world into a story and yourself into someone memorable.

We know the world through our words. When you enrich the language, you enrich the known world. That makes you more than just memorable. It makes you heroic.

APPENDIXES

APPENDIX

I

WHAT TO DO NEXT

IF YOU'RE READY TO flex your figurative muscles, you can find more exercises at wordhero.org. Discover your oratorical type, then play with the tools that best suit your personality and situation. Take quizzes testing your knowledge of figures. Try your wordplay wits against other readers. A section on the site lets teachers share tips with others. And the site links to Figarospeech.com, where I dissect the rhetoric in politics and the media.

To pursue traditional figures, you'll find a list of technical terms in Appendix IV. A much longer scholarly list exists on the venerable website "The Forest of Rhetoric," http://humanities.byu.edu/rhetoric/Silva.htm. No other resource does better at linking figures to rhetorical theory. Richard Lanham's *A Handlist of Rhetorical Terms*, published by the University of California Press, remains the bible of scholarly figuring.

Over the years I've met a surprising number of nonscholars as geekily in love with the ancient figurists as I am. To gain a deeper, primary-source understanding of our rhetorical forebears, you can start with Cicero's *Rhetorica ad Herennium*, which offers a list of figures used in ancient Rome. You'll find more comprehensive coverage in *The Institutio oratoria* of Quintilian. The Loeb Classical Library publishes both works. One of my most prized books is Henry Peacham's *The Garden of Eloquence*, a facsimile of a 1593 volume held by the Bodleian Library in England and published by Scholars' Facsimiles & Reprints. The book is out of print but still available in limited numbers on Amazon. Once you get past the Renaissance typography, Peacham's book is more gold mine than garden: the first scholarly, complete book of figures written in English. Shakespeare almost certainly studied Peacham. His contemporary, George Puttenham, wrote a book, *The Arte of English Poesie*, that's available for only ten dollars on Amazon. Puttenham combines discussion of figures with advice on how to use them with appropriate gestures and tone of voice. Unless you're training for a Renaissance fair, you might find his tips a bit old-fashioned; but I like knowing just how those ruffed sweet talkers were employing their figures.

The single most useful follow-up of all, though, might be contained in the book you're reading now. Check off the tools that you can see using most, and review the exercises. Then get out there and be memorable.

WHEN YOU WANT TO . . .

WHICH TOOLS TO USE WHEN

THESE ARE THE BEST, though not the only, tools for each purpose. Once you find the figures or tropes you need, find an index for each one in Appendix IV.

Accuse someone: catalog, getting medieval, paradox (to accuse of hypocrisy), word repeater

Apologize: euphemism, for want of a shoe, litotes, multiple synonyms, sound repeater, word repeater, understatement

Brand a product, service, or project: analogy, belonging trope, catalog, definition, descriptive label, metaphor, Mr. Potato Head, multiple synonyms, onomatopoeia, personification, portmanteau, pun, repeat changer, Russian doll, simile, slogan, sound repeater, sound symbolism, verbing

Charge up your team: getting medieval, kindergarten imperative, last person on earth, metaphor, mirror image, multiple synonyms, word repeater

Compare or contrast: analogy, belonging trope, contraster, if-then clause, like . . . only technique, metaphor, mirror image, Mr. Potato Head, Russian doll, simile, word repeater

Connect widely different things or ideas: analogy, belonging trope, contraster, like . . . only technique, metaphor, Mr. Potato Head, paradox, pun, Russian doll, sound repeater, venereal language

Console someone: analogy, belonging trope, contraster, descriptive label, euphemism, kindergarten imperative, litotes, mirror image, slogan, sound symbolism

Describe a character: analogy, belonging trope, catalog, descriptive label, feigned precision, hyperbole, like . . . only technique, metaphor, Mr. Potato Head, multiple synonyms, onomatopoeia, oxymoron, paradox, portmanteau, Russian doll, simile, slogan, sound symbolism

Describe a place: analogy, belonging trope, catalog, descriptive label, feigned precision, hyperbole, like . . . only technique, metaphor, Mr. Potato Head, multiple synonyms, onomatopoeia, paradox, personification, portmanteau, Russian doll, simile, sound symbolism

Explain a difficult strategy or procedure: analogy, belonging trope, for want of a shoe, like . . . only technique, metaphor, Russian doll, verbing

Give a speech (see chapter 15): analogy, contraster, descriptive label, for want of a shoe, getting medieval, metaphor, mirror image, paradox, repeat changer, simile, venereal language, word repeater

Label a friend: descriptive label, metaphor, Mr. Potato Head, multiple synonyms, slogan

Label a group: belonging trope, definition, descriptive label, feigned precision, like . . . only technique, metaphor, Mr. Potato Head, oxymoron, paradox, portmanteau, pun, simile, slogan, venereal language

Label an issue or argument: analogy, belonging trope, definition, descriptive label, feigned precision, metaphor, Mr. Potato Head, oxymoron, paradox, personification, portmanteau, pun, reductio ad absurdum, Russian doll, simile, slogan

Label an opponent: belonging trope, descriptive label, like . . . only technique, metaphor, Mr. Potato Head, multiple synonyms, oxymoron, paradox, simile

Make a card: catalog, pun, sound repeater (rhyme)

Make an outcome seem inevitable: repeat changer ("boys will be boys"), for want of a shoe

Make things seem bigger or smaller, more or less important: analogy, belonging trope, definition, descriptive label, euphemism, feigned precision, hyperbole, last person on earth, litotes, multiple synonyms, reductio ad absurdum, simile, understatement, venereal language

Say a lot in a few words: catalog, contraster, definition, like . . . only technique, metaphor, oxymoron, portmanteau, verbing

Sound poetic: belonging trope, catalog, descriptive label, metaphor, mirror image, onomatopoeia, oxymoron, personification, portmanteau, pun, simile, sound repeater (rhyme), sound symbolism, venereal language, verbing

Sound witty: analogy, belonging trope, definition, descriptive label, euphemism, feigned precision, if-then clause, irony, last person on earth, like . . . only technique, litotes, mirror image, Mr. Potato Head, multiple synonyms, oxymoron, portmanteau, pun, reductio ad absurdum, repeat changer, Russian doll, venereal language, verbing, Yogism

Tell a story (see chapter 14): belonging trope, catalog, descriptive label, feigned precision, hyperbole, personification, pun (Feghoot), slogan, sound symbolism, venereal language, Yogism

Win an argument (see chapter 16): Contraster, descriptive label, if-then clause, irony, kindergarten imperative, mirror image, portmanteau, pun, reductio ad absurdum, repeat changer, sound symbolism, understatement

TECHNICAL TERMS

acyrologia (a-KEER-o-LO-gia), "unauthorized speech." The fortunate use of the wrong words; malapropism. The figure forms some of the best Yogisms, including "It's not the heat, it's the humility."

adianoeta (ah-dee-ah-NEE-tah), "incomprehensible." An ironic figure of hidden meaning. ("Oh, you shouldn't have.")

adynata (a-din-AH-ta), "helpless." The last-person-on-earth figure. It links a series of impossibilities as a form of hyperbole.

alliteration. A sound repeater that repeats the first letter of succeeding words with the same letter, usually a consonant. See *paroemion*.

anadiplosis (an-a-di-PLO-sis), "redouble." The for-want-of-a-shoe figure. Uses the last word in each phrase, clause, or sentence to begin the next series.

analogy (an-AL-oh-gee), "proportional thought." The figure of parallel cases.

anaphora (ann-AH-for-ah), "carrying back." The first-word repeater.

antanagoge (an-tan-a-GO-gee), "against a leading up." A form of contraster, balancing a negative aspect with a positive one.

anthimeria (an-thih-MARE-ee-uh), "substitute part." The verbing figure.

antistasis (an-TIH-sta-sis), "opposite stance." The repeat changer; repeats a word in a way that changes its meaning.

antistrophe (an-TIS-tro-fee), "turn against." See *epistrophe*.

antithesis (ann-TIH-the-sis), "against a position." The figure of contrasting ideas. The contraster is a subset of this figure, using contrasting examples to change the perspective on an object.

antonomasia (an-to-no-MAY-sia), "substitute name." The descriptive nickname—a term for the descriptive label. Also see *periphrasis* and *circumlocution*.

autophasia (auto-FAY-sia), "speaking of oneself." Catch-22; a rule or act that can only be carried out by its contrary.

chiasmus (kee-ASS-mus), "crisscross." The mirror image figure.

circumlocution (cir-cum-lo-CUE-tion), "speak around." Using words that circumvent a subject. The descriptive label is a form of circumlocution.

conduplicatio (con-du-pli-CAT-io), "doubling with." A word repeater that makes its repetition in different clauses to make a point.

diaphora (die-AH-for-ah), "**difference.**" A word repeater that emphasizes the properties of the word; e.g., "Boys will be boys," and "Number two is number two."

diasyrmus (die-ah-SIR-mus), "**tear apart.**" The figurative use of the reductio ad absurdum, belittling the opponent's argument with a ridiculous analogy.

diazeugma (die-ah-ZOOG-ma), "**separation.**" The play-by-play figure. It lets you catalog a series of actions by eliminating the conjunction between each. ("Gretzky lines up the shot, shoots, scores!")

enantiosis (en-an-tee-O-sis), "**opposing.**" Called *contrarium* by the Romans. Uses a contradiction to prove a point. "You wouldn't eat like that at a restaurant, would you?"

enargia (en-AR-gia), "**made manifest.**" The special effects of figures: vivid description that makes an audience believe the scene is taking place before their very eyes.

epistrophe (e-PIS-tro-phee), "**a turning around.**" A word repeater that uses the same word to end successive phrases, clauses, or sentences. Also known as *antistrophe*.

hyperbole (hie-PER-bo-lee), "**throw beyond.**" The figure of exaggeration.

litotes (lie-TOE-tees), "**meager.**" A figure of ironic understatement, which usually denies a hyperbole.

malapropism. A humorously misapplied word; see *acyrologia*.

metallage (meh-TAL-ah-gee), "**swap.**" The getting-medieval figure. It uses a word or phrase as the object of a sentence.

metonymy (meh-TON-ih-mee), "name change." One of the two belonging tropes, along with *synecdoche*. The metonymy takes a quality of something or someone and makes it stand for the whole; e.g., calling a red-haired woman "Red."

neologism (NEE-oh-loh-gism), "new word." A freshly minted word.

onomatopoeia (onna-motta-PEE-ah), "name maker." The noisemaking figure. It takes a sound and makes it a word. I call it the ono for short.

palilogia (pa-lih-LO- ja), "speaking again." A word repeater that uses the same word twice for emphasis, with no words in between. ("Terrible. *Terrible*.")

paradiastole (pa-rah-die-ASS-toh-lee), "send along." A kind of euphemism in which a bad thing is spoken of in flattering terms—such as my calling our foulmouthed, angry culture our *frank, passionate* culture on page 204.

paradox, "against common wisdom." A trope that pairs two or more contradictory things.

paroemion (pa-RO-mee-on), "nearly the same." Alliteration.

paronomasia (pa-ro-no-MAY-sia), "altered name." The near pun. It plays on words that sound or mean the same but aren't identical.

periergia (per-ee-ER-gia), "overworked." The sin of overfiguring. Even the ancient Greeks, who loved figures, spoke against too much of a good thing.

periphrasis (per-IF-ra-sis), "speak around." The descriptive label. It swaps a descriptive phrase for a proper name, or vice versa. Also see *antonomasia*.

polyptoton (po-LIP-to-ton), "multiple grammatical cases." A sound repeater that uses the root of a word more than once, with different beginning or ending. Robert Frost said, "Love is an irresistible desire to be irresistibly desired."

portmanteau (port-man-TOW). The hybrid word.

prosopopoeia (pro-so-po-PEE-uh), "to make a person." Personification.

reductio ad absurdum. Taking an opponent's argument to its illogical conclusion.

symploce (SIM-plo-see), "interweaving." A word repeater that uses the same word at the beginning and end of each phrase, clause, or sentence.

syncrisis (SIN-crih-sis). "decide with," "compare with." Compares or contrasts things in like-sounding clauses.

synecdoche (sin-ECK-doe-kee), "take one thing for another." One of the two belonging tropes, along with *metonymy*, the synecdoche makes a part stand for the whole, or a member for the group; or vice versa. Joe Sixpack, representing average working-class Americans, counts as a synecdoche.

APPENDIX
IV

THE TOOLS

DESCRIPTIONS AND INDEX

USE THIS APPENDIX to review the tools. After each description, you'll find an index of examples.

Analogy (166 to 168)

A multiple simile in which the comparables, or "analogs," have more than one matching characteristic. Translated from the Greek, *analogy* means "proportional thought," or, more loosely, "template." That's what an analogy is: a template for something else. The analogy reveals itself as an analogy—unlike the metaphor, which pretends that the analog is the real thing. But the line between analogy and metaphor can get pretty blurry. For instance, "word-powered chords" (page 74) could be considered either an analogy or a metaphor. That's why I consider the analogy to be a close relative, even a spin-off, of the trope.

Belonging Trope (182 to 194)

This most under-the-radar of tropes takes a member of a group, a part of a whole, or characteristic of a thing and makes it represent the whole shebang; the trope also works the opposite way. In rhetoric, the belonging trope splits into two subtropes: synecdoche and metonymy. *Synecdoche* (sin-ECK-doe-kee) translates unhelpfully into "takes one thing for another." It's the representational trope, taking a member or part and making it stand for the whole, or vice versa. The White House is a synecdoche, a single building standing for a whole presidency. The *metonymy* (meh-TON-ih-mee) takes a characteristic or container and makes it represent the thing it characterizes or contains "The bottle" for alcohol is a metonymy. But the two devices over ap so much that in the real world we can combine them into the belonging trope.

Catalog (120 to 124)

A list used for rhetorical effect. You can employ a catalog to describe, to emphasize a key concept, or to surprise your audience with an unexpected item. Catalogs have the advantage of being easy to follow, letting your audience pay attention to the details you provide them. You don't actually have to list every item; you can imply some items by stating a range (from . . . to . . .).

Contraster (225 to 228)

A figure of relativity, the contraster brings in an object of contrast to make a subject look bigger or smaller; more or less important; or more or less ridiculous. Formal rhetoric has many figures that compare and contrast; I combined a raft of them to create the contraster. The one that comes closest, the *syncrisis* (SIN-crih-sis), puts contrasts next to each other: "A typist types; a writer stares out windows." The *antanagoge* (an-tan-a-GO-gee) balances good and bad in the description of a person or thing: "Yes, he's stupid, but completely loyal." The *antithesis* (ann-TIH-the-sis) sticks contrasts together, often in paradoxical ways: "She was both beast and fowl, animal and vegetable." The *enantiosis* (en-an-tee-O-sis), or *contrarium*, uses a contradiction to prove a point: "You couldn't possibly bring a woman so diet-obsessed to a Taco Bell."

Definition (138 to 139)

The definition uses a description or action to define the subject. It's really a sneaky form of description. The ancient Greeks and Romans used this device, but I don't see any name for it in the rhetorical literature.

Descriptive Label (133 to 135)

This figure makes the description of a thing stand for the thing itself. A form of *circumlocution* (cir-cum-lo-cue-tion)—literally "speaking around" in Latin—this figure lets you apply a stark label to your subject. Belonging tropes compose great descriptive labels by making a single part or member serve as the description. Technical name for descriptive label: *periphrasis* (per-IF-ra-sis), Greek for "speaking around."

Rhetoricians say that another form of this figure takes a formal name and makes it stand for a type: "You're no Jack Kennedy." But I put that device under the rubric of the belonging trope.

Euphemism (202 to 204)

Like most rhetorical terms, this one also comes from the Greek, meaning "substitute something pleasing." Not all euphemism is ironic; the military term "collateral damage" to mean civilian death and destruction lacks irony. But that just shows why it's best to stick to euphemistic irony: people resent a serious euphemism.

Feigned Precision (150 to 152)

By giving an exact-sounding exaggerated number, feigned precision coats your hyperbole with a figurative patina of accuracy. It's usually most useful for humorous effect. Otherwise it comes awfully close to a lie.

For Want of a Shoe (113 to 115)

One of the most enjoyable word repeaters, for want of a shoe layers its repetition by using the last word in the previous phrase or clause to begin the next one. The figure has its origins among the ancient Greeks, who named it *anadiplosis* (an-a-di-PLO-sis), meaning "redouble." Use it to explain a complex process or to make an outcome sound inevitable.

Getting Medieval (96 to 98)

This figure works like verbing in that it makes words play unaccustomed parts of speech—in this case, creating an ungrammatical object in a sentence. ("I've heard enough 'No's' for the day.") Technical term: *metallage* (meh-TAL-ah-gee), Greek for "to change over" or "swap."

Homonymnastics (78 to 80)

A four-step method for crafting puns: (1) suss out the pith and key words of what you want to say; (2) list relevant synonyms, looking for like-sounding words called "homonyms"; (3) combine the homonyms in phrases to see whether any make sense; (4) use the successful homonyms in context.

Hyperbole (141 to 142)

Greek for "throw beyond," the hyperbole is the supertool of exaggeration. Because it twists reality without lying, the tool qualifies as a trope along with metaphor, belonging trope, irony, and personification. For a variation of hyperbole, see *feigned precision*.

If-Then Clause (146 to 149)

A form of reductio ad absurdum, the if-then clause claims that if *a* is true, then a perfectly ridiculous *b* must also be true.

Irony (196 to 202)

The term comes from the Greek *eironeia*, meaning "dissimulation" or—to put it crudely—"bullshit." The sixteenth-century rhetorician George Puttenham called irony "Drie Mock." That's exactly what irony is: dry mockery.

Kindergarten Imperative (208 to 211)

Expresses a desire in terms of a need while posing as someone in authority. Author Ben Yagoda invented the term, claiming that the figure showed the decline of the imperative mood—the kind of language contained in the Thou Shalt Nots of the Ten Commandments.

Last Person on Earth (143 to 144)

Even under the most extreme circumstances, this hyperbolic figure alleges, your interlocutor's scenario would not play out. Technical term: *adynata* (a-din-AH-ta), Greek for "helpless" or "without power." Presumably, the Greeks meant that even the gods would be powerless to affect the outcome. Use the last person on earth to state an impossibility or to praise someone lavishly.

Like . . . Only Technique (164 to 166)

A variant of the simile, the like . . . only points out a difference or exception. You won't find this figure in the classical literature, but I find myself using it frequently.

Litotes (155 to 157)

Pronounced "lie-TOE-tees," this offspring of understatement denies an exaggeration. The word comes from the Greek *litos*, meaning "plain" or "meager." (Hardly an over-the-top name, what?) You might call it an ironic form of hyperbole; by denying an exaggeration, the litotes tends to make an exaggeration of its own. An overstated understatement, if you will.

Mad Lib Protocol (40 to 44)

A trick for borrowing the technique from a great quote. Use unwriting to find the key words. Then write down the parts of speech those key words represent; the result should look like the Mad Libs game. Now fill in those parts of speech with your own words.

Metaphor (159 to 164)

A trope, or type of nonliteral language, that pretends one thing is something comparable to it. Usually better in formal or poetic speech, the metaphor can sound fancy in day-to-day conversation. P. G. Wodehouse's character Bertie Wooster was beleaguered by a young woman who liked to refer to stars as "God's daisy chain." When you're on a date, better let stars be stars.

Mirror Image (228 to 231)

An elegant device that states the reverse of a phrase, clause, or sentence. Called *chiasmus* (kee-ASS-mus) and *antimetabole* (anti-met-AH-bo-lee) by rhetoricians, the mirror image lets you state a paradox or argue against a point by flipping it over.

Mr. Potato Head (125 to 127)

A catalog that compares each item with something analogous to it. Like the toy that lets you stick a ridiculous nose on a starchy face, the figure offers opportunities for surprise. Sound objective with a few flattering analogs, then throw in an unflattering one to turn the whole description south. As you might have guessed, the Mr. Potato Head is one of my own named figures—a highly useful one nonetheless.

> agility of a tank   125
> brains of aging invertebrate   126
> clothing sense of cheerleader   127
> music playlist of aging hair-band roadie   125
> suspense of phone book   126
> talent of a meat packer   125

Multiple Synonyms (129 to 132)

This repetition-like catalog uses items of the same meaning. Use it to pile on a key concept or piece of persuasion. Multiple synonyms constitute a form of amplification, turning up the volume on your point. The figure therefore works best at the extremes, helping you exaggerate or emphasize. For once, the technical term here seems natural: *synonymia*.

> linebacker huge, refrigerator huge   130
> nerdy, bookish, law-abiding, sexually late-blooming   73
> painful, agonizing, arduous, and most fun   131
> parrot is no more . . . 129
> sound and fury, and not a single believable character   130
> stabbed, stuck, pricked, pierced, punctured   80
> strode like a grenadier   130

Onomatopoeia (55 to 61)

A sound effect that grew up and became a word. The ono turns up the volume in a story or argument—don't use it if you want to sound subtle. A good ono can add cartoonish humor; it can also convey the drama of recent disaster, or a future crashing or melting apocalypse.

Oxymoron (221 to 223)

A paradox expressed in a two-sided phrase. The term means "sharp dullness" in Greek—an oxymoron in itself.

Paradox (215 to 220)

A trope that claims the truth of a contradictory statement.

Personification (205 to 208)

This role-playing trope pretends that an animal, thing, or abstraction is a person; or that an absent person is in the room.

Ancient Greek and Roman educators considered personification an important part of school exercises. Students would mimic the voices of past historical figures in a practice called *prosopopoeia* (pro-so-po-PEE-uh). Personification lets you imitate another person, live or dead; or anthropomorphize (make human) an animal or object. The ancients talked to dead people all the time, moaning things like "Oh, Caesar, what you would think of us now?" They weren't delusional; they were bringing in a free celebrity endorsement of their beliefs.

Pith Method (14 to 25)

Boil down what you want to say, until you have two or three key words. Then use those words in a sentence.

Portmanteau (87 to 92)

Mashes up two words to create a single new word. The term comes from Lewis Carroll, whose 1871 novel *Through the Looking-Glass* stars a word-coining Humpty-Dumpty.

The portmanteau is especially useful when you're describing a novel situation or a new political issue. You can stick standard suffixes onto existing words to make new ones: *-asize* or *-gate* or *-tron*. But the more clever will marry two stand-alone words. You're creating figurative nuptials for neologisms: neoluptials, as it were. Or nuptialisms.

Pun (72 to 82)

A device that uses homonyms—words that sound the same—to imply more than one meaning. While in our culture we employ them mostly as a crude form of humor, I believe that every kid should be encouraged to pun as often as possible. Puns' regular use in wordplay creates verbally sophisticated adults, if occasionally annoying ones. Puns do have their serious uses as well, as Shakespeare proved—not to mention Madison Avenue.

Reductio Ad Absurdum (145 to 146)

The "reduction to absurdity" follows an opponent's logic out the window, reducing it to absurdity; hence the name. If rendered in the form of an if-then clause ("If you're a plumber, then I'm a rocket scientist"), the ad absurdum takes the technical name of *disasyrmus* (die-ah-SIR-mus), meaning "tear apart."

Repeat Changer (110 to 13)

This tool repeats a word with a different meaning second time around. (Technical term: *antistasis*—an-TIH-sta-sis, meaning "opposite stance.") The repeat changer can make you look remarkably witty for very little effort; just listen for the opportunity to repeat your interlocutor's words in a different context. Because of its boomerang effect—its ability to throw an opponent's words back at her—the figure makes an excellent weapon in argument.

Russian Doll Figure (127 to 129)

A catalog with packaging, making each item wrap the next. While the items need not be literal coatings or wrappings—Churchill, after all, managed to wrap a mystery in an enigma—the Russian doll generally comes off better if the wrapping seems natural. If there's a diaper for your baby's temper, this is the figure for you.

Simile (164 to 166)

A comparison, *a* is like *b*. The simile forms a soft-core metaphor, openly admitting the comparable. What's the difference between an analogy and a simile? A simile usually matches just one characteristic, while the analogy has multiple comparables.

Slogan (136 to 137)

Follows or precedes a name with a one-phrase description. The word "slogan" comes from the Gallic words for "army" and "cry." The first slogans were war cries, just as the word "campaign" originally meant a military effort. Early marketers picked up the language of war because they understood the equal importance of guns and blabber.

Sound Repeater (61 to 69)

Employs the same sound at the beginning, middle, or end of consecutive words. A repeated consonant is called *consonance*; repeated letters at the beginning of consecutive words are *alliteration*. A repeated vowel sound is *assonance*. You don't have to repeat the sound just at the beginning of a word. A sound repeater helps you maximize sound-symbolic letters in descriptions. I count rhyming as the ultimate sound repeater, since it repeats ultimate (last) sounds.

Sound Symbolism (51 to 54)

The position of your mouth makes things seem big or small, significant or unimportant. Use it to create special effects in a story, or in persuasion to play up or down an object or character. Sound symbolism proves that almost all language is rhetorical to some degree; when we choose our words, we choose the value-laden, emotionally charged sounds to go with them.

Understatement (152 to 157)

The opposite of exaggeration.

Unwriting (35 to 40)

A tool for discovering the art behind a great quote. Write it in your own words. Edit them into the simplest terms. Compare your simplified version with the original. Now zero in on the key difference, looking especially for sounds, pictures, or associations—the SPA memory keepers.

Venereal Language (98 to 100)

Words that describe collections of animals and things. "Venery" is an antique term for hunting—from the Latin *venari*, to hunt or pursue.

Verbing (92 to 96)

This device takes a noun and turns it into a verb. In fact, the figure can recruit any part of speech—noun, adjective, adverb, whatever—and transform it into any other part. Technical term: *anthimeria* (an-thih-MARE-ee-uh). From the Greek, meaning "part switch." As with the portmanteau, verbing helps you create new language.

Word Repeater (103 to 109)

The most common type of word repeater duplicates the first word; the technical name for this figure, *anaphora* (ann-AH-for-ah), is Greek for "carrying back." You can also duplicate words at the end of phrases, clauses, or sentences—a device the name-loving Greeks called *epistrophe* (e-PIS-tro-phee), or "a turning around." Naturally, words can repeat in the middle as well. Repetition in general is useful in speeches or when you're accusing someone—any time you want a strong emotional effect.

Yogism (211 to 213)

An ironic, role-playing expression that seems foolish on the surface while containing a higher wisdom. Named after the witty-idiot savant Yogi Berra.

ACKNOWLEDGMENTS

IF ANYONE COULD MATCH the stereotype of the lonely writer in a garret, it would be me. I wrote this book sitting in a cabin in rural New Hampshire, in the tolerant company of moose and wild turkeys. In the winter I allow no visitors, not even loved ones, unless they're willing to ski out from our house. The deep snow forms a virtual moat.

And yet when I think of the people who provided friendly support while I wrote, it's as if I worked in an especially highbrow coffee shop. My children, Dorothy and George, practiced wit with me even while I wrote about it. My agent, Cynthia Cannell, proved indefatigable throughout my stops, starts, and deadline extensions. David Beals of NASA helped me explore the effects of words on extremely left-brained audiences. Rhetoricians across the country challenged me on my less scholarly forays into figurative language, as did the loyal subscribers to Figarospeech.com. Thanks also to Kevin de Miranda, Debbie Dunkin, Craig Waller, Barri Tucker, Marilee McInnis, and David Kaufmann. Ambassador Bonnie McElveen-Hunter connected me to Wynton Marsalis, a man who truly understands musical figures. Who else would ask the audience at a jazz concert to define an epistrophe

Even the wittiest, best-turned words couldn't express my gratitude for my wife, Dorothy. She listened patiently to every draft, offered indispensable editing advice, and refused to let me admit defeat. It's traditional to say that a book would be impossible without one's partner. Without Dorothy, *I* would be impossible.

ABOUT THE AUTHOR

JAY HEINRICHS is a journalist, persuasion expert, and media consultant whose clients have ranged from Southwest Airlines to NASA. His previous book, *Thank You for Arguing*, is the best-selling work on rhetoric. He gives numerous lectures and workshops on persuasion and "witcraft." As an editorial director at Rodale, Jay supervised five newsstand magazines. After beginning his career as a conservation journalist in Washington, DC, he served as deputy editor of *Outside* magazine and group publisher of the Ivy League Magazine Network. The Council for Advancement and Support of Higher Education awarded him three gold medals, and his persuasion writing has earned him a National Magazine Award nomination. Jay lives with his wife, Dorothy Behlen Heinrichs, on 150 acres in central New Hampshire.

Thank You for Arguing is your master class in the art of persuasion, taught by professors ranging from Bart Simpson
to Winston Churchill. The time-tested secrets the book
discloses include strategies and tricks from Cicero, Honest Abe, and Yoda. Whether you're a lover of language books
or just want to win a lot more anger-free arguments, *Thank
You for Arguing* is for you.

Thank You for Arguing
$14.00, paper (Canada $17.99)
978-0-307-34144-0

Available wherever books are sold